Managing
Organizational
Performance

Michael Nash

Managing
Organizational
Performance

Jossey-Bass Publishers
San Francisco · Washington · London · 1984

MANAGING ORGANIZATIONAL PERFORMANCE
by Michael Nash

Copyright © 1983 by: Jossey-Bass Inc., Publishers
433 California Street
San Francisco, California 94104
&
Jossey-Bass Limited
28 Banner Street
London EC1Y 8QE

Library of Congress Cataloging in Publication Data

Nash, Michael M.
    Managing organizational performance

    Bibliography: p. 335
    Includes index.
    1. Management. I. Organizational behavior. I. Title.
HD31.N254   1983   658.4   82-49049
ISBN 0-87589-561-1

Manufactured in the United States of America

The paper in this book meets the guidelines for permanence and durability of the Committee on Production Guidelines for Book Longevity of the Council on Library Resources.

JACKET DESIGN BY WILLI BAUM

FIRST EDITION
    First printing: April 1983
    Second printing: November 1984

Code 8312

A joint publication in

The Jossey-Bass Management Series

and

The Jossey-Bass Social
and Behavioral Science Series

$19.95

Preface

Only here in the introduction of a book should a writer's own voice be audible to the reader. For a brief moment he can tell the story of how the book came to be written, and, if he chooses, he can reveal something of its craft.

The why probably should be told first. After ten years I find I can make a vision a reality. I wanted to write a book about American Business, to tell what I had learned and to point out those things I felt were important. This book has taken a long time and a short time to write. I began thinking about the subject matter in the early 1970s, shortly after joining the Hay Group, when I outlined a work I tentatively titled *The Psychology of American Business*. For ten years I carried that outline in my briefcase.

Managing Organizational Performance thus had its beginning over a decade ago. The reading for it began in the stacks of the University of Chicago library shortly after I joined the Hay

Group. It continues even as I write now—in my personal library during California's predawn hours.

In the early 1970s as a clinical psychologist, I helped companies select hundreds of executives through psychological assessments. Later as a partner and general manager of the Hay Group, I thought frequently about the strategy and performance of my clients' companies as well as my own. In 1980, Milton Rock, managing partner of the Hay Group, suggested I write a book and shared ideas he had gathered during a three-year period. Using this as the catalyst, I gathered more material from my own experience and from a review of applied psychology entries in Psychological Abstracts, a compendium of the world's research literature in that field. I did this manually since I felt compelled to read and think about each entry and to decide for myself what was relevant. My experiences reading business books have never been as valuable to me as going to the original literature and synthesizing it by using my own conceptual framework. This approach plus my consulting experience may be responsible for any novel features of my work. References to the literature are made where they yield information useful to managers. Advice is offered where, in my experience, I am fairly certain that the suggestions will work.

This book could not have been written when I first put together my psychology of business outline in 1970. I realize that now. I needed the experience of being a consultant and a line manager. Both roles taught me things that reading and research never could. Having done the things I write about gives the work whatever authenticity it may possess.

The topic of the book is the planning, measuring, and controlling of organizational performance. The task I have set for myself is to try to contribute to the solution of one of the principal problems of management: How do you establish, implement, and achieve the goals of the organization? The challenge is central not merely for companies wishing to change their strategies but also for those who believe that their organization's performance is less than optimum.

The purpose of the book is to discuss organizational performance in all its various aspects from the strategic to the personal. While there are textbooks on organization control, performance appraisal, and corporate strategy, each takes up the subject of managing corporate performance from that single perspective. The approach taken here can be compared to a funnel; the view is broad and general in the book's beginning at the corporate level and specific toward the end at the individual level.

Once a novel idea, corporate planning is now an established management tool. Performance appraisal is also not a new subject. Rather, it is a task that management does often if not well. What is new in this book is a clear exposition of the links between the conceiving of an idea for a business enterprise and its successful accomplishment through the combined efforts of all the people in the organization.

The book covers performance from corporate planning at the top to individual goal setting and performance appraisal at the base. Typical books focusing on human resources have chapters on motivation, ability, perception, learning, groups, and leadership (Steers, 1981; Luthans, 1981; Kerr, 1979; Kelly, 1980), but they tend to be written from a group point of view and touch only tangentially on how to integrate corporate, group, and individual performance. *Managing Organizational Performance* shares with Potter (1980) a goal common to consultants—to show readers how to use scientific knowledge to manage people effectively. Potter has a behavioral orientation, as do several other consultants who apply operant conditioning and behavior modification to managing people in business organizations (Gilbert, 1978; Connollan, 1978; Miller, 1978). My approach is eclectic.

Although organizational behavior texts cover input and process issues, only a few emphasize output and performance (Szilagyi and Wallace, 1980). The declining productivity of American organizations has become a national issue, of concern not only to for-profit businesses but also to budget-driven not-for-profit organizations faced with fewer resources. There is a growing concern over performance, calling for books that are shorter on theory and longer on application, scholarly but practical.

This work is written for thinking managers who find most textbooks protracted and the popular "how to . . . for success" paperbacks superficial. Corporate specialists in organization development and in management and human resources development, while familiar with some of the concepts, nevertheless should find interesting new material because of the author's consulting knowledge data base. It is also intended that the book will be useful to professors and graduate students in business management, public administration, organizational behavior, and industrial and organizational psychology as a refreshing alternative to standard texts and books of readings. An effort was made to write about the business world with clarity and euphony, to give pleasure while giving instruction.

Part One consists of seven chapters. All deal with performance at the corporate level. By beginning the book this way the reader can deal first with the sum before tackling the parts. The genesis of a successful corporation lies in first defining its mission and formulating an overall enterprise strategy. Only when this broad sense of purpose has been articulated does it then make sense to establish specific goals and evaluate performance. The introduction places the book in context by providing a brief overview of the subject and the position *Managing Organizational Performance* occupies in that context. Chapter One, "Strategic Business Planning," analyzes the various stages in a company's life cycle and demonstrates how the challenge to management differs depending on where in that cycle the company finds itself. At the conclusion of the chapter, the reader is presented with the first of several case studies. These are disguised to protect the identity of clients but are based on actual consulting experiences. Each case illustrates a particular problem that managers confront and the processes and tools that can be used to help them solve it.

The subject of Chapter Two is the elusive notion of reputation or image. The corporation's image can be managed if the chief executive officer asks himself, "Who are we, who should we be, and how do we get there?" Chapter Three describes the kind of internal corporate climate found in profitable, growing companies that sustain excellent performance over time.

Chapter Four deals with quantitative measures of performance for profit-making organizations—such readily available measures as profit, size, and growth. Various indices and sources are compared to show that although quantitative measures do help the executive understand and manage his business any single measure of performance may be misleading. Companies can also be measured qualitatively and Chapter Five on supplemental measures of corporate performance provides these yardsticks.

Next, two chapters on the performance of the not-for-profit organization are included. The first discusses performance in government, explains why there is more than a normal amount of inefficiency there, and talks about what business techniques might help improve it. The next chapter examines the cost-control aspect of the health care field and shows how a particular tool—incentive compensation—can help contain hospital costs.

Part Two is about appraising and achieving performance from the divisional to the individual level. Once the course of the ship has been set, all hands must get the word and work toward the achievement of the corporate goal. This is far more easily said than done. In Chapter Eight line units and staff units are discussed, especially the problem of how to measure the performance of the staff department. Illustrations are drawn from such functions as research and development, engineering, finance, and the legal department.

Having decided on the enterprise, picked a strategy, and set goals, how does the manager get real people to perform? With a review of measures of corporate and unit performance complete, Chapter Nine considers the appraisal of the individual employee. This is followed in Chapter Ten by a brief review of the literature on the psychology of goal setting and performance appraisal—what works and what doesn't.

Part Three wraps up the book by bringing together all the links in performance management. Chapters Eleven and Twelve are on the subject of participatory management, a management tool that takes into consideration the concepts and techniques discussed so far. It is a performance assurance planning and control system that integrates company mission, corporate goals, unit objectives, and individual efforts into a workable whole. The subject is treated at length and in some detail because of its importance to the primary topic of the book—measuring and controlling organization performance—and the role that individual performance must play in it.

The next to the last chapter of the book returns to the beginning, and in a long case study it forges together all the links in the performance chain. Expository observations are made throughout to make sure that major points are not missed. Finally, Chapter Fourteen serves as a review of the book, echoing the theme of a few chapters and the leitmotif of the entire work. How can organizations establish, implement, and achieve worthwhile goals and, through this successful realization of the vision of their business, ultimately ensure success?

There are some special people at the Hay Group who deserve acknowledgment. Pallas Johnson and Diana Beachboard produced the manuscript. James Williams reviewed it and made helpful suggestions. Daniel Stix, general partner, worked with me as I learned about business and management. Milton Rock, managing partner, convinced me that I could write about organizational performance and encouraged me to trust my own voice.

Palos Verdes, California   Michael Nash
February 1983

2	0
He	
4.0026	

Contents

The Author

Michael Nash, previously a partner with the Hay Group in Los Angeles, is currently with the consulting firm of Heidrick and Struggles in the Los Angeles office. He is also president of *Network Information Services.* He received a B.S. in chemistry from the University of Michigan (1964) and a Ph.D. in clinical psychology from the University of Chicago (1969).

At Chicago he was given the Temple Award for his research and was elected to Sigma Xi. He has taught at the University of Chicago and the University of Illinois at Chicago Circle. Nash speaks frequently on topics in the management field and has written on various topics in psychology and in management.

In consulting with hundreds of corporations, he has worked with all the techniques described in the text. Case studies, although fictional, are based on actual consulting experiences. Industrial clients have ranged in size from companies in the Fortune 100 to those barely out of organization; from multinationals to local distributors; from oil wells to airplanes, hard goods, soft goods, no technology, and high technology. Nash has developed corporate goals for financial companies and spoken to the Hay Partnership on its own image. He has designed hospital bonus plans and has conducted workshops on incentive compensation in both for-profit and not-for-profit organizations. His experience in the public or almost-public sector ranges from the classification of thousands of county and municipal employees to organization studies of utility companies. For thirteen years he linked together, for manufacturing and service companies, the individual achievement, goal-setting, and strategic planning tools discussed in *Managing Organizational Performance*.

Managing Organizational Performance

Introduction: Linking Performance from the Corporate to Individual Level

"Water, water, everywhere
nor any drop to drink"

Samuel Taylor Coleridge (1772–1834)
Rime of the Ancient Mariner

A captain of industry decides to sail his ship to a chosen port and there conduct trade on behalf of the ship's owners. So, perhaps as a mere notion, he begins his enterprise. Wouldn't it be interesting and fun and profitable to embark on this particular venture? A business, and the organization it takes to manage it, is first just a thought in someone's mind (Schein, 1980). After starting off, the corporate mariner will encounter storms, lulls, and crew members who seem to hinder more than help. Unless he is courageous, uses navigational aids, and holds firm to the wheel, his ship may founder before it reaches safe harbor.

1

Within this metaphor lie several assumptions. First, the voyage is a success if the ship reaches the chosen port and not some other. Second, the faster the ship sails, the better. Third, getting there is not without its cost but is worth it (Evans and Bartolomé, 1980). This is a log book for captains, crews, and owners interested in how to sail their ships quickly to their chosen port.

The theme of this book is the defining, measuring, controlling, and achieving of the goals of the business enterprise. It seeks to link those organizational behavior tools that are useful in planning and controlling corporate performance. This book deals with the conceptual and quantitative structures that constitute successful business. This is only part of what our captain of industry needs to know to get his ship safely to port. Ideally, he would also have us tell him what kinds of people, managed by what means, will help him to his destination. This would require advice on the selection, training, organization, satisfying, motivating, and promoting of people. That must await another book, except for a section on the psychology of performance appraisal.

The theme of managing corporate performance is how the executive begins with the idea of an enterprise, shapes its image, creates its climate, sets its goals, motivates its people, and measures individual performance. The leitmotif is achievement, the achievement of goals from the corporate through the divisional and functional down to the individual. It is a vertical integration of achievement linking organizational levels through the use of organizational behavior tools: strategy, climate, goal setting, incentives, performance appraisal.

Organization is a word of Latin origin that made its first appearance relatively late in the English language, around 1700, meaning an organized body, structure, or being. For purposes of studying business enterprise, here is a definition that will do: "A coalition of interest groups, sharing a common resource base, paying homage to a common mission, and depending upon a larger context for its legitimacy and development" (Miles, 1980, p. 5). *Corporation* here is used as a synonym for *organization* and in the broad Webster sense of the word—"United body;

a legal, municipal, mercantile, or professional association"
(*Webster's Dictionary for Everyday Use*, 1981).

   Managing Organizational Performance integrates fraction-
ated material and uses it to carry out a theme. Although some
material in the text is presented here for the first time, it is not
experimental or theoretical. It is experiential, derived from consulting engagements and from a review of the literature.

   The purpose of the book is to bring together most of the
major facets of organizational performance. My objective is to
help executives manage better by giving them an increased understanding of the attributes of companies that successfully
achieve their mission and how these attributes are interrelated.
The book's thesis is that successful organizations take an *integrated* approach to the challenge of performance. They do not
rely on a single tool such as corporate planning to achieve their
ends, or even on several, such as planning and performance appraisal. Although the book stops short of advocating a particular system, it does argue that managing organizational performance means performing several distinct tasks more or less in
sequence, each linked to the others.

Organizational Performance in Context

Peter Drucker believes that there are three major tasks of management: to decide the purpose and mission of the institution,
to make work productive, and to manage social impacts and responsibilities. This book deals with the first and second of these
managerial tasks. About the second, Drucker says, "The second
task of management is to make work productive and the worker
achieving. Business enterprise (or any other institution) has only
one true resource: man. It performs by making human resources
productive. It accomplishes its performance through work"
(1973, p. 4).

   The major responsibilities of executives are to plan the
work of the organization and to be sure that the organization
achieves the plan. The business of management, put plainly, is
organizational performance. Admittedly this is an oversimplification—not because it contains contradictions or exceptions but

because it does not go far enough. Management must do more than plan, execute, and review quantitative corporate results in order to be successful. It must do the same for its image and climate, for line and staff, for business units and functional departments. It must understand the psychology of goal setting and performance appraisal at the individual level and must be able to involve its human resources through a process of true participation. Successful management is *holistic management.* Each decision or action is taken with insight into its effect on the other parts of the corporate body.

The Challenge Facing Management

Performance remains one of the classic problems of management: how to get the people in the organization to achieve its goals. The problem is enduring and timeless, as old as management itself.

Performance: Management's Primary Function. The word *perform* means to do, to accomplish. The act of performing means to carry out a goal or responsibility. Performance is the thing done. At one time the word *perform* meant to discharge one's function, to do one's part. Later the word *performance* was used to mean the accomplishment, carrying out, or doing of work. It was also used with the connotation of carrying out a command or duty.

In his book *Management: Tasks, Responsibilities, Practices* (1973), Peter Drucker is unequivocal in his view that the primary function of management is to make the organization perform. "The test of an organization is the spirit of performance" (p. 455). For Drucker, performance is the pure essence of management, independent of time, place, or type of business. *To manage* is synonymous with *to perform.* "Management is independent of ownership, rank, or power. It is objective function and ought to be grounded in the responsibility for performance. It is professional . . . a task to be done" (p. 6). Drucker was one of the first to realize that successful management is integrated, balanced, holistic. "The manager [must] consider simultaneously the performance and results of the enterprise as a whole and the diverse activities needed to achieve synchronized performance" (p. 399).

The Right Combination. I make no claim to originality. Instead, my inclination is to believe, with the author of Ecclesiastes, that "there is no new thing under the sun."

What I hope to show is that existing management tools—reconsidered, better used, and used in the right combinations—will help managers achieve the organizational performance they seek. The typical reader no doubt will be quite familiar with some techniques described here, familiar in passing with others, and relatively untutored about the rest. No other book appears to have taken the common theme of performance and carried it through from planning to image to climate to goal setting to individual performance, all within a participatory management framework. "Business managers do not think in terms of . . . overall performance . . . managers who expend mental effort for this . . . will almost certainly be well repaid" (Koontz and O'Donnell, 1968, p. 713).

The Chapters Pass in Review

Chapter One, "Strategic Business Planning," begins by asking the obvious—why plan? The essence of planning is described, as are the characteristics of good plans and bad plans. There is a hierarchy of business planning from enterprise through corporate down to product and market strategy. The kinds of planning matrixes favored by some companies and their consultants are illustrated. Selecting the right strategy for each business unit is explained. A case study about Caro Products, a consumer goods company, closes the chapter.

Chapter Two is "The Organization's Image." It is unreasonable and inefficient to formulate a business plan without knowledge of the organization's external reputation, its image. A good plan will be in harmony with that image and will enable the company to do the things it does best even better. Where a plan calls for achievement outside the organization's current image of competence, this must be recognized and allowances made. Neither Rome nor General Motors was built in a day or even a generation. Changing a corporation's image to accommodate a new strategy is extremely difficult and is seldom achieved without great cost. One's strengths are one's limitations. It is best if the strategic plan is congruent with and amplifies the corporate image. Chapter Two helps executives understand how to identify their organization's image and how to manage whatever change may be required. You may insist that your employees get water from stones, draw blood from turnips, and make silk purses from pigs' ears, but understand what you are asking for. Once established, an image influences everything, including performance and strategy. Chapter Two begins with a general overview of how image is communicated. How does one analyze the corporation's image, what tools are available, what questions do you ask, and whom do you talk to? Once data have been gathered about the image of the organization—once you know how you are seen—how do you decide what your image should be? Which images portend success and which predict failure? Can you change your image? How can you tell if your image is changing? In an extended case study of the Lunada Bay Bancorporation, these and other questions are answered and the interplay shown between strategy, image, and performance.

Chapter Three, "Organizational Climate," begins by defining climate as a kind of internal image. Climate is the perceptions that employees have about their organization's practices and operating principles. Climate, too, strongly influences corporate performance. Although the measurement of climate is still developing, some of the better-known techniques are reviewed. A climate audit is described and the relationships explained between organizational performance and each of eight climate variables: clarity, decision making, integration, style, performance orientation, vitality, compensation, and human resources development. Climate must be understood before strategy can be implemented. Measures and standards of performance will depend in part on what the climate data tell you your employees believe to be the current internal state of affairs. Some climate dimensions correlate more highly with sustained profitability than others. The executive whose climate is deficient in these characteristics may need to set goals and measures so as to create them. The case study, National Business Machines, illustrates the didactic material. This was a company that needed to change both its strategy *and* its climate.

Chapter Four is an exhaustive review of quantitative measures of corporate performance. The typical manager concerned with performance usually begins, and sometimes even stops, by identifying a few key quantitative indexes of performance—usually profit and growth. By Chapter Four, the reader will probably be convinced that an integrated approach to the challenge of performance requires three prior steps before the right quantitative measure can be chosen at the right level of difficulty. A holistic approach says that the manager should ask: (1) What business do we want to be in? (2) What business does the public think we are in? (3) How do our employees feel about the organization? Having answered these questions, either formally or informally, the manager can begin the search to find the right quantitative measures of performance. This chapter and the next deal with all the traditional indexes of performance and many of the experimental ones. Profit and growth are defined and debated. Historical performance standards are reviewed and particular industries highlighted.

Chapter Five continues the discussion begun in Chapter Four. The subject is supplemental measures of performance. Two special statistical techniques useful in appraising corporate excellence are explained: the Hay Performance Compensation and the Value Line data base. The remainder of this long chapter is devoted to the topic of supplemental and more subjective measures of organizational performance established by the American Institute of Management: economic function, corporate structure, health of earnings, research and development, directorate effectiveness, fiscal policies, production efficiency, sales vigor, executive quality, and service to stockholders. The chapter ends with a case study of a utility company—Appalachian Power and Light.

Chapter Six is a change of pace, the subject being performance in the not-for-profit organization—specifically, government. Although the principles enumerated in the previous five chapters are applicable to both for-profit and non-profit organizations, the weight has been on the former. Here, and in the next chapter, the country's most pervasive type of institution receives some of the attention it deserves. About 30 percent of the American work force is employed by a not-for-profit, when government is included. The chapter begins with background material about differences between nonprofit service organizations and organizations in the private sector. The argument is made that tools used by managers striving for profit and growth can be modified and used by those seeking service and cost containment. The chapter goes on to describe business planning, resource allocation, budgeting, and measuring performance. Finally, a particular management style is advocated for public-sector managers struggling to motivate a contentious civil servant.

Chapter Seven looks at another nonprofit organization: the hospital. Of the challenges facing health care institutions and their clients in the 1980s, the most acute and potentially terminal problem is cost containment. Hospitals have struggled to find legitimate quantitative measures of performance while preserving their primary mission: to provide quality care that enhances and preserves life. Chapter Seven reviews the missions and some of the better-accepted quantitative measures for an essentially qualitative and subjective industry. It describes how at times a single measure of performance can be used correctly in the management of an entire enterprise. The positive side of cost containment in a hospital is net operating income. The case study of San Miguel Hospital illustrates how a technique like incentive compensation, typical for a hospital, can bring improved performance to an institution already considered one of the best in its field.

Chapter Eight, on performance of divisions and departments, takes the issue of managing performance from the corporate level to the middle of the organization. The theme is the performance of various business units and job families within the organization. After a brief introduction, the goals and measures of groups and divisions are described. Then a few select functions are chosen and performance for them defined.

Included are the functions of marketing, research and development, engineering, finance, audit, and legal. The case study of Pitkin Manufacturing is a fictionalized version of an actual consulting assignment where the development of measures for a functionally organized equipment manufacturer was the mandate.

The focus on performance moves next from the functional and unit level to the individual level. Chapter Nine is called "Individual Performance." It is a review of the more common methods of performance appraisal and their limitations. After beginning with administrative matters, the chapter continues by cataloguing and describing different appraisal techniques—employee evaluation, performance comparisons, performance descriptions, results-oriented evaluation. Because of its popularity and the controversy surrounding it, management by objectives is covered at greater length. The didactic part of the chapter concludes with a review of the problems of appraisal. Although it deals with the individual, Chapter Nine is still written from the vantage point of management. What tools can you use to determine the presence of performance at the individual level? What are the pluses and minuses? Are some methods better than others? What technique is best for what purpose? The case study is a panel discussion on the do's and don't's of appraising the individual.

Chapter Ten is "The Psychology of Goal Setting and Performance Appraisal." Topics covered include needs to achieve, goal difficulty, time, participation, rating reliability, validity, employee perceptions, employee traits, and changing behavior. The point is made repeatedly that to successfully manage corporate performance, the executive must make the individual employee feel a part of the organization. A business organization, like any whole, is never more than the sum of its parts. Often it is much less. People who believe in organizational synergy have not studied much chemistry. It is important to capture the commitment of each employee. Although the cooperation of employees will not guarantee corporate performance, its absence can make success impossible.

Chapter Eleven is the first of two chapters that show how

to link corporate, functional, and individual performance to the company's overall strategy. The approach described is called "participatory performance management" (PPM). Chapter Eleven covers the concept of PPM and then accountabilities, measures, and standards. PPM goes beyond performance appraisal, beyond management by objectives. It attempts to integrate the individual employee into each major component in the performance cycle: strategy, image, climate, measures, goals.

Chapter Twelve concludes the description of participatory performance management by discussing goals, action plans, and appraisals. The remaining concepts are described and examples given: goals, action plans, participatory goal setting, and performance reviews.

Chapter Thirteen is a case study of participatory performance management. The chapter provides an example of an organization trying to involve its employees in the management of the organization, from challenging strategy to setting their own goals. After a brief introduction to the bank, the organizational structure is shown. Top officers participated in formulating the bank's corporate mission, and this exercise and its output are described. Then the strategy and goals for finance and marketing are reviewed. The reader sits in on the training the bank provided for its employees in participatory management and performance appraisal. Through the case, the integration of performance is demonstrated, tying the major concepts together.

The last chapter, Chapter Fourteen, provides some final bits of advice on selected major topics. Subjects given a final emphasis are strategic strategy, corporate image and corporate differentiation, coming of age in the not-for-profit, the future of performance appraisal, managing productive people, the lessons of Japan, and productivity.

An Emphasis on Planning

Planning has become a field of specialization within management with subspecialties of its own. Besides the usual general planning books, there are texts on selected topics (Denning,

1971), on integrated planning (Rothschild, 1976), and on companywide approaches to planning (Cotton, 1970). Among the special aspects of planning that have received book-length treatment are its measurement (Ferguson, 1974), strategy and effectiveness (Collier, 1968), long-term profit planning (Weinwurn, 1971), systemic approaches (Argenti, 1974), and alternative approaches (Rothschild, 1979). Finally, there are books that link corporate planning to other things: tactics (Hutchinson, 1971), policy (Mockler, 1971; Kins, 1978), forecasting (Cooper-Jones, 1974), and management (Ansoff, Declerck, and Hayes, 1976). Few books link strategy to image, climate, goal setting, performance appraisal, and participatory management. Planning should be viewed as a long-range strategy for corporate effectiveness, but in fact it is not. Both specialists in the field and top management seem to lack the strategic perspective (Beer, 1980).

Planning is an issue of worldwide proportions. There are many problems inherent to the world of work and indigenous to all industrial societies. Since these irritants are structural ones within any enterprise, they are not likely to be eliminated by choosing one politicoeconomic system over another. Rather, the task is to develop universally applicable problem-solving processes to deal with these dilemmas. Proof that they are ubiquitous and not merely a capitalist malady is their occurrence in the management literature of other nations. At least one Russian, writing under the auspices of the USSR Academy of Sciences, believes that "the central issue of the psychological study of managerial activity is preparing and putting into effect a system of collective acts. Hence, planning in social systems constitutes the key to understanding individual planning activities" Lazarev (1980, p. 25). For Lazarev the key to successful output is planned input.

The Japanese appear to plan in ways that yield superior productivity. According to Bryan (1982), five factors are principally responsible for their success: (1) a group quest for knowledge, (2) willingness to sacrifice short-term profitability for long-term gain, (3) an emphasis on quality assurance, (4) company loyalty, and (5) participatory management. Does corporate planning really improve performance, or is it merely a wizard's abracadabra?

Does corporate planning improve corporate performance? Thune and House (1972) report that "companies that engage in formal long-range planning have historically outperformed a comparable group of informal planners" (p. 82). Formal planners did better than informal planners in corporate performance as measured by improved earnings per share (+44 percent), return on equity (+38 percent), and return on capital (+32 percent). The before-and-after performance of companies adopting corporate planning showed sales up 38 percent, earnings per share up 64 percent, and the price of the companies' stock increasing by 56 percent. Formal planning was most helpful for medium-sized companies and those in rapidly changing industries.

Although corporate planning aids some enterprises more than others, it appears to be a universally applicable management tool. Rather than being appropriate only for large American corporations, a strategic approach to the management of a business can be successfully applied in any situation (Taylor and Hawkins, 1972).

These few comments and citations do not exhaust the subject of corporate planning. A proper full chapter on strategic business planning follows next. It, in turn, is succeeded by sections on image, climate, measures, applications—each a variant on the theme of performance in the corporation.

Performance Appraisal

Another time-honored management tool is the appraisal of individual performance. It preceded corporate planning and management by objectives by almost a generation, and its development paralleled the personnel research being conducted in job evaluation and salary administration. Between 1926 and 1946 alone, over 600 books, articles, and pamphlets were published on the subject of merit ratings and appraisals (Mahler, 1947).

The appraisal of the performance of the individual used to be a simple one-way communication in which the boss told the employee what he thought of the employee's performance, behavior, attitudes, and habits. During the 1930s, 1940s, and 1950s, performance appraisal plans were routinely used to (1) make decisions about salary increases, promotions, and terminations, (2) tell employees how they were doing, and (3) coach employees and help them develop. Unfortunately, this approach, according to some critics, placed management in the position of being judge and jury over employees (McGregor, 1957, 1960). The to-be-expected segmentation of the subject of performance appraisal occurred. There are, for example, books on efficient performance (Becker, 1975) and optimum performance (Mahler, 1975). Performance appraisal has been linked to human development (Smith, 1977) and greater productivity (Olson, 1981).

One of the first scholar-practitioners to argue that individual performance needed to be linked to corporate strategy was Arch Patton (1960). He recommended a technique he called "planned performance," which was a composite approach to appraisal. It related a person's individual performance targets to the short- and long-term goals of the enterprise. Later Sloan and Johnson (1968) identified what they believed was a trend toward a "systems" approach in personnel. They foresaw the use of performance appraisal more as a tool for corporate planning and less as a device to control performance. Unfortunately their prescience now seems premature. Although there have been more calls for an integrated approach to the problem of performance, there have been few responses.

Goal Setting

Another major organizational behavior tool that has stood the test of time is goal setting. George Odiorne (1965, 1979) is usually called the father of management by objectives, although Peter Drucker was one of the first to write on the subject (1954, 1964). In *The Practice of Management*, Drucker recommended that subordinates establish their own short-term performance goals and that performance be analyzed (separated into its constituent elements) but not appraised (have a value put on it).

For about a decade goal setting using the management by objectives technique enjoyed explosive growth and uncritical acclaim. Then two separate trends began to emerge. After the appearance of more books outlining goal setting and its benefits (Raia, 1974), "how to" books were written (Humble, 1973; McConkey, 1976). Scholars and practitioners tied MBO to other concepts in business: accountability (Marvin, 1968), action (Humble, 1970), profit (Mali, 1972), and results (Morrisey, 1977). Because setting goals is a more natural and therefore an easier task for line units than for staff, there appeared books on line and staff (Gruber, 1976) and line (Holtz, 1981). Specialized texts were written treating the subject of management by objectives as it applied to staff managers (McConkey, 1972), nonprofit organizations (McConkey, 1975), and human service systems (Budde, 1979).

Management by objectives as a technique was initially received with enthusiasm by executives because it met a need. It provided a system by which executives could plan and review—by which they could manage. But it dealt with just one element of the whole of the management challenge, and so it failed to become the panacea of performance. Even when done well, MBO has weaknesses. There is a tendency to set goals at the top of the organization and force them on the rest of the company. Those charged with carrying out the programs are inclined to make them too complex. Finally, like many new techniques, MBO is often well planned and implemented but poorly monitored and controlled. After a few years, half the companies that install MBO quietly drop it.

But the more telling criticisms of a "pure" management by objectives approach were of the sort first expressed by McGregor when he wrote about performance appraisal (1957) and in his classic, *The Human Side of Enterprise* (1960), where he first put forth in a book his Theory Y, Theory X. According to Bennis (1972), for whom he was a teacher, colleague, boss, and friend, McGregor echoed throughout his work the belief that all must actively participate in the management of the company and, where necessary, the occasional conflicts between individual needs and organizational goals must be resolved.

By the early 1970s, criticism of MBO had become more virulent. Listen to Harry Levinson writing in the *Harvard Business Review* (1970): "The typical MBO effort perpetuates and intensifies hostility, resentment, and distrust between a manager and subordinates . . . MBO as a process is one of the greatest of managerial illusions." Within a year, books were being written on making MBO more effective (Redding, 1971), and a decade later a book was published called *MBO Can Work!* (MacDonald, 1982).

MBO can work, but not in a vacuum. Goal setting is useful in managing organizational performance when done in conjunction with other processes and in the right internal and external environments. Linked to strategy and image, based on a true spirit of participation, goal setting is an important part of management. Levinson's most important point is probably in the title of his article "Management by Whose Objectives?" If the answer is not "By *our* objectives," then goals and objectives are really just Frederick Taylor revisited, industrial engineering in a new bottle. Goal setting alone does not work if individual goals are not linked to corporate goals so they become shared and become "ours." MBO, wrote Levinson, often "fails to take adequately into account the deeper emotional components of motivation."

There is a psychology of goal setting and performance appraisal that managers must take into account (Chapter Ten) as well as an art to appraising individual performance (Chapter Nine). If management remains blind to these performance components, it will have its hands full of hostile or indifferent employees who see performance standards and goals as pressure and punishment. Levinson suggests some solutions: (1) forge a true partnership between people and the organization, (2) let people set their own goals, (3) include group goal setting, (4) appraise the appraisers. These recommendations cut across the grain for many top executives. Yet, this is the direction in which successful companies that use MBO-type goal-setting programs will travel. Unquestionably, goal setting does have the potential to become coercive, a kind of pseudo participation masquerading as the real thing (Oberg, 1972). For goal setting to work, for it to perform, participation must be genuine, and goals must mesh with a sound corporate strategy, a facilitating climate, and a congruent external image.

Little is available in the literature on how to link corporate strategy and employee goal setting except for isolated chapters in books devoted to other subjects (Wilkens, 1972). The notion of having employees participate in the accomplishment of corporate goals can be described as participatory management or a collaborative leadership style. The guiding principle is that if people are informed and involved, they will do better by the company than if they are not.

Why does goal setting with employees help manage corporate performance? Bass (1970) believes that the CEO can better accomplish corporate objectives by pushing certain parts of the planning process far down into the organization. Bass asked 600 managers to evaluate their own plans and those given them by others. Invariably they felt their own to be superior and felt more of a sense of responsibility for them. Of course, employees do not provide strategy for the whole organization, but involving them increases their motivation and therefore increases the likelihood that the corporate goals will be achieved. The assumption, supported by research, is that productivity is a multiplicative function of motivation and ability (Odiorne, 1965).

Worker involvement in corporate matters is popularly called *industrial democracy* in Europe. Worker representation is required by law and focuses on issues of compensation and job security. The more familiar phrase in the United States is *participative management,* and the advantages of this form of management are said to include increased job satisfaction. In neither form of management, however, do employees formulate corporate or functional strategy. That must be done by the chief executive and other top executives. Instead, employees are involved in translating corporate and functional goals into unit and personal goals (Bass, Shackleton, and Rosenstein, 1979). Not having employee support means a rough voyage for the ship, but with it you can sail close to the wind.

The success of a corporation depends on its ability to satisfy individual needs while meeting common goals. Since employee interests, education, and skills differ at various levels up and down the organization, it is easy for the same corporate goal to be differently perceived and pursued by people working at these various levels. Communications and coordination are important.

Simply telling people to do their best is not as effective as assigning them subtasks or having them participate in carving out their share of the overall objective. Improvements in performance are significant when corporate strategy is linked to individual goal setting, but the effects are evanescent, evaporating in six to nine months unless there is a later intervention (Ivancevich, 1977). Managers who are trained in goal setting have subordinates who are more satisfied and effective than managers who are simply given goals and told to go ahead (Ivancevich and Smith, 1981). Something complex and fragile is at work here.

Integration of Performance

There have been a few attempts to provide management with an integrated approach to the challenge of performance. One of the earliest was developed by McKinsey, as described by Goetz (1949). The approach was an organization audit to appraise the enterprise in all its aspects. McKinsey's audit first studied the firm's industry. Next it appraised the position of the firm within its industry. Then it examined the basic objectives of the company to see where it wished to be in five to ten years. Finally, it could conduct an examination of organization, policy, procedure, programs, facilities, financial position, personnel, and management. The last step is similar to the technique used by the American Institute of Management (1970) described at length in Chapter Five.

By 1955, General Electric had tried to develop a comprehensive system for overall organizational performance in eight areas: profitability, market position, productivity, product leadership, personnel development, employee attitudes, public responsibility, and integration of short- and long-range goals. The effort failed (Controllership Foundation, 1955). In 1958, in a widely read and reprinted article in the *Harvard Business Review,* Kelly argued that "the foundation of successful performance lies in a triad of individual ability, job structure, and total job or organizational relationships." His major topic, however, was individual performance appraisal, and he did not go on to advocate an integrated or systems approach to managing corporate performance. One of the earliest book-length attempts at the kind of integration attempted here was a text by Wickert and McFarland (1967), *Measuring Executive Performance.* They stated the proposition that personal effectiveness is an interrelated amalgam of functional processes. Their focus, however, was on individual performance, not organizational performance. Also writing from the perspective of improving individual performance, Kellogg (1967) described methods of encouraging employees to accept responsibility for planning and evaluating their contribution to the organizations's goals and emphasized the importance of integrating the employee into the organization.

In 1967, Nadler published a book describing a true systems approach to the problem, called IDEAL, intended to increase productivity and develop management effectiveness. In IDEAL, the idea is that the individual stands as part of a unit and his performance should be evaluated in terms of what he contributes to the unit and the organization. In their textbook *Principles of Management,* Koontz and O'Donnell (1968) shared with Sloan and Johnson (1968) the dream of an integrated and systematic approach to the challenge of managing organizational performance: "It is not possible to be precise about . . . control without, at the very least, reference to a given plan, to the personality of the manager involved, and to specific enterprise goals. . . . Planning and control are being increasingly treated as an interrelated system" (p. 694). I hope this book will be remembered as one which helped make that vision a reality.

If knotting together all the components of performance works so wonderfully, why isn't everyone doing it? Curiously, management seems reluctant to involve the entire organization in the achievement of the corporation's objectives. In one study of 366 executives, Buchholz (1977) found that the top management was not in favor of participative management structures. Managers may say they want to involve workers in improving performance, but they fail to give them enough information to participate intelligently.

> *Alone, alone, all, all alone;*
> *Alone on a wide, wide sea.* *

The executive has help available for managing corporate performance. There are many good tools and good people to assist him. He need not go it alone. Planning and controlling organizational achievement is the subject of this book. The first chapter deals with the question "Where do we want to go?"

*Rime of the Ancient Mariner.

1

Strategic Business
Planning

To avoid the mistakes of the past and realize opportunities as yet only dreamed about, the future must not be allowed to just happen; it must be crafted. Creation of an acceptable future requires vision, allocation of resources, and a willingness to work now for what is desired later. Strategic business planning assumes that the future can be shaped to the desired image of the corporation. In strategic business planning a company works today to create for itself an acceptable tomorrow.

To shape its own future, management must make choices that concern its longer-term survival. Because the successful chief executive is anticipating the future, he tries to get the right mix between return on assets today and investing in his business of tomorrow. A primary accountability of the chief executive officer is to think regularly and systematically about the future of his company.

The idea behind strategic business planning is simple. Strategic business planning is an anticipation of the future and a determined effort to shape it according to the strategy formulated by the company. The primary question in long-range planning is "What should our business be?" The answer to this question is often different from the answer to the question "What is our business?" For a few businesses, the future should be a repeat of the present. However, most businesses must evolve over time. By looking five to ten years into the future, the enterprise can identify those businesses that should be abandoned and the new and different ones that should be started.

One of the first companies to use the term *strategic business planning* to describe this look into the future was General Electric. For General Electric the ultimate purpose of strategic business planning was to identify new and different businesses for the company and the technologies and markets required.

Strategic business planning is the process of determining a company's long-term goals and designing the plans necessary to achieve them. It is a process that involves risk because it bets on what the future will be. Strategic business planning decisions must be more than intellectual. They require investing financial and human resources in tomorrow. A company that is successfully performing strategic business planning has clear, specific objectives about what its business is now and what it wants it to become. If diversification is an important part of the long-range plan, then the diversification strategy should include the role of every new business within the enterprise. Each business must have its own mission, goals, and measures of performance.

Though a conceptual, not an operational, activity, strategic business planning done badly can be fatal to the future of the corporation. The chief executive officer, as strategic business planner, tries to answer three questions: "What should our business be?" "How much business should we be doing?" "When should we be doing that business?" Strategic business planning is not model building, forecasting, or research. Although such tools are useful in aiding the strategic business planner, successful long-range planning is possible without them.

One of the first steps in a successful strategic planning process is deciding what business to quit and when to quit it. The company must also decide which of many possible new businesses it should enter. All organizations have limited resources, there being only so much money and talent that an organization can invest. Successful companies are those that do a few things well. This requires careful selection of investment opportunities and commitment of the necessary people and capital to achieve mission, profit, and growth objectives.

Of the limited resources consumed by the strategic goals

of a corporation, it is managerial talent that is usually in short-est supply. Few companies have the depth of talent that will allow major mistakes in the allocation of their best people to the pursuit of current and strategic objectives. From strategy decisions flow decisions about organizational structure and the assignment of people. By working backward from business-strategy goals, the chief executive can determine the type and number of management jobs required to achieve corporate ob-jectives as well as the characteristics and skills of the people needed to fill the jobs.

Why Plan?

Sometimes even the obvious should be asked and answered. Argenti (1969, p. 35) said, "If a company does not know what it wants, it cannot decide how to get it." Planning is the process of deciding what you want, of picking your port. In the 1950s more firms became convinced that their problems, at least some of them, were strategic problems. There was a mismatch be-tween the firm's products and the demands of the marketplace. If that was the problem, then strategic planning, it followed, was the solution. This planning process was a rational analysis of market opportunities and of the company's strengths and weaknesses and the selection of the best fit between opportuni-ties and strengths that was harmonious with the company's overall objectives. Choosing the strategy was considered the hard part, achieving it somewhat easier. But thirty years later the problem appeared more complex (Ansoff, Declerck, and Hayes, 1976).

Planning is, or should be, the first task of business. As early as 1963, Moreno wrote: "Obviously the first step in effec-tive management is the determination of the needs and goals in all the key areas and for the company as a whole. Management's continuing question should then be: 'What is it that we are try-ing to accomplish?' Once these needs and goals have been estab-lished it is up to the various responsible members of the line organization to make them tangible, giving them the proper fo-cus and direction by their actions and decisions, and up to top management to evaluate the performance and results by the application of reliable yardsticks of measurement keeping in mind the overall and long-term aims of the business" (pp. 21–22).

To the question "Why plan?," Cantley (1972) answers that planning serves three purposes: (1) to rank courses of action, (2) to serve as a yardstick for monitoring corporate performance—in other words, to provide targets—and (3) to provide a common framework of reference to ensure operational consistency—to be a control. Actually, the rhetorical question is now not often asked, for what was once an orphan has become fortune's child. Many companies plan formally and almost all plan at least informally. Size does not matter. All companies must plan (Ewing, 1972). Again quoting Moreno (1963, p. 20), "All business organizations entertain certain policies and objectives which they follow either consciously or unconsciously to assure the growth and development of the company, but greater success can be achieved where these policies are based on predetermined and well-defined objectives."

Having answered "Why plan?" and "Who plans?," it may be helpful to back up and better answer the question "What is planning?" Strategic planning is a process of deciding on the company's basic mission and objectives and on how it will choose to deploy the resources at its disposal (Steiner, 1969). And it is more.

The Essence of Planning

The words *corporate* and *strategic* have gradually replaced the word *long-range* preceding the word *planning.* Although some scholars can see differences among the three words, *corporate* and *strategic* will be used here as synonyms. *Planning* is derived from the Latin word *planum,* meaning a flat surface. As first used in English, it meant drawing on a flat surface, most often a blueprint or a map. To plan, then, was to capture on paper the essence of a thing and to use that essence in building reality from image; or, in travel, to find one's way about the real physical world from a figurative representation of it. *Strategy* is also a word of classical origins, coming into English from the Greek *strategos,* which meant general. *Strategy* meant the art of the general.

So much for etymology. What *is* corporate strategy? First the simple, from a vice-president of The Boston Consulting Group: "A strategy is a set of goals and major policies. The definition is as simple as that" (Tilles, 1963, p. 49). Now the serpentine, from America's foremost management consultant: "[Planning is] the continuous process of making *present entrepreneurial (risk-taking) decisions* systematically and with the best possible knowledge of their futurity, organizing systematically the efforts needed to carry out those decisions, and measuring the results of those decisions against the expectations through *organized,* systematic feedback" (Drucker, 1972, p. 6).

If that is what planning is, how well are we doing it? Not too well, apparently. At the first International Conference on Strategic Management, held in 1973, Ansoff, Declerck, and Hayes (1976, p. 39) said, "Today only a handful of leading firms employ genuine strategic planning to manage their forward thrusts. A majority still employ the simpler and earlier long-range planning techniques based on extrapolation of the past and lacking the systematic generation and analysis of alternatives required in strategic planning."

In the experience of the author, writing a decade later and having worked personally with hundreds of organizations, this is still pretty much the current state of affairs. Some of the very largest companies have small but established planning departments. Others use an executive who is being permitted to retire on the job by puttering about on special assignments in corporate planning. A few more have someone accountable for acquisitions or new-product planning, which is euphemistically called "corporate strategy." A good number hire a consultant who does a corporate strategy study, and does it well, but this is then promptly filed and forgotten a few months after the consultant last snapped his briefcase shut. For most, corporate planning is a sometime activity of the chief executive officer musing on the freeway or in an airplane.

Good Plans

A corporate plan need not be fuzzy. There are criteria for good plans against which a company can evaluate its own to see how it is doing. Good plans are internally consistent and are consistent with the environment. They are appropriate given the company's current and readily accessible resources. The risk in the plan is satisfactory, neither too little nor too much. Time spans are appropriate. The plan feels workable (Tilles, 1963).

There are also logical steps in the planning sequence. Skipping a step will usually weaken a corporate plan. First, determine the overall objective. This amounts to asking why the company is in business anyway. The second step is to decide how much profit is required, including specific profit targets for competent, commendable, and distinguished performance. Third, prepare a forecast and estimate the probable error. Fourth, identify who needs to do what and the possible constraints that could hinder plan achievement. Fifth, write it all up in a formal plan. Last, implement the plan and monitor performance (Argenti, 1969).

What, precisely, does one plan? Here is a limited list: (1) optimal profits, (2) survival-level profits, (3) ownership, (4) size, (5) market position, (6) management succession, (7) public responsibility.

Steiner (1969) surveyed 250 chief executive officers who told him that the following were the ten strategic factors they believed were the most important for managing corporate performance: (1) raising low-cost short-term working capital, (2) raising low-cost long-term debt, (3) raising low-cost equity participation, (4) financing diversification by acquisition, (5) attracting and maintaining high-quality top management, (6) improving present products, (7) motivating a managerial drive for profits, (8) improving service to customers, (9) improving executive thinking (judgment and creativity), (10) establishing better personnel relations.

Since almost all companies want and need to grow, any corporate plan needs a section that addresses growth. There are four possible growth vectors (Litschert, 1972). Some companies need emphasize only one; others need to pursue all four. Put neatly, growth comes either from marketing or from product development. Marketing growth means selling more of what you have where you are. That's one vector. The second is to sell your product where you currently are not. To maximize this type of growth, you obtain the maximum share of each market you are in, and you expand geographically. A company doing business regionally would next try national sales and then become international. In some businesses there is an advantage to having a local presence. You save transportation costs, you can respond more quickly to customers and prospects, and so on. Of course, there are disadvantages too. Multiple locations are harder to control, overhead increases. The situation is similar for companies seeking growth through international expansion. Operating in a country other than your own is enormously more difficult than establishing yourself nationally. Not only are control and expense problems multipled severalfold, there are different cultures and laws with which to contend. Nonetheless, market growth is still easier than growth through product development or diversification.

In product development growth, current products are refined and improved, and new products in the same line are created and brought into the same market. One goes from chocolate, vanilla, and strawberry to thirty-one flavors; or one offers ribs and chicken instead of just chicken. Although this is somewhat risky—customers may prefer someone else's ribs, or your sale of higher-margined chicken may drop as total sales remain unchanged—the idea is that you stick with products or services that are more similar than different.

With growth through acquisition you change your mix dramatically. You offer ribs, chicken, and bicycles; or ribs, chicken, and bath towels. Occasionally you combine them within one unit, but more often you keep them apart. And nine times out of ten you will fail in the bicycle business because you got in too late, you didn't understand the business, the management of the acquired company was poor—but most often because your success in one business works against you in the other. Your image in the public's eye is that of a leader in *consumable* consumer goods, not *durables.*

So the safest growth strategy is: Sell more, sell in more places, sell similar products, and finally sell different products. Risk increases in that order. If your environment is characterized by rapid change, then a product development strategy is best. If the environment is stable, then the preferred strategy is one that is marketing-oriented. Bigger companies tend to need research strategies, and companies with research strategies usually require a complex planning process.

Good corporate plans, it can be seen, are realistic, complementing current corporate resources. At the same time, they are sufficiently aggressive to inspire and motivate investors and employees. They are specific enough to permit conversion into working capital and debt/equity requirements. Good plans are ubiquitous, covering the whole enterprise—all functions and strategic business units. Like anything worth doing with a hope of permanence, they require occasional looking after—review and modification. If conditions require it, a plan should dissolve if you need it to, giving way to new plans. Finally, a good plan is susceptible to measurement. These suggestions are Moreno's (1963).

What should a good plan not be? A good plan is broad rather than narrow, deals in major issues, not minor points, is more qualitative than quantitative, is more strategic than tactical. A good plan is written. It is formal. It is both rational and intuitive, it is flexible, and, not last, it makes good economic sense (Steiner, 1969).

Bad Plans

If the preceding are planning's virtues, consider its capital sins. Bad corporate plans are stamped "top management" only and are not made practical for the rest of management. They are viewed as a fad, not an integral part of the business. They are more fantasy than possibility, so vague as to defy quantification (Dowd, 1972).

Some mistakes are common in the corporate planning process (Steiner, 1969). Perhaps the greatest sinner is the chief executive officer who completely delegates the responsibility for planning or who does not believe in planning because the company is currently successful. Lesser (venial) sins include overemphasizing numbers, trying to be too precise, and undervaluing intuitive judgment. Trying to give all parts of the plan equal weight is futile but not potentially fatal, as is the practice of extrapolating the future rather than thinking it through. Like fancy underwear, a plan should be used, not merely kept in a drawer, and, of course, needs changing from time to time.

Hierarchy of Business Strategies

An organized approach to strategic business planning requires a systematic analysis of the present and the future. Several such systems are available, and it is not particularly critical which of these conceptual frameworks the CEO chooses to support his corporate strategy. What is important is that thinking about the future proceed methodically, that the future be directed rather than haphazard.

One systematic way of doing long-range planning looks at the total business strategy of an organization at three levels: enterprise strategy, corporate strategy, and product and market strategy.

Enterprise Strategy. Enterprise strategy is typically the responsibility of the chief executive officer. It is the development of a defined theme that places the total business in the proper relationship with its multiple environments. Enterprise strategy means charting the shape and direction of the total enterprise while anticipating fundamental changes in the economies and politics of the world in which the business will operate.

Enterprise strategy is the entrepreneurial vision of the chief executive officer, his values and aspirations, his leadership and style. The time frame of enterprise strategy is long, at least five to ten years into the future, sometimes longer. Enterprise strategy focuses on the determination of what kind of enterprise the company is to be and what fundamental changes are required in the business to achieve that result. Of necessity, the perspective must be broad—the nature of business generally and of the society in which the particular business operates. Enterprise strategy includes thinking about the company's social responsibility, the kind of image the corporation should have, and the kind of internal climate it wants for its employees. More than anything, enterprise strategy is a vision, a dream, a sense of what you want to be rather than what you are.

Few companies, especially larger ones, excel at enterprise strategy. Of all the forms of planning, enterprise strategy requires the most imagination, daring, and enthusiasm. Small companies are successful enterprise strategists, particularly those still run by their founders. It is their faith in themselves and the future that gives them their vitality and excitement. Companies need enterprise strategy to generate excitement, commitment, and a continual striving for excellence. History abounds with examples of whole nations willing to die for a dream, but there are few cases of people willing to die for compounded increases in earnings per share. Enterprise strategy is the company's religion. The chief executive officer, as enterprise strategist, is the prophet leading his people to the promised land.

A company's enterprise strategy is an extension of the personal values and interests of the person at the top. Those values might be prestige, profit, or preference for type of business. One company in the semiconductor business had an enterprise strategy that amounted to its "nine commandments." The first commandment was to always be ethical, giving fair, honest, and full value to customers. The second was to make low-cost, high-volume products—which led the company to the third, which was to emphasize return on investment (ROI) as the main measure of success. The fourth commandment was to stay in the top five companies in sales in that industry by following the fifth commandment—"Research and Development shall produce at least one new salable product each year." The sixth, seventh, and eighth were marketing imperatives: be international, participate in both the military and the commercial markets, and sell on a contract basis. The ninth and final commandment was to provide employees with a satisfying place to work (Branch, 1962). The foundation of this company's strategy was that conducting a scrupulously ethical business would give it a competitive edge to build on. With the exception of the

ROI measure of profitability and the mandate to enjoy one's work, this company was one whose concept of enterprise was a philosophy of marketing.

According to McDonald (1964), Sears Roebuck made about ten major strategic decisions over a fifty-year period. The first was top management's decision to add retail stores to the catalogue business. The second was the decision to centralize merchandising. Having goods made to Sears's own quality specifications had a major impact, as did its aggressive geographical expansion after World War II. In the mid 1950s a strategic choice was to expand into soft-goods lines. The sixth key choice was to emphasize style and fashion over economy. This was a poor choice, which the company later reversed. A better decision was to set up a service organization to support the sale of durable goods even if the business had to be run at break-even. It is too soon to know whether the diversification into financial services or the decision to invest in supplies corporations was a good idea. Only time will enable us to determine the accuracy of management's judgment.

Corporate Strategy. Most organizations, when speaking of business strategy, mean corporate strategy. This is the part of the total planning process devoted to developing a portfolio approach for the existing business units of the enterprise. The CEO is almost always involved in corporate strategy, and other members of top management, such as the chief operating officer and group executives, may also participate. The perspective of the corporate strategist is more narrow than that of the enterprise strategist but broader than those of people concerned with product and market strategy. The corporate strategist focuses on industry sectors and expected economic conditions. He makes decisions on resource allocation among existing operating units and recommends new businesses in which to invest. The chief executive officer, as corporate strategist, is a business portfolio manager. He examines the existing yield from his various investments, sells or folds his losers, and gives his winning units more resources. The time horizon of the corporate strategist is intermediate. He plans three to five years ahead and reviews overall operating results annually.

When the chief executive engages in corporate strategic thinking, the focus is multifaceted, but the image is still singular. Comparable data permit historical performance comparisons, and economic forecasts can be used to project the demographics of the future. Corporate strategic decisions, while complex, are still relatively cold-blooded. Model building, statistical analysis, and numerical decisions are all possible.

Product and Market Strategy. The focus of business strategy thinking is clearest at the product and market level. The thinking challenge is analytical. Voluminous numerical data are available to guide decisions, and the wisdom of alternative choices is quickly ascertained.

Product and market strategists think mostly about today and a little bit about tomorrow. They are concerned with understanding how to compete in the corporation's marketplaces. Their perspective is markets and competitors, and their primary goal is to position the business within the market and against competition. Profit and growth are monitored quarterly, and immediate corrective action is taken. Planned results are usually expected within a year. Product and market strategic thinking can and should take place at many levels within the enterprise. Any executive with profit-and-loss accountability necessarily concerns himself with how effective his product is in the marketplace.

A company's product and market strategy is determined mainly by the attractiveness of the market and the competitive strength of the corporation. There are many characteristics that make a market attractive, including the sales growth and profitability of the industry and its pricing structure. Because government has become such an important variable in business, the regulatory climate and the social and legislative environment for that market must also be taken into consideration.

The level of opportunity for a particular product or service depends on its competitive strength. Many factors make up

competitive strength. Among them are intangibles such as corporate image, product quality, and the managerial depth of the
organization behind the product. Other variables that are part
of comparative strength are market share, price, the distribution
network, and operating expenses.

Business Strategy Selection. A popular systematic device for
strategic business planning is to use a matrix to aid in allocating
capital resources to business units. By displaying strategic planning factors along the X and Y axes, the strategist can determine where in an overall field the corporation currently stands
(see Tables 1, 2, and 3).

For example, it is possible to characterize a corporation
by the stage of its market development. Typically, a corporation goes through a sales cycle that takes the company from
emerging to developing to maturity and finally to decline and
liquidation. Another matrix uses the variables of competitive
strength and market attractiveness to make product and service
decisions. Here competitive strength is placed along the Y
(vertical) axis, and market attractiveness is the X (horizontal)
axis.

When both competitive strength and market attractiveness are high, the chief executive should elect to invest in the
business and to seek growth. An investment-and-growth strategy
means a determined effort to improve market share by expand-
ing the sales force and distribution system, by developing new
products for the market, and by increasing manufacturing capacity.

An earn-and-protect strategy is best when both the competitive strength of the product or service and the attractiveness
of the market are moderate. Here the CEO is not trying to score
major gains or to achieve above-average returns on her investment. Instead, she is satisfied to earn a predictable return on investment and to protect her current market share. She optimizes
her margins by increasing operating efficiency and reducing the
cost of goods produced. Typically, market share is protected
through segmentation and differentiation and positioning of

Table 1. Business Assessment Matrix.

	Stage of Market Development			
	Emerging	*Developing*	*Mature*	*Liquidating*
Growth Potential	Extremely high	High	Average for all businesses	None
Industry Structure				
• Size tendency	Small	Small to medium	Large	Large
• Number of firms and trend	Small but increasing rapidly	Many but mergers and casualties occurring	Moderate and stable	Moderate and declining
Product-Market Characteristics				
• Price structure	Low price elasticity	Some price elasticity	High price elasticity	Very high price elasticity
• Demand structure	Small, homogeneous customer base	Expanding buyer segments	Highly segmented demand	Saturated demand
• Product characteristic	High differentiation	Moderate differentiation	Limited differentiation	Commodity
Financial Characteristics				
• Typical profitability	Negative to low	Low to moderate	Moderate to high	Declining
• Cash-generating capability	None	Modest	Excellent	Declining
Technological Availability	Limited possession of proprietary know-how	Expanding base	Public knowledge	Practical know-how

Table 2. Organization Assessment Matrix: Climate and Process.

	Stage of Market Development			
	Emerging	*Developing*	*Mature*	*Liquidating*
Delegation • Freedom to act • Risk • Innovation • Conflict openness • Support	Limited delegation by strong leadership; variety of schemes are possible	Highest degree of delegation and freedom supported	Delegative to controlled; flexibility in meeting fixed goals	Very limited delegation and freedom
Decision Making • Information • Clear goals	Formalized goals virtually nonexistent Information limited	More information for decisions General goals exist	Information-based decisions High degree of clarity	Rigid goals Control information
Planning and Control Systems	Informal, highly qualitative (milestone-oriented)	Capable of setting broad goals and measuring results (program-oriented)	Supportive of careful goal setting and control (P&L-oriented)	Deemphasize long-term planning; quantitative controls (balance-sheet-oriented)
Responsiveness to External Conditions	Limited responsiveness at first; focus on establishing a position	Highly responsive; adapt to market opportunities	Less responsiveness required because of decreasing rate of change in markets	Responsive but under very limited conditions
Integration and Differentiation	High degree of differentiation Integration at top	Decreasing differentiation Integrative function becoming more "local" to markets, products	Continuing decrease in differentiation Integration "local"	Low differentiation Integration at the top (corporate)

Table 3. Organization Assessment Matrix: People.

	Stage of Market Development			
	Emerging	Developing	Mature	Liquidating
Leadership	Entrepreneur, strong leader	Entrepreneur/business manager	Sophisticated manager	Administrator
Motivations	Venturesome; accepts unaccustomed risks	Venturesome to conservative; accepts accustomed and unaccustomed risks	Primarily conservative; generally risk-adverse	Conservative, risk-adverse
Reward Management	High base compensation to attract people; discretionary bonus	High levels related to job; incentives for building results	More average levels related to job; incentives for results above high goal	Average level; incentives for cost control
Know-how Development	Know-how depth important near top; development needed to support expected expansion	Ever-broadening scope and increasing numbers of managers required	Development needs and know-how becoming specialized, static	Specialized depth and scope of know-how

existing products. The goal is to do the best one can with existing resources and to allocate limited resources to business ventures with more promise.

Not all the company's products will be strong, nor will they all be in attractive markets. In some of its businesses, the corporation will find itself faced with a low product strength and low market attractiveness. Here the most successful strategy is to harvest and divest. Existing profit margins must be protected by holding prices where possible and increasing operating efficiency. A declining market share is acceptable as long as profit margins are maintained. When the market is saturated or shrinking, ruthlessly prune marginal product lines. Resources freed as a result are committed to invest-and-grow situations. The management skills required of the successful harvest-and-divest manager are much different from those of earn-and-protect or invest-and-grow managers.

In summary, the total strategic business planning cycle of a company has three parts. Where both market strength and product strength are high, the corporation should invest available resources and aim for growth of the business in order to strengthen its profitable position. Where product strength and market attractiveness are moderate, the right strategy is to earn income and to protect market position. Finally, low-attraction markets should be harvested for maximum profits and eventually be sold off.

The strategic business plan is the navigation plan, the ship's log of the enterprise. It lays out where the organization is going, how quickly it intends to get there, and what style it intends to maintain during the journey. Strategic business plans should also indicate why the voyage is being made and what it will accomplish. The fact that a plan has been filed does not mean the chief executive officer loses the right to change direction. But an overall plan is important if the enterprise is to contribute meaningfully to the quality of life and the economy of the nation under whose flag it sails and if it is to provide exciting and useful work for the individuals who commit themselves to serving on board.

CASE STUDY
Caro Products, Inc.

This case study illustrates the hierarchy of corporate strategy: enterprise, corporate, and product. The three situations were quite different. In Menswear an earn-and-protect strategy made most sense. Outerwear was going nowhere, and a harvest-and-divest posture was best. Sportswear was Caro's growth opportunity, the only business worth investing in.

The top management of Caro Products took a portfolio approach to business strategy (Haspeslagh, 1982). In this method of planning each strategic business unit (SBU) is considered according to the attractiveness of its products and markets. Resources are then allocated according to the SBU's position on the grid, or matrix (Table 1). Using this rationale, Caro executives decided to invest in Sportswear, gradually liquidate Outerwear, and maintain the status quo in Menswear. This was the combination of strategies that would maximize cash flow over a three- to five-year period.

Caro Products, Inc., was founded in 1919 as a manufacturer of bar soaps. The founder was John Boerhaave, the son of a Dutch chemist, Herman Boerhaave. Herman had immigrated to the United States in 1880, joined du Pont, and eventually reached an upper-level management position with the company. He sent his son John, his youngest, to Cornell University, where the boy rowed crew and also studied a little chemistry. After graduating from Cornell with three varsity letters, a C average, and a spattering of chemical knowledge, John went to work for du Pont in a job procured for him by his father.

After four years of learning the chemical business, John was staked by his father to $3,000 and a one-way railroad ticket to Philadelphia. The young man had decided to move there because of the rowing clubs that, every weekend, competed up and down the Schuylkill River. His father had advised him that bar soap was a highly profitable and chemically simple product with an unlimited future. John rented a small plant in Camden, idle because of a drop in demand for horse liniment. He converted the production equipment to the manufature of hand soap. Weekdays he was a capitalist. Weekends he was third oar in the fastest shell on the East Coast.

Over the next forty years Caro Products expanded its line to include detergents, fabric softeners, industrial cleaners, and solvents. From 1960 to 1970 it diversified into processed foods and soft drinks. Then, between 1975 and 1978, the company acquired three companies in the apparel industry: Menswear, Inc., Outerwear, Inc., and Sportswear, Inc. By 1979 Caro Products had a sales volume of $1.5 billion and a net after-tax income of $75 million. The Boerhaave family, through various trusts, owned less than 5 percent of the company stock, which was selling at a modest 6 times earnings. The grandsons of John Boerhaave still lettered in crew for Cornell.

Overall Corporate Strategy

The chief executive officer of Caro Products had established as part of his overall corporate strategy the goal of building a mix of businesses that would provide at least 14 percent return on equity and sustained growth in earnings per share. The overall strategic direction of the company was to build on the basic strengths of the organization and its consumer products. The five-year growth plan emphasized internal growth at a real rate of 6 percent per year rather than additional growth through acquisitions.

Overall Organizational Structure

The organizational structure of the corporation was decentralized. Corporate staff positions provided overall policy and advice to operating groups and subsidiaries. Group vice-presidents for food products and cleaning products headed businesses of $600 million and $700 million. Annual sales for Menswear, Outerwear, and Sportswear were $82 million, $33 million, and $75 million. A decision had been made to create a new position of group vice-president for the clothing business, and a search was being conducted outside the organization to identify the executive who could best fill this job.

Menswear, Inc.

The Menswear division manufactured and distributed medium-priced men's tailored suits and sportcoats. These were distributed through department and specialty stores to American males in all age groups whose dominant buying motive was to buy acceptable quality at moderate prices. Over the past five years, the division's average sales growth was 10 percent per year, its average return on equity 13.5 percent per year, and its average unit sales growth 2 percent. The medium-priced men's-wear market was expected to grow at 8 to 10 percent per year. The best market opportunity was in the popular-priced suit market, which was expected to grow at 17 percent per year.

The strength of the division was its modern, integrated, and highly engineered manufacturing facilities. The division also had depth in merchandising know-how and two labels with high market identity accounting for 75 percent of its overall operating volume. The major problems of the division were the potential obsolescence of its current labels, the threat of imports, and a need to reduce costs to maintain competitive prices.

The Menswear division was a ho-hum business—medium market strength, medium competitive strength. The best strategy was to earn and protect, with some additional allocation of resources for the more attractive segments of the market. This could be accomplished by (1) increasing market share of existing products through lower production costs and more aggressive marketing strategies, (2) developing new businesses in the lower-priced products, and (3) reducing cost of goods produced.

Outerwear, Inc.

The Outerwear division was a $33 million company manufacturing and distributing men's high-quality overcoats, raincoats, and jackets. The distribution network consisted of department stores and selected specialty stores. The primary customers were fashion-conscious men in the upper income bracket. Over the past five years, the division had a 10.9 percent return on equity, an average sales growth of 1.6 percent, and an average unit sales decline of −3.6 percent.

The higher-priced market for quality men's outerwear had been dropping 3–4 percent per year. It was progressively harder to demonstrate a quality difference between the company's coats and those of its competitors. Some opportunity for growth existed in the women's market if the company was willing to use its name and reputation without major capital outlays for equipment conversion.

The division's strength was a reputation for quality, for service, and for strong relationships with distributors. The major weaknesses of the Outerwear division were its high labor costs, low productivity, and low utilization of existing capacity.

This was a harvest-and-divest business. The company's products had moderate competitive strength, and its marketplace attractiveness was low. A sensible strategy for this division was to (1) reduce costs through the use of more automated equipment, (2) prune low-margin, low-volume product lines and squeeze profits from higher-volume lines, and (3) resist allocation of additional resources to the division, with the exception of possible entrance into women's wear through licensee agreements using the corporation's name and labels.

Sportswear, Inc.

The Sportswear division of the apparel group of Caro Products was a $79 million business whose average return on equity was 7.9 percent. Average sales growth was 15.3 percent and average unit sales growth 7.5 percent. This division manufactured and distributed four product lines, which were priced above average for sportswear. The product lines were jogging, golf, tennis, and ski clothing. Distribution was through department stores and selected specialty stores to high-fashion, quality-conscious men and women.

The active-sportswear market was the fastest-growing segment of the apparel industry, with overall market growth expected to average 15 percent over the next five years. Competition was strong from large, established corporations as well as from small casual-clothing manufacturers eager to enter the market.

This division's strengths were (1) quality products with strong consumer brand identification, (2) aggressive, knowledgeable salespeople, and (3) substantial market share in a rapidly growing segment of the apparel industry. The major weaknesses of the division were (1) low productivity and technical capability and (2) high administrative overhead.

This was an invest-and-grow business with high market attractiveness and moderate current corporate product strength. A good strategy recommended for this division was to (1) increase existing market share, (2) invest in new products for boating and sailing wear, (3) invest in new products for country and western casual wear, and (4) reduce cost of goods produced and increase return on investment through the introduction of new automated equipment.

Conclusions

What are some of the points about strategic business planning that the Caro Products case brings out? Had the company answered the questions that needed to be asked in the beginning of the planning process: "What business should we be in?" "How much business should we be doing and by when?" Although the organization was much different from the bar-soap company founded by the young oarsman from Cornell, it was still a consumer products company. The product mix had shifted from consumables to semidurables, but the strategy adopted for the clothing group said that the company was still in business to provide consumers with the basic necessities of life.

Caro Products had taken some of the steps essential in developing an overall corporate strategy. The answer to the question "How much profit?" was 14 percent. To the question "How much growth?" the company had decided 6 percent per year and from internal development. These are not the simple numbers they may appear to be; they have the kind of complex consequences that Cantley (1972) describes.

The company was weak in the area of enterprise strategy. This was to be expected because it was a multigroup and multidivisional organization where the chief operating officer was a woman with a strong financial background who really believed in the portfolio-of-strategic-business-units approach to management. She had risen rapidly through the ranks by running things by the numbers and was known for her ability to cut her losses and invest in winners. Her yields were always the best in the company. Nor was the CEO especially imaginative. So the company's strategic plan seemed a cold-blooded and rather dull exercise, correct in concept but uninteresting.

No one could quarrel with the decision to quietly and gradually liquidate Outerwear. The division did not meet the strategy goal of 14 percent ROE profit and 6 percent growth, nor was it ever likely to. A matrix approach to planning said that this was a moderate/low business, and so only a sentimentalist would invest in the product lines. Still, it seemed a shame to squeeze the business, because it was the group's highest-quality line. The problem was that although there would always be a small market for very high-quality men's wear, the buying public did not see Caro in that light.

Sportswear represented a real opportunity. Although profitability at 7.9 percent was well below what was wanted, management correctly decided to invest in the business. Market attractiveness was quite high, and the company had a fairly strong position in the market. Here the challenges were investing the right amount of money in the right lines at the right time. Because the market was so attractive, Caro knew that eventually it could expect overcapacity, price cutting, and a consolidation of companies in the market. It had to get strong enough fast enough to be sure it could take advantage of this expected cycle and survive beyond it.

The Menswear division was like most businesses—not so bad you should quit, but certainly not one with excellent prospects. The best strategy here was to mind the store and not to change much except to set goals to improve current profit, sales, and production performance. The future here was simply more of the same, but better.

2

The Organization's Image

Corporate image, the impression of a company held by its various publics, is one of the more subjective aspects of an organization's performance. That image often is based not on experience but on stereotype, hearsay, and preconception.

Despite these problems, corporate image is important because people act on impressions, whether accurate or not, and both external publics and employees are affected by image. The chief executive must deal with three elements of image: how his company is perceived, what the image should be, and how to get there. Unless a true and consistent image is developed, a company will be constrained in reaching its potential. Managing the corporation means managing its image.

Image Communications

Although the sources of corporate image are often vague, it is possible to measure a company's current image among its several publics. The resulting information allows the company to construct communications programs that provide specific plans for achieving the company's image goals.

Care must be exercised in choosing a desirable image and deciding how much corporate communications can reasonably be expected to achieve in any given time period. The ability to favorably affect image varies by type of public and requires a different emphasis for each. Successful image management will have three positive outcomes: strengthening positive attitudes where they already exist, changing neutral or negative attitudes to positive ones, and changing the frame of reference in which the company is viewed so that opposition is reduced and support is increased.

Image Analysis

The first step in image management is to determine what impressions, positive and negative, correct and incorrect, each public has about the company. With this information, the organization can prepare a comprehensive plan for its communications activities to fulfill specific goals. The determination of current image will serve as a baseline to assess how completely image-change goals have been achieved.

In surveying current image, specific questions should be asked:

- *Awareness and knowledgeability.* How aware are the publics of the company and its activities? How correct is their knowledge? How do the publics vary in their interest in gaining more information?
- *Involvement.* What role does the company play in the mind of each public? How does its image vary based on the dealings each public has with the company?
- *Competition.* For each public, what other companies are seen as the company's competition? What are the perceived strengths and weaknesses of the company when viewed against its competition?
- *Evaluative criteria.* What criteria does each public use in reaching its judgments about the company versus competition? What is the relative importance of these criteria? Have these criteria changed in the past? Are they likely to change in the future?
- *Credibility of sources.* Which sources of information are like-

ly to be most credible for each public? Do they vary by message content?

- *Expectations about the future.* What are the public's expectations about the future of the company's industry and about the company's relation to the economy and to important social issues?

Beyond these questions, which apply to every public, there are questions unique to each public being studied. Although the publics appropriate to the study of a given company differ, the following list is representative:

- *Internal management.* How does the company's management view itself? How would it prefer to be seen?
- *Customers.* What is the customers' image of the company? How can it be improved?
- *General public in local communities.* In local areas, how aware is the public of the company's presence? What is its image there?
- *Media.* How do the media influence the image of the company? To what extent is their knowledge of the company accurate? How much knowledge do they have?
- *Competition.* What is the company's image among its competitors?
- *Financial community.* What is the financial community's view of the company's growth potential and its understanding of the company's current financial condition?
- *Regulatory agencies.* What perception of the company is held by those who establish the regulations under which the company operates?
- *Educators.* What are the impressions of the company held by academia?
- *Intellectual leadership.* Are writers and speakers who have influence with the public knowledgeable about the company? What are their opinions of it?

The variety of these objectives emphasizes the need for companies to develop comprehensive, cohesive themes for their communications programs.

Formulating a Corporate Image Strategy

The chief executive officer should assign responsibility for determining current image to his own internal communications specialists or to an outside agent. To determine current image and formulate an image strategy, it helps to start with some research.

Such research usually begins with interviews with company management to develop issues that should be explored with external publics. The interviewing is done in two steps—personal interviews with a selected group of executives and a specially designed questionnaire to be completed by the remaining executives.

Interviewing strategies are then developed for each particular public, usually telephone interviews but often some in-person interviews with representatives of certain publics. For example, sampling of the general public might consist of a certain number of telephone interviews analyzed by age, sex, and other characteristics, while the study of the business community might involve personal interviews conducted with top managers of a select number of the largest companies in the same communities as the company being researched.

The measurement of corporate image often reveals that a range of opinions about the company is held by various publics. By untangling the themes underlying the opinions, the study enables a company to work to correct misconceptions and to clarify its image of itself.

Measuring Change in Corporate Image

Part of the challenge in managing change is determining whether the desired change has actually occurred. It is the review step in the managerial sequence of plan, organize, execute, and review. Detecting change in image is difficult because corporate image is a soft concept that resists quantification. Change here must, at times, be operationalized as the presence or absence of an impression or event. Scalar measures are too hard to construct.

More Inquiries. Changing the corporation's image to one that is more desirable in the public's eye should result in more inquiries from the public about the company's services. This is probably one of the more direct and easier-to-detect indexes of change.

Increased Awareness, Changed Perceptions. As image changes, a company should be able to detect shifts in perception in the public. At time A, the public thought X; now, at time B, public sentiment is Z. Not only should perceptions change positively in content, they should also change in intensity.

Favorable Publicity. References to the company by word of mouth and in the media should become progressively more favorable as image changes for the better. Adverse publicity, when it occurs, should have a less negative effect and a briefer impact.

Easier Recruiting. Good people want to be teammates on a winning crew, and even rats leave a sinking ship. A successful company with a good image should have an easier time finding competent recruits and should be better able to persuade them to join the organization.

Lower Turnover. Together with easier recruiting, the company should experience lower turnover. As the company's image improves, so does internal climate. Employees feel better about the organization and their place in it. Although the relationship is indirect, improved image aids in employee retention.

Executives Quoted Topically. As the organization develops a more favorable image locally, its senior executives will be sought out as spokespersons on various topical issues. This will be due partly to the company's own efforts to cultivate the media but partly, also, to the company's positive image.

Technicians Quoted Technically. Finally, if the company is successful in constructing a better image for itself in its industry, its specialists should be sought out to report on technical developments specific to the company's business. In the public's mind, technical excellence is identified with a positive organizational image.

CASE STUDY
The Lunada Bay Bancorporation

The Lunada Bay Bancorporation is the seventeenth largest multibank financial holding corporation in the United States. It can trace its origins to the original Rancho Palos Verdes, to the days of whalers and cattle ranchers portrayed by Richard Henry Dana in *Two Years Before the Mast*. The original Lunada Bay Merchant's and Seaman's Bank was organized in 1849 in Lunada Bay, California, and has grown to an international financial organization of over $20 billion in assets. The company's principal business is commercial lending, although as a holding company it also has substantial operating subsidiaries engaged in mortgage lending, consumer finance, leasing, insurance (primarily credit insurance), and data processing.

The bank occupies a unique position in U.S. banking. It owns thirteen member banks located in nine Western states. Additionally, it is a major international bank with over half its assets overseas and 45 percent of its profits derived from foreign operations. It conducts its international business from regional centers in London, Frankfurt, Paris, Milan, and Hong Kong. The Bancorporation is commonly perceived as a commercial bank with a substantial international capability. Its deposits have been growing at a rate of 18 percent per year over the last five years, and it has returned .80 on average assets over the same period.

The Bancorporation's chief executive officer was Pero Nazarko, a fifty-one-year-old chairman with twenty years of corporate experience, primarily in commercial lending. Traditionally the Bancorporation had avoided publicity, preferring not to have a highly visible public image. But now the chairman was convinced that for the corporation to continue its success into the 1980s and 1990s, it must broaden its image and reduce its reliance on commercial lending. He commissioned a study of the Lunada Bay Bancorporation's public image to develop a strategy that would properly position his company.

Mandate

The Bancorporation needed to answer three questions about its corporate image: (1) "What is it?" (2) "What should it be?" (3) "How can it get there?"

The question "Who is the bank?" gets at the issue of the Bancorporation's current image. How is the corporation seen currently by its publics? What the corporation should be depends on obtaining information about the future of banking. It depends, too, on vision, the image the corporation's policy makers want it to have. After identifying the current and desired images, a commitment to action is necessary to close the gap between actual and ideal.

As is true for all corporations, the public image of Lunada Bay Bancorporation was multifaceted. The corporation's advertising emphasis was on its founding date, its size, and its commercial-bank relationships. It intentionally fostered the image of a solemn, sober businessperson's bank, the type of place where John D. Rockefeller would have gone for a loan.

An organization's image comes partly from the communications pieces it produces—annual reports, news releases, and so on. It is made up, too, of people's opinions of it. These opinions are based on direct experience, on word of mouth, and on how the organization performs against its promises. The factors that constituted Lunada Bay's current image included direct experience, written communications, informal talk, and promise versus performance.

There were several sources of data about image, summarized in Table 4. One source was interviews conducted with the company's officers, primarily a few senior executives who represented major business units and geographical locales. These interviews were semistructured in format. The same questions were asked of each officer, but interviewees were encouraged to

Table 4. Survey Data Base.

Where	What	Who
United States	Lunada Bay–Sierra Pacific Mortgage	Residential and commercial brokers
United States	Corporation	Lunada Bay officers
United Kingdom	Northern Europe operations	Customers
Hong Kong	Asia Pacific operations	Customers and targeted prospects
United States	U.S. operations	*Fortune* 1,000 chief financial officers

respond freely and to add any additional observations they believed to be useful. The company's mortgage corporation supplied more information through an extensive third-party telephone survey of major residential and commercial real estate brokers to determine their perceptions of the mortgage banking company.

A survey was also made of the corporation's operations in Hong Kong. A questionnaire was mailed to current customers of the Bancorporation as well as targeted prospects throughout the Pacific Rim area from Japan to China, the Philippines, Indonesia, Malaysia, and on down to Australia. Lunada Bay's Northern European operations, headquartered in London, conducted their own survey of active clients, using questionnaires and interviews.

The largest group surveyed was Lunada Bay's U.S. banking operations. The chief financial officers of the top 1,000 U.S. corporations (as identified by *Fortune* magazine) were sent a questionnaire on the current image of Lunada Bay versus its competitors and were asked what characteristics they felt to be critical to banking in the last two decades of the twentieth century.

Survey Results

The survey of chief financial officers showed that the company was the third-preferred commercial bank. The Golden State

Bancorporation was most preferred, 29.1 percent choosing it as the bank they would like to deal with. Sepulveda National Bank was second choice, preferred by 23.6 percent. Lunada Bay was chosen by 19.6 percent of respondents. The remainder of the preferences were scattered among a dozen other banks.

The survey results were puzzling. Lunada Bay was the bancorporation most widely used by the companies surveyed. This finding could be attributed in part to its size and its age, factors that gave it the largest market share. It could also be due to the bank's status. Although Lunada Bay was not the highest-status commercial bank (a few smaller East Coast banks that dealt primarily with blue-chip, old-money companies had more status), it had a high-prestige image. The disturbing finding was that it was ranked only third in preference.

The reasons for this poor showing were subtle. Lunada Bay's commercial lending officers were viewed by corporate financial officers as technicians first and businesspeople second. They were thought to be overly dependent on a technique Lunada Bay had for determining a company's line of credit. The size of the loan, the compensating balances, and the other loan terms were derived from a classical model of merchant lending the bank had developed years before. Corporate treasurers would seek out the loan officers of other banks who were believed to be more creative and flexible in financing their companies' needs.

Senior management at Lunada Bay, however, suspected that if the survey had queried the chief executive officers of the *Fortune* 1,000 rather than the financial officers, the results would have been more favorable. A loan from Lunada Bay was testimony to a company's financial soundness. Lunada Bay was fussy about whom it lent money to and was quick to intervene in situations it thought had the potential to deteriorate. A member of the board of directors of a company felt a sense of assurance when the company's bank loans were with Lunada Bay. It was a vote of confidence in the company's corporate financial structure and in its management.

Overall, Lunada Bay's image among financial officers was neutral to slightly negative. Besides its conservative approach to granting loans, the bank was seen as slow in processing the inevitable paperwork required in lending and as inconveniencing its customers by missing deadlines. Fees were judged about right, and the bank's technical expertise was viewed as a plus. Pero Nazarko suspected that his customers thought the typical Lunada Bay lending officer was an unexceptional banker and a less than impressive businessperson—but he couldn't be sure. He did know that his people didn't understand business as well as they did the application of the bank's well-known test of creditworthiness. Their narrowness worried him as he looked forward a few years, trying to plan the bank's future.

Nazarko had been the force behind Lunada Bay's extensive geographical diversification and its modest service diversity. Ignoring the fears of his board, in the 1970s he had taken a series of calculated risks and opened offices in the major money centers of the world. His judgment had proved correct, for in less than ten years over half the bank's assets and almost half its profits came from overseas. Now he was pushing even harder to broaden the bank's service base beyond its traditional strengths in commercial lending. It was tougher than he had expected. Even after several years of intensive efforts to broaden its services, Lunada Bay was still perceived as a commercial house.

The findings of the U.S. operations survey did not surprise Nazarko; they merely confirmed his judgment. The survey showed that corporations preferred to use different banks for different services. They were most likely to come to Lunada Bay for a commercial loan. Then they would call in someone else to handle their trust business, transfer business, and leasing and mortgage lending. It was like any other business, he supposed. If you got too good at selling fried chicken, you were going to have a hard time convincing the public that you were also a good place to get a hamburger.

Northern Europe Operations: Survey Results

One of the company's earliest overseas ventures had been to establish a Northern European operations headquarters in the money center of London. During the fifteen years since, Lunada Bay had built a large and successful business that included banks in the major countries of Northern Europe: Britain, Denmark, Sweden, Belgium, the Netherlands, and Germany. The rest of continental Europe was served from a regional office in Paris.

Lunada Bay's image among its customers in Northern Europe was broader than it was in the United States. Here Lunada Bay was viewed as a full-service bank. Customers felt it was especially helpful in restructuring and in consortium lending, in which more than one bank would join together and work with a company in repackaging its debt. Although Lunada Bay did a modest amount of institutional advertising in Northern Europe, most of its customers had sought it out because of referrals from other companies and a reputation for professionalism.

The company's strengths, as seen by its Northern European customers, were the depth and accuracy of the analysis its loan officers conducted in determining the best financial package for customers. Its officers were viewed as agreeable people, and its rates and terms were considered fair and competitive. Among its major weaknesses were its loan-administration capability, including accuracy, completeness, response time, and follow-up.

Lunada Bay–Hong Kong: Survey Results

Two years after opening in London, the company commenced operations in Hong Kong, another major money center. Smaller and less profitable than its European counterpart, Lunada Bay–Hong Kong mirrored the characteristics of its region. Geographically it was extraordinarily diverse, making loans to mining companies in the Australian outback, to oil exploration ventures in Indonesia and New Guinea, and to agricultural conglomerates in the Philippines. The regional senior vice-president served as one of several export advisers to the People's Republic of China. The Tokyo branch even did sale/leaseback deals for rolling stock between the Takamatsu Railcar Company in Japan and a group of high-tax-bracket Japanese-American physician investors in Los Angeles.

Besides complexity, the region was known for corruption. Embezzlement, counterfeiting, currency manipulation, bribery, and general corporate intrigue resulted in a substantial potential for loan losses, and Lunada Bay experienced its share of them. Still, it was an exciting area of the world in which to conduct business, and Nazarko was optimistic about his company's future there.

The survey of current customers and targeted major prospects confirmed what had already been discovered in the United States and Europe. Companies preferred to use different banks to serve their financial needs rather than to rely primarily on a single bank. Lunada Bay's fees were about right. There was a marked preference for dealing with only one account manager from Lunada Bay, who would coordinate the bank's efforts to provide an array of services to its customers.

The Hong Kong survey found that foreign banks, such as Lunada Bay, were used mainly for export financing and, to a lesser extent, for commercial loans. There was little demand for lease financing or trust services. Depending on the regulations of the host country, there was some use of personal banking services—taking in deposits, offering checking accounts, and making loans to individuals. But even where the law allowed it, foreign banks were infrequently chosen for such activities.

In deciding which bank to use, two factors that should have mattered proved not to be important. One negligible element was fees and terms; the other was location. What did concern customers was the reputation of the bank and the expertise of the account manager—and the chemistry between the account manager and the customer.

Sierra Pacific Mortgage: Survey Results

In 1970, Lunada Bay Bancorporation acquired a U.S.-based mortgage banking company, Sierra Pacific, and operated it as a wholly owned subsidiary. Nazarko's strategy for this division was to place a mortgage banking officer in each of the bank's major operations and to use moral and monetary persuasion to encourage Lunada Bay managers to encourage customers to use the service.

Sierra Pacific remained a small part of the total activity of Lunada Bay. Its officers, arrogant by tradition and training, had not mixed well at Lunada's social affairs. Each group tended to denigrate the other, and mutual disdain kept them from achieving the reciprocity that would have come from friendlier relations. Sierra Pacific was running a distant third behind Golden State, the leader in the field. Sierra had a much smaller market share in mortgage lending than Lunada did in commercial lending and little name recognition in its field.

Nazarko was interested to find that his strategy of pursuing Lunada commercial customers as the highest-potential customers for Sierra Pacific Mortgage was both right and wrong. The survey found that Lunada customers were more willing than non-Lunada customers to try Sierra's services. However, the characteristics of noncustomers (smaller, less sophisticated, more remote) actually made them better prospects.

Lunada Bay Officers: Survey Results

Interviews conducted with senior Lunada Bay officers painted a self-portrait of Lunada, a picture of how its people perceived themselves and their organization. They believed the bank had become synonymous with its approach to commercial lending. The Lunada Bay corporate credit analysis was its major asset and its major liability. The bank's lending officers were considered mere technicians by the treasurers of its customers.

Lunada Bay's officers understood why the bancorporation needed to become a full-service bank, but they also realized it was still primarily a commercial bank that also did some personal banking, mortgage lending, leasing, and trust work. They saw themselves as conservative, which was acceptable, but also as narrow. The typical Lunada Bay officer knew commercial lending in great depth and had a passable grasp of full-service banking but was ignorant about business. This self-image was changing gradually as the bank recruited M.B.A.s fresh from the better schools and managers with nonbanking experience. But it was still true that its average officer felt most at home spreading a financial statement and fell silent when talk changed to managing a corporation.

Nazarko's predecessor, Jonathan Yarmouth, had believed strongly in having the bank keep a low profile. Lunada Bay's dominance in commercial lending gave it a special status, and Yarmouth enjoyed having the company's name be both instantly recognizable and mysterious. The business community thought about commercial lending and Lunada Bay in an almost generic way, just as consumers thought of soft drinks and Coca-Cola, facial tissues and Kleenex, photocopying and Xerox.

Yarmouth's penchant for enigma was not shared by his officers. They resented the greater media exposure their competitors received in the business periodicals. Lunada Bay officers would find themselves calling on a prospect on a given morning and have the customer push the *Wall Street Journal* at them across the desk and ask, "Did you read what Sepulveda's Brown said? He said the prime rate should drop about 2 percent over the next quarter because demand is softening." Lunada Bay may have been saying the same thing to clients for the past sixty days and may already have had its prime rate 1 percent below Sepulveda's, but Sepulveda had a Brown, and he was always being quoted someplace. It made Lunada Bay's field people feel second-rate.

Lunada Bay deliberately avoided building up any of its senior officers as spokespersons or stars. It gave the bank a sense of security not to have to worry about departing spokespersons or falling stars. Its people were well hidden within the company. Nazarko himself ran little risk of being sought out by the media. Everyone knew his company, but few people knew *him.*

Personally, Nazarko didn't care about the lack of superstars. What upset him was that his officers felt the company lacked a marketing strategy. He knew exactly what he was doing to diversify and protect the company. Anyone who said they didn't understand this obviously had not been listening to Nazarko's speeches at the company's annual meetings for the past five years. He was going to create, through geographical and product diversification, the world's largest full-service bank, with a reputation of being first in quality in each of its service areas. It was as simple and as difficult as that.

What Should the Bank Become?

Part of the study of the corporate image of the Lunada Bay Bancorporation was a look into the future, the world of banking in the 1980s. The 1980s were going to be dominated by larger and more specialized banks. As the United States entered the twenty-first century, there would emerge a few banks doing a few things well for many clients.

Nazarko's strategy to diversify his bank beyond commercial lending was going against the current of change in his industry. An easier course to steer would allow the bank to become even stronger in the commercial lending field, to be the dominant force in merchant banking throughout the world. Under that strategy its strength would be derived from its geographical diversity and from its numbers of customers—strength based on size and resource dispersement, not service segmentation.

Asked what they looked for in selecting a bank, the chief financial officers of the *Fortune* 1,000 emphasized that what was most important to them was to feel they were dealing with competent people. This competence factor included the bank's reputation and its knowledge of the company's industry, region, and country. After competence, the next most important factor in selecting a bank was flexibility. The customer wanted a bank that would be reasonable in determining the terms and size of its loan and could be creative in meeting the company's capital needs. This flexibility was more important than the cost of the loan. As in most business transactions, people were willing to pay a little more if they felt they were getting special treatment.

During their interviews, Lunada Bay officers were asked how they wanted the company to be viewed—what kind of image they thought was desirable. They responded with seven descriptive characteristics. First, officers wanted the company to be seen as the best in quality. They wanted Lunada Bay to occupy the premium position among banks, to be both most used and most preferred. In addition to a reputation for excellence, the officers wanted to deal with large companies, which they found more prestigious and satisfying than working with small organizations. They wanted outsiders to see Lunada Bay as a bank that served big and successful companies. Furthermore, the survey showed that Lunada's current self-perception was that of technicians serving treasurers of corporations; ideally, they wanted to be seen as advisers serving the chief executive officer.

Other desirable image characteristics were size and complexity. Lunada Bay officers were proud of their company's good record of growth and wanted it to continue, along with an international variegation. Agreeing with Nazarko, they felt the company should continue to diversify and present itself as having many linked businesses. His officers definitely wanted more media exposure, although Nazarko was still ambivalent on this point. They saw this happening as a result of improved public relations.

For optimum success in banking in the 1980s, the officers believed the bank would need to become both more specialized and more diversified. It would have to be sensitive to the political environments of host countries. Demonstrating in-depth understanding of particular industries would be important. Finally, the officers were convinced that the bank was going to have to do a better job of strategic planning if it was going to manage its future.

Its best strategy for shaping a successful image would be to communicate to its publics an image that emphasized the following:

> Lunada Bay Bancorporation has *competent* people with *deep technical* expertise who *understand your business* and are *responsive to your needs.*

Because of Lunada's current geographical diversity and its intended service diversity, it was going to be necessary to position the bank's image somewhat differently within its different market targets. The market targets were the different audiences, such as boards, CEOs, chief financial officers, and treasurers, who were potential buyers of the bank's services. Each had the capacity to see the company's business units, its services, differently. For example, Sierra Pacific Mortgage was a separate business unit of Lunada Bay and did not even share a common name with the parent. A source of controversy within the company was whether all the bank's business units ought to have a common linking name or whether distinct names better served the goal of rapid growth. Nazarko favored commonality of names and, at a minimum, wanted the word *Lunada* in each business unit's title. Some senior officers disagreed. They argued that the survey results showed that customers wanted to use different suppliers for different services. Sierra Pacific had the best chance of meeting its growth goals, they believed, if it had an identity distinct from Lunada.

Each business unit needed a frame of reference, an identifying label. The name *Lunada Bay Bancorporation* meant commercial lending to most people; that was the frame of reference. *Sierra Pacific* didn't mean much, but it should have meant mortgage lending. To position a company's image, a distinguishing characteristic was needed, a point of difference to plant in the minds of its market target. Ideally, this point of difference should be one that customers had identified as making a difference to them when they selected a bank.

It would be foolish to select price as a point of difference —"loans at competitive rates"—when the bank's customers and prospects had indicated that terms were much more important to them than rates, that they were looking for flexible financing. A better point of difference would be "creative solutions to your financing problems."

Positioning itself within the overall market was to be a gradual process for Lunada Bay, carefully managed so that the image conveyed at any given time was consistent with the bank's performance. The point of difference selected would be targeted to deliver the most meaningful benefit to users or to correct their biggest problem. It would positively segment the bank from its competition.

With existing customers, Lunada Bay needed to strengthen the relationship between the account manager and the financial officers in the customer company. Besides more personal closeness, there was a need for more product separation. The

bank offered several services with separate reputations. The
ideal image to have was not that of a generalist. Rather, the best
image was that of a group of linked specialists, each backed by a
large, resourceful, and prestigious institution.

Changing Lunada Bay's Image

The first two phases of the study for Lunada Bay Bancorporation were complete. The company had successfully answered
for itself the questions "Who are we?" and "Who do we want to
be?" Now it faced the last and most difficult task: It had to develop an action plan to change its image. The company had
found out how it saw itself and how it was seen by its various
publics. Looking forward, it envisioned its world over the next
ten years and the kind of bank that would perform best within
that world. Now the challenge was to decide on a plan, commit
the necessary resources, and implement the plan. Different communication tools were available to the company, and it would
have to be selective to be sure it was achieving the maximum in
image change from the dollars and hours it was devoting to
managing its corporate image.

Nazarko didn't care for the idea of deliberately managing
his company's image, because it struck him as contrived. He
would have preferred to simply let the actions of the bank
speak for it. Image building seemed manipulative to him. Yet,
he couldn't disagree with the major findings of the study—the
bank was not properly positioned. What it all finally boiled
down to, he decided, was this: To become what you wanted to
be, you had to get a firm picture of your desired image in your
mind and pretend that that was who you were. Gradually the
difference between reality and fantasy would dissolve, and you
would be what you had imagined. Well, if that's what it took,
fine. He wanted to get on with it. Change always took too much
time, as far as he was concerned. The faster they got this done,
the better.

The survey of the *Fortune* 1,000 sought to determine
how companies learned about banks and their services. Almost
three fourths of the companies indicated that word of mouth

was the most frequent method. This included referrals received from counterparts in other companies, from members of the board, or from friends in the business community. The next most frequent source of information was actual previous experience someone in the company had had with the bank.

This finding had enormous implications for Lunada. The bank's relationships with its current customers were by far the most important factor in predicting its future business. All the other instruments of change available to it—advertising, media campaigns, sales calls, and so on—wouldn't matter as much as the bank's own performance. The surest way for the bank to succeed in the future was to do a good job in the present.

It wasn't that advertising didn't matter; it just didn't matter much. Advertising created an awareness in the prospective customer about the bank. The awareness was followed by the prospect's inquiring within its circle of peers about the bank's performance. A well-conceived advertising campaign might persuade the less sophisticated to use the bank without this inquiry step. But the more savvy prospect phoned around and asked about the bank's reputation.

What was true of advertising was true of marketing as well. Sales-call programs by well-trained marketing officers using slick point-of-sale materials could create an image, and a favorable one. But the seasoned buyer would stall on making a commitment until he could check out the bank. If what he heard was favorable, he would phone the Lunada Bay officer, ask him back, and let him make the loan.

The irritatingly low profile of Lunada Bay was similarly unimportant to its success in getting business. The hard evidence showed that being quoted in the newspapers and in magazines did help create an image of expertise (if a company is quoted, it must be good). But there was not much evidence that a high profile in the press sold any business.

Nazarko was reminded of a friend of his who was the president of a large architectural firm. The friend had hired a public relations company that placed an article about him and his company in a Los Angeles business newspaper. The article was a nicely done piece on the do's and don't's of planning a new office building. After the article appeared, the friend received exactly two phone calls in response to it. One was from Nazarko, complimenting him on his positive press. The other was from an insurance agent, trying to sell him the additional life insurance that was sure to be needed by someone of such obvious importance.

The bank's communications department devised an action plan for Nazarko's review and approval, a strategy to close the gap between actual and ideal image. Its first recommendation was for a program of contacts with chief executive officers. The bank needed to give a higher priority to developing personal relationships with CEOs. Many customers still had interlocking directorates; that is, the chairmen or presidents of companies sat on each other's boards. Some of the bank's best customer relationships had come from referrals at the board level.

To build more of these relationships, the bank decided on a series of special informal seminars for CEOs only. The topics were to be financial in nature, and the meetings were off the record so people could speak freely. The seminars flopped. No one attended. Next, the bank's communications people advised writing a series of pieces addressed just to CEOs, a succession of booklets specially printed and issued in limited editions. Nazarko thought this was pretentious and instead had his economist supervise the preparation of an irregularly published monograph on financial issues of interest to a broader cross-section of the corporate community.

The company had to decide whether to continue to have different names and logos for its business units or to adopt a policy of uniformity. The board wanted Nazarko to begin immediately to create a greater cohesiveness among the bank's operating units. Taking Sierra Pacific as an example, they asked why the name of the company shouldn't be changed to Lunada Bay Mortgage Company or Lunada–Sierra Pacific or Lunada Pacific Mortgage. And the company's logos were as diverse as its names. There was no single type style, color, or symbol that ran consistently throughout the company's letterheads, its sales literature, or even its advertising.

Feelings on the subject of names were more deep and intense than Nazarko had expected. His international officers and those running subsidiary companies worried that uniformity would mean loss of their identity and autonomy. Nazarko resented their parochialism, but he had worked hard to build geographical and service diversity, and so he was willing to compromise and wait.

Eventually he settled on the strategy of letting his board insist that the word *Lunada* be part of each business's name and that a uniform logo and color scheme be used wherever the company did business. The communications department designed several blue-and-white logos with a globe, a mountain, and a moon. Nazarko chose the one he liked best, and the company began to use it around the world. Although the operating groups and subsidiaries were told to accept the standard logo, they were allowed to keep their individual identities and were encouraged to market themselves as separate services.

Reluctantly, Nazarko approved a plan of more media coverage. He remained unconvinced that it would bring the bank more business, but he understood its importance to morale. He hired a public relations pro from a business magazine and gave him responsibility for getting the company's name into print more often. Several senior officers were encouraged to improve their speaking skills and to take time off to write and deliver speeches. Editors of the more prominent business publications were cultivated, and the company began to make the news more often. Nazarko took care to spread interviews around and, where possible, to have more than one officer's name mentioned. He was still nervous about superstars and preferred that his company, rather than particular executives, be in the news.

The survey data had shown to the bank that, more than any other single factor, its future depended on its people and how they interacted with the bank's customers. Because customers most often learned about the bank from referrals, what current customers said about Lunada Bay today made a difference in getting more customers tomorrow. Customers ranked the competence of the loan officer as one of the most important characteristics in using a bank. Lunada Bay officers did not have a good self-image. They saw themselves as narrow technicians who were at a loss when it came to understanding business. It was clear that the bank had to invest in the training of its officers to improve their self-image and the image held of them by customers.

Several programs were recommended to the chief executive. The first was an internal communications campaign to inform and motivate officers. Next, managers were encouraged to emphasize more teamwork and less competition between officers. The internal climate at Lunada was more entrepreneurial than colleaguial. To enable officers to learn from one another, a shift in management style was necessary, encouraging sharing and trust.

Content-specific training courses were also recommended. The courses covered general business, service-segment management, and the vocabulary and issues of individual customer industries. The intent of the training was to make each officer a credible expert not only in lending but also in the customer's business and in business generally. Quality and responsiveness were discussed over and over in the training programs to build an image of professionalism. Additionally, the bank changed its loan-administration procedures, adding staff and automating certain functions to substantially reduce the time it took to process a loan. Loan authority was decentralized further into each region, so that a prospective customer received a yes-or-no reply to his loan request a full twenty-four hours faster than in the past.

The most difficult challenge was modifying the use of the company's loan-analysis technique. Many officers believed that this unique approach to credit analysis had much to do with the company's success. The "Lunada Bay system" was known throughout the world as the acid test of corporate creditworthiness. Yet, even the bank's best customers criticized the system as mechanical and unimaginative. It was hard to convince them that the technology could at the same time be both systematic and flexible.

Eventually a compromise was reached. Senior loan officers were taught alternative methods of loan analysis and the financing techniques of competitor banks. They were also encouraged to bend or even drop the traditional system if, in their judgment, the customer would be best served by other than their classic approach. Because of the public's many years of experience with Lunada Bay's system, it was still too early to determine how well this new multisystem approach would work.

Nazarko realized that the "Lunada Bay system" was important to the bank's future. He decided to invest in it rather than treat it as a cash cow. This was accomplished mainly by giving it higher visibility, more academic prestige, and the appearance of greater flexibility. Senior bank officers published articles in prestigious business journals showing the usefulness of the technique, especially for high-technology companies experiencing explosive growth. Lunada Bay offered a research prize for the best work done that year in the field of banking. It sponsored an annual symposium at Aspen in August on "Trends in International Finance" and published its proceedings.

All these activities helped to greatly modify the organization's image. Yet, they did not truly change it into what Nazarko would have liked it to be. Still, he felt, it was an improvement. Maybe you couldn't become exactly what you wanted to become by just deciding you were going to go out and do it. But you could get close enough to make it worth the effort.

3

Organizational
Climate

Climate—the perceptions employees have about their organization's practices and operating principles—strongly influences corporate performance. Until recently, the connection between climate and performance has been a matter of speculation and intuition, with various rules of thumb taken for granted because they seemed reasonable. Many of these assumptions proved inaccurate after a systematic method was developed of untangling the factors of climate, measuring them in a company, and determining their relation to performance. It is now known that there are a few critical climate factors that are essential to managing successful corporate performance.

Climate analysis is as much a technique of performance appraisal as it is a management tool because it reveals organizational strengths and weaknesses and because it can be translated into a program of corrective action. Although research has resulted in general guidelines about climate, data from each corporation must always be considered in relation to that company's industry, its stage of development, its objectives, and its internal operations.

Climate is more than management style. It is the perceptions managers and other employees have of the mixture of formal and informal policies, structures, and systems that guide management behavior and influence overall organizational performance. Corporate climate is the result of the interaction between two sets of conditions: (1) the organizational structure and other formalized management practices, policies, and procedures and (2) the character of people and their informal structure. Climate is an expression of the prevailing ethos within which managers make decisions. Climate analysis measures people's perception of the effectiveness of internal procedures; it tells the CEO how well the corporate mission is being understood and implemented. The technique can identify present and potential problems in employee organization and motivation, assess internal readiness for programs of change, identify where change is needed, measure the change brought about by new programs, and assess whether the organization's climate will support corporate goals. Because climate measurement can be segmented by specific units, it can be used to identify what is happening throughout the organization and at various levels of management.

Climate Defined

Climate is not synonymous with morale, and high morale, in turn, does not ensure productivity, although the three are related (Herzberg and others, 1957). Neither should executives and organizational behavior specialists assume that a positive organizational climate is synonymous with job satisfaction. "Corporate climate" is an abstract concept encompassing practice and procedure. Whereas job satisfaction is emotional and individual, climate is descriptive and organizational (Schneider, 1975). Climate is also not merely the attitudes of a company's employees.

Generally speaking, what constitutes a successful climate? Participation in management seems to be one criterion that differentiates positive climates from negative ones. In a study of upper- and middle-management employees in a health care company, Welsch and Lavan (1981) found that a participative climate was related to organizational commitment. Sense of teamwork was related to satisfaction with work and promotional opportunities.

An effective climate is one that emphasizes achievement,

personal goal setting, and a sense of individual responsibility. Litwin (1968) found that the people in an organization will experience the climate created by its leader. The most satisfactory climates for productivity and job satisfaction that executives can create are ones that stress achievement, positive motivation, involvement in goal setting, and sense of individual responsibility. In a later study using the Improved Climate Questionnaire, designed by Litwin and Stringer, reward was an important predictor of improved climate and perhaps the most important climate dimension. Concerns and feelings about pay are important factors in climate. The poorer the organization's climate, the more its people are likely to demand more money, again suggesting that pay tends to be either a cause or a symptom of pervasive dissatisfaction. Negative climate can have serious practical implications. For example, the climate created by supervisors can be a significant predictor of the intensity of unionization activity, and employees dissatisfied with a company's climate are more likely to participate in union activities.*

Measuring Organizational Climate

The measurement of climate has especially challenged organizational behavior specialists. There are a few ways to analyze climate. One method is to use information-processing models, individual decision theory, and role theory and to show the implications for organizational climate (Naylor, Pritchard, and Ilgen, 1980). But probably the most popular climate-measurement tool is the questionnaire, a deceptively simple-looking device that actually operates at four levels: (1) the hypotheses behind the information requested, (2) the questionnaire layout and format, (3) the questions themselves, and (4) the exact wording of the questions. Opinion polling is prevalent in business research and gives every indication of increasing (Labaw, 1980).

*In addition to the work reported here, performed by the Research for Management division of the Hay Group (Gordon and Cummins, 1979), the other major work in climate surveys has been conducted by the Survey Research Center of the University of Michigan (Taylor and Bowers, 1972).

One measure of climate developed by the Hay Group (Gordon and Cummins, 1979) consists of forty-eight questions evaluated on a scale of 1 to 7 (see Exhibit 1). The forty-eight questions were selected from hundreds after an analysis of multiple samples obtained in a survey of sixty-five organizations in 1974 and 1975. This analysis identified eight dimensions of climate.

Exhibit 1. Items Included in Each of the Climate Dimensions.

Organizational Clarity

> To what extent do goals provide a useful context for the everyday functioning of this organization?
>
> To what extent does this organization have clear goals?
>
> Planning for the achievement of goals in this organization tends to be formal.
>
> Planning for the achievement of goals in this organization tends to be complete.
>
> Planning for the achievement of goals in this organization tends to be oriented toward the long term.
>
> Decision making in this organization tends to be based on a long-range view.
>
> To what extent does this organization have defined plans to meet its goals?

Decision-Making Structure

> To what extent does the current reporting structure facilitate or hinder implementation of the organization's strategies?
>
> To what extent does the current reporting structure facilitate or hinder the achievement of the organization goals?
>
> To what extent do the systems in this organization provide a manager with the information he needs for decision making?
>
> To what extent are decisions in this organization based on adequate information?
>
> To what extent does the current reporting structure facilitate or hinder coordination of efforts?

Organizational Integration

> To what extent do the various units in this organization understand each other's problems and difficulties?
>
> Communications laterally to you from others at the same organizational levels tend to be extremely good.
>
> Everything considered, communications in this organization tend to be extremely good.
>
> How clear are managers concerning the interrelationships of their own jobs with those of others?

(continued on next page)

Exhibit 1. Items Included in Each of the Climate Dimensions, Cont'd.

To what extent do the various units in this organization understand each other's objectives and goals?

To what extent do various units in this organization truly cooperate with one another?

To what extent do you feel that you are sufficiently aware of things that are happening in other areas of the organization that might have an effect on how you do your job?

Management Style

To what extent are people in this organization free to take independent actions that are necessary to carry out their job responsibilities?

To what extent are managers encouraged to take reasonable risks in their efforts to increase the effectiveness of this organization?

To what extent is open discussion of conflicts encouraged?

To what extent are managers encouraged to innovate in their jobs?

To what extent is constructive criticism encouraged within this organization?

Communications downward to you from above tend to be extremely good.

To what extent do managers receive the support they need from higher levels of management to successfully carry through their job responsibilities?

Performance Orientation

To what extent are managers held personally accountable for the end results they produce or fail to produce?

The measures or yardsticks used to judge managerial performance in this organization tend to be very clear.

To what extent are managers within this organization expected to meet demands for high levels of performance?

To what extent are the goals in this organization truly challenging?

How clear are managers about the end results that are expected of them in their jobs?

Organizational Vitality

To what extent is this organization responsive to change in its business environment?

Goals in this organization tend to be venturesome.

Decision making in this organization tends to be innovative.

Decision making in this organization tends to be timely.

Relative to its competition, this organization is a pacesetter.

What is your estimate of the overall vitality of this organization as reflected by such things as a sense of urgency and a rapid pace of activities?

Compensation

To what extent are managers in this organization offered benefits that are competitive with similar organizations?

Exhibit 1. Items Included in Each of the Climate Dimensions, Cont'd.

Considering the work you do, how satisfactory is your present compensation?

To what extent is your pay high compared to others in this organization with similar responsibilities?

To what extent is your pay high compared to people in other organizations with similar responsibilities?

The relationship in this organization between compensation and individual performance tends to be very strong.

Human Resources Development

Overall, how would you rate the opportunities for promotion within the organization?

When a management vacancy exists, the search within the organization to fill that vacancy tends to be very broad.

How successful is this organization in developing people from within for bigger jobs?

To what extent does this organization provide opportunities for individual growth and development?

To what extent does your job present a significant challenge to you?

To what extent are the talents of managers appropriately matched to the demands of their job?

Note: Items have been slightly reworded to account for the response scales.

The responses to each of these questions are averaged and compared against percentile norms of more than 20,000 managers from more than 450 companies who have responded to the same question. In addition to responses of the total organization, results may be analyzed for separate units, management levels, and respondent characteristics (such as age or years with the company). Demographic segmentation such as this permits significant internal comparisons.

High and low scores for each of the eight dimensions have specific implications. I now define the eight climate factors and what it means when an organization is high or low on a given factor.

Organizational Clarity. Organizational clarity is the understanding of the organization's goals and plans held by the people in the company. Organizational clarity is present when people perceive the company's mission, objectives, processes, and activities as purposeful, rational, and fully communicated. In such a setting, people experience these characteristics as unifying influences that enhance cooperation. Clarity is increased by the use of planning and goal setting to provide a clear purpose and a context for performance.

In companies scoring *high* on organizational clarity, people feel that the organization has clear goals and complete, well-defined plans to meet them. They understand what the organization intends to accomplish, how the objectives influence their own goals, and what they must do to contribute effectively to organizational performance. People in *low*-scoring companies are unsure of the purposes of the company. They may be unclear about their own jobs, the effectiveness of managerial planning, or the future of their unit. This uncertainty about aims, objectives, and future directions may result either from a lack of adequate goals or from a failure to communicate them effectively.

Decision-Making Structure. The factor labeled "decision-making structure" measures the nature of the flow of information through a company. It refers to the process of rationally choosing a course of action from a group of alternatives and then implementing and systematically evaluating that choice.

High ratings on decision making indicate confidence that the company is able to make effective decisions, implement them, and evaluate their impact. Decisions are perceived as relevant, rational, and effective. *Low* ratings mean that information systems are poorly conceived or ineffectively used or that decision making is not taking place at the appropriate management levels. Lack of clarity in organizational accountabilities can cause low ratings, as can the failure of management to implement or evaluate decisions.

Organizational Integration. Organizational integration is the extent to which various subunits cooperate and communicate to achieve overall organizational objectives.

High ratings on organizational integration indicate people believe that units understand one another's objectives, needs, and problems and that communication, cooperation, and collaboration exist among units. Such scores tend to accompany a participative management style if the latter is reflected downward from top management. *Low* scores indicate poor communications, unclear relationships, and an unwillingness of people to expend effort in support of other units. Organizations differ in the degree of integration required for effective overall performance.

Management Style. Management style is the pattern of delegated authority throughout a company and employees' perceptions of freedom and constraint. This factor measures the extent to which people feel encouraged to use their own initiative and to question authority and how much support they sense from higher levels of management.

In companies scoring high on management style, managers have considerable freedom to determine and take the actions they believe necessary to perform their jobs well. High ratings indicate a delegative style under which managers are encouraged to think innovatively, to take responsible risks, and to speak up about problems or constraints. A *low* score, which indicates a centralized, more directive management style, is not necessarily negative, because different types of environments require different management practices. But a style more directive than is necessary may be reflected in low ratings that signal frustration over inadequate participation.

Performance Orientation. Performance orientation is the degree of emphasis placed on accountability for clearly defined end results and high levels of performance.

On this dimension both very low scores and very high scores are negative indicators. A reasonably *high* rating shows that people know their accountabilities and the standards of performance. *Low* ratings may indicate that accountability is diffuse and unclear or that no one is clearly responsible for producing specific end results. Therefore, too low a rating can reveal toleration of poor performance. However, too high a score can indicate a tendency to focus only on immediate profit-producing activities, with inadequate attention to long-range development.

Organizational Vitality. Organizational vitality is the extent to which people see the company as dynamic and responsive to change, with venturesome goals and innovative decisions.

In companies with *high* scores on organizational vitality, people feel that a dynamic management will recognize and seize opportunities as they arise and will maintain a fast pace of activities. This type of environment is generally preferred by competent, venturesome, achievement-oriented individuals. But many mature, slow-growth companies are best served by moderate vitality, focusing on proven methods and know-how rather than on risk taking. In these instances, *low* scores indicate a relatively conservative organization rather than dissatisfaction with the company's business approach. Low scores can also indicate such problems as inadequate delegation or an overly cautious decision-making style.

Compensation. The compensation factor reflects perceptions about the rewards available and how they are perceived—whether the compensation system is seen as equitable, competitive, and related to performance.

High scores on compensation mean employees believe that a company's compensation plan is competitive compared with other employers', that the system is internally equitable, that rewards are commensurate with performance, or perhaps all three. *Low* scores suggest that people believe their compensation is unsatisfactory compared with what others receive within or outside the company. Such scores may accurately reflect the facts or may arise from inadequate communication of the real situation.

Human Resources Development. The factor of human resources development measures the extent to which employees perceive opportunities within the company that will allow people to develop to their full potential.

High scores on human resources development indicate an emphasis on the realization of individual potential through policies and programs of career development and the availability of growth opportunities. *Low* scores can arise when individual development is ignored or misdirected or when developmental and promotional opportunities are limited.

Although the preceding generalizations can be made about the indications of certain ratings in each dimension, the raw data have meaning only in the context of the company's particular situation. Each organization must be considered in relation to its industry, its stage of development, its objectives, and its internal operations.

Climate and Performance

A climate analysis can provide the organization with useful data. The information is most valuable when the chief executive understands what type of climate will result in long-term profitability and growth. Different climates correlate with different performance results. By discovering these relations, a company can work to develop a climate that leads to the goals it wants.

Each company has a unique climate resulting from the character of its leaders, its business environment, its history, and its strengths and weaknesses. Corporate climates are like fingerprints: Each company has its own.

What is the relation between a company's climate and the results it achieves? How is corporate performance influenced by the common climate factors in companies? The five-year average annual rate of growth in net income (compounded growth rate) is a good measure of long-range achievement. It also reflects the typical time span of climate change, which can take from three to five years.

Twenty-nine of the sixty-five organizations originally surveyed between 1974 and 1975 had profit data that they made available for analysis. The average compounded net-income growth of fourteen of the companies was more than 10 percent; for fifteen companies it was less than 10 percent.

The study discovered that companies with high profit and growth are clearly similar on three climate dimensions and dissimilar on others. *Organizational clarity, organizational integration,* and *compensation* show a much greater correlation with performance than the other dimensions (see Figure 1). High-performance companies develop clear objectives and pursue them through a well-understood planning system. They have a strong communications network that integrates the efforts of units to

Figure 1. Correlations Between Climate Dimensions and
Five-Year Growth in Net Profit.

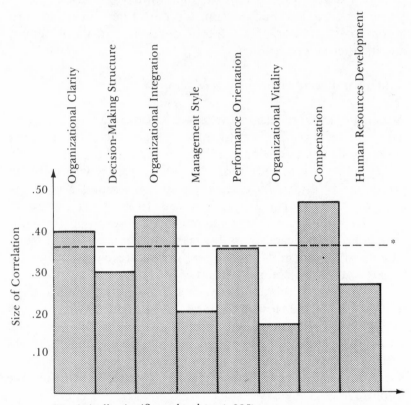

*Statistically significant level (p < .025).

Source: After Gordon and Cummins, 1979; the Hay Group, Philadelphia.

achieve goals. The high compensation levels may be explained
by one of two reasons: Companies doing well pay well, or companies that pay well demand high performance for what they
pay.

Surprisingly, performance orientation does not have a
statistically significant relation to performance results, nor does
management style. Management style relates closely to morale,
which itself has little correlation with results. However, some
climate elements relate to both performance results and morale,

especially good communications, efficient information systems, clearly defined interrelationships, and success in developing people (Table 5).

Table 5. Climate Characteristics Associated with Five-Year Growth
in Profitability and Morale.

Climate Dimensions	Organizations Having Sustained Profitability	Organizations Having High Morale
Clarity	• Complete planning process • Clearly defined goals • Goals provide a useful context for management • Clearly defined end results expected of managers	• People aware of events • High degree of communication
Management Style	• Freedom to act and reasonable risk taking encouraged • Constructive criticism and open discussion of conflicts encouraged	• Support from higher management levels when needed
Human Resources Development	• Talents matched to jobs • Good promotion opportunities	• High job security
Compensation	• Compensation related to performance	• Compensation externally competitive
Leadership	• Company leaders aware of problems • Leaders take actions to solve problems	• Few management problems exist

Source: After Gordon and Cummins (1979); the Hay Group, Philadelphia.

For factors correlating with performance an analysis of items within the factor was done. These items within a factor have a significant relation to profit:

- *Organizational clarity:* Clear goals, formal planning, complete planning, and existence of defined plans.
- *Decision-making structure:* Information available for decisions and information used for decisions.

- *Organizational integration:* Lateral communications, overall communications, and units' understanding of one another's goals.
- *Performance orientation:* Clear performance measures and clear end results.
- *Compensation:* Competitive benefits, competitive salary, and relation of compensation to performance.

Many of these items are related to goal setting. A company that is profitable has clear goals and communicates to employees their role in achieving them. For example, compensation and performance-orientation items indicate a clear understanding of what constitutes performance. Thus, a successful company identifies objectives, makes plans to achieve them, and measures performance, all with widespread communication of relevant information. In profitable companies:

1. Goals are part of the corporate climate.
2. Clear corporate goals are established and communicated.
3. Specific measures are used to judge overall performance.
4. There is a well-defined planning system: missions, functional goals, unit goals, personal goals.
5. Clear interrelations among jobs exist.
6. Clear limits of managerial authority and results expected of individuals are communicated.

Besides these findings concerning the general relation of climate to performance, other studies have shown that successful companies in particular industries share specific climate profiles. For example, manufacturers tend to stress short-term considerations such as changes in products, schedules, or marketing, while financial institutions pay more attention to long-range implications of decisions (Figure 2). A company must measure itself in the context of its own industry.

A high or low score on one item is not necessarily good or bad. What benefits one company may not help another, depending on the industry, the company's stage of development, its mission, and other factors. For example, a highly delegative,

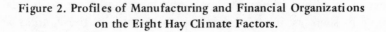

Figure 2. Profiles of Manufacturing and Financial Organizations
on the Eight Hay Climate Factors.

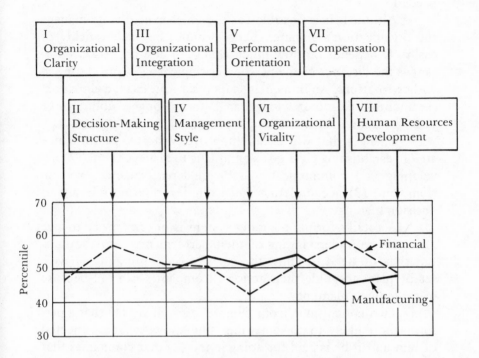

Source: After Gordon and Cummins (1979); the Hay Group, Philadelphia.

demanding climate may produce superior results when management is achievement-oriented but might inhibit performance in
a company with many security-oriented employees. Here a
more centrally controlled, structured management style would
be better.

Climate differences between industries are often descriptive of the operations of the industries. Some differences indicate the existence of problems. For example, a comparison of
manufacturers and utilities indicates that utilities have information systems with strong capabilities in information generation
and transmission, allowing managers to quickly attend to problems involving more than one department or division. But compared with managers in manufacturing, utilities managers are

less clear about company goals and plans, and company planning is seen as inadequate. Improvements in these areas are
needed.

Although it is possible for the chief executive to manage
the organization's climate, changes cannot be made quickly or
easily. It depends on how much change is desired. Also important is the distance of the person desiring change from those she
wishes to affect. An immediate supervisor can change climate in
six months. Corporatewide change takes longer, about three
years for a medium-sized company.

Changes that will usually improve corporate performance
are (1) establishing clear goals and plans to achieve them, (2) developing and communicating individual performance expectations, and (3) accumulating and using information relevant to
decision making.

A totally formal planning system is not necessary to give
managers an understanding of their performance contributions.
But they do need to know the goals of their unit and to have a
set of plans to guide their actions. Companies can fail because
of inadequate planning.

Two conclusions from climate research are (1) that a person is more likely to do something if he knows what is expected
of him and if he is paid for doing it and (2) that companies that
have clear goal-planning systems are more successful than those
that do not.

In a way, these two simple rules of thumb are the essence
of managing organizational performance.

CASE STUDY
Managing Climate:
National Business Machines

In this case study we find an example of the use of climate data to
help a CEO change both the behavior of the people in the organization and the basic strategy of the corporation. Here the CEO, Andrew Somerville, was faced with a company that must change
both its direction and its character if it is to survive. It lacked or-

ganizational clarity, with no clear goals or plans or much of a planning process. Divisions and major functions in some cases had a general idea of what they individually were trying to accomplish but were ignorant about the goals of their corporate neighbors. NBM was really in three distinct businesses that were at different stages of maturity and required different strategies. Its traditional business, cash registers and accounting machines, was in the harvest-and-divest stage; the goal was to maintain current market share and to maximize profit margins as long as possible. So the first challenge facing the CEO was *organizational clarity*—to decide on the nature of the company's business and to communicate these decisions throughout the company.

The second major problem the company had was the disintegration that existed in certain functions. Somerville wanted better balance in his organization's structure. The weakest staff function was finance, but research and development also had to be upgraded. Organizational integration also suffered because overall communications horizontally and vertically were poor.

To Somerville his third major task was to renew a sense of performance orientation in his company. Climate research said that performance orientation was two-edged—both too much and too little were bad. The research also said that it was not a factor that significantly divided the profitable from the unprofitable. Still, Somerville wanted people who wanted to achieve and expected to be paid well for doing so. His company's climate results showed that NBM's employees believed their company lacked management talent and needed more high achievers who demanded competitive pay.

The National Business Machines case study exemplifies several of the components required to successfully manage organizational performance. First, the organization must know where it is going. It needs to decide on the nature of its business and to share these decisions with its people. Next, it needs not to be afraid to understand its culture and how the climate inside the company will facilitate or hinder the accomplishment of its mission. Finally, it must pay special care to the profit-sensitive climate factors: organizational clarity, organizational integration, competitive compensation, and the right performance orientation. The effective corporate mariner decides where the ship is going, makes sure everyone gets the word about the intended port, divides the crew's duties but has each member understand what the others do, has them participate in deciding how fast they want to go there, and pays well for a ship that outperforms the others.

National Business Machines is a leading producer of electronic business equipment, accounting for about 25 percent of the U.S. office equipment market. NBM products include electronic cash registers, computers, automated banking equipment, and a small line of high-quality programmable hand calculators. The company's headquarters are located in a square, yellow brick building in an old section of Detroit, surrounded by working-class homes.

The company was founded in 1889 by Charles Cooper, a thin, asthmatic, sour man who believed fervently in the Protestant ethic. At one time Cooper owned a small dry-goods store. Profits were small because of the constant pilferage that he suffered at the hands of his employees. His brother-in-law told him of a mechanic who had invented a business machine that was guaranteed to reduce thefts and increase profit. It was called a cash register. Cooper was desperate enough to buy one.

The machine did everything his brother-in-law had promised it would. On learning that the inventor/manager wanted to sell his little garage factory and his rights to his invention, Cooper eagerly bought him out. With the profits from his store, which was now thriving, he expanded the cash-register production facilities and began hiring the sons of immigrant families to sell the machines on a straight commission basis. Between 1890 and 1918, the year Cooper died, the company's growth was outstanding, and the NBM cash register was sold everywhere in the United States and in most large countries in Europe.

Cooper's initial success was due to his sales and marketing tactics. His corporate strategy was simple. The best companies did the best sales job. His credo was that with God's help any hardworking salesman could acquire some wealth, and he preached this mission constantly to his sales force. Cooper insisted that his salesmen maintain a professional appearance, and an NBM man could be recognized in the country stores, on the highways, in the train stations, and in the hotel restaurants of every small town in America. The uniform was a white shirt, a brown suit, and a solid black tie. A choice of either black or brown shoes was permitted. Cooper discouraged his men from chewing tobacco while on the job and counseled them to save at least 10 cents of every dollar they earned. Over and over, he urged them to work hard and achieve for themselves and their families. Those who took his advice to invest that dime in NBM stock eventually came to see their investments pay handsome dividends and appreciate enormously in value. A few of the more abstemious and chaste even accumulated the wealth that Cooper had promised. Thus Cooper created a corporate climate that emphasized marketing, rapid growth, and personal income tied directly to individual production. While the business was still immature and the products technically simple, this was an ideal corporate strategy supported by a complementary climate.

It was during World War II that the other person who would come to leave his mark indelibly on NBM, Andrew Somerville, learned some of the lessons that would help him take the company through its period of adversity. Somerville saw extensive combat duty as a Marine Corps captain during the island campaigns of the South Pacific. His experiences there against the Japanese developed in him a great respect for discipline, loyalty to an idea larger than one's own welfare, and the ability to take unpopular but necessary action under adverse circumstances.

When Somerville took over NBM as president and chief executive officer in 1970, he was faced with eroding profit margins, a shrinking market share, a lackadaisical sales force, and antitrust lawsuits against the company's cash register division. Determined to arrest this terminal decline, he decided to realign and restructure his business. He had three immediate objectives:

1. Develop for NBM an enterprise strategy plus individual strategies for its business units to position them properly.
2. Identify and implement divisional organizational structures that would best support the achievement of the corporation's strategies and objectives.
3. Provide the corporation with a management continuity plan to identify internal talent and the series of develop-

mental experiences necessary to help executives actualize their potential.

To achieve these objectives, it was necessary first to gather information about the company's current situation and to develop recommendations for change. Somerville commissioned a climate study of NBM. First a group of executives representing major functional units, geographical areas, and divergent points of view were interviewed to gain an understanding of the company's business, its problems, and its opportunities. Next, a questionnaire was designed and distributed and an analysis of climate conducted at all levels of management. Finally, an executive retreat was held for the top ten executives, who met over three days to discuss the corporate mission and to prepare a draft of the company's mission statement and business strategy.

The initial interviews, conducted with anonymity, helped the climate consultants gain an understanding of the issues that were important to NBM corporationwide. After the interviews a questionnaire was constructed to survey systematically the fields of concern identified in these private talks with executives. The consultants provided fifty to sixty standard survey items, based on dimensions considered important in the literature and previous experience. These items were selected as a standard practice. Another fifty tailor-made items were written and added to the questionnaire. A few of these latter items were opinion questions, and they often elicited very candid material. All executives at the four organizational levels below the president were sent the questionnaire at their homes, filled it out without identifying themselves, and mailed the document back to the consultant for tabulation and analysis. This previously tested method worked best in achieving the maximum number of responses from a client population, usually at least 85 percent of the sample.

This effort gave Somerville a far better understanding of NBM's position in its industry as well as the viewpoints of his most important managers. It permitted him to begin work developing strategies and structures and to identify the personnel who could be counted on to help the company prepare for the future.

First, Somerville needed to decide on the business he wanted to be in. He needed a corporate strategy and goals. In a systems-oriented industry such as NBM's, there is considerable overlap in products. This makes it difficult to separate the systems companies into distinct businesses. However, for NBM, it was possible to identify three major and distinct enterprises: freestanding equipment, dedicated systems, and general-purpose systems.

Freestanding equipment was NBM's traditional business. It included electromechanical cash registers and accounting machines. Although the business accounted for the bulk of the company's sales, its products were considered to be liquidating. Despite their current prominence, these products were eventually going to be divested, and the company's strategy was to simply attempt to maintain existing market share and profit margins for the time being. To achieve organizational clarity, Somerville made it clear he did not intend to invest much in the cash register business. His goal here was to "maximize profit."

A dedicated system is any combination of terminals, communications equipment, and mainframe units whose processing capability is limited to a few applications. This market could conceivably represent NBM's greatest growth opportunity, but NBM had to compete with American Systems, Inc., the world's largest manufacturer of computers and related systems. Marketing dedicated systems requires extensive knowledge of the problem to be solved by the system, ability to design a system that will solve the problem, engineering know-how to make the system work, and skill in training the customer in its use. Buying decisions are normally based on price, performance, and service capabilities. Because competitors offer similar hardware, the main selling point is the price and performance of software packages.

General-purpose systems are computer systems capable of performing a wide variety of applications. Price and performance are still important elements in the customer's buying decision, but because such systems are intended for general use, processing capability and flexibility are also important, along with software support and service support. The key to competing effectively was to segment user markets, focusing on those areas in which NBM's software was superior. The company wanted to persuade customers who did not yet use a computer to buy NBM's as their first one.

Regarding NBM's freestanding equipment, this was the chosen strategy: The company first decided to work only to maintain current market share and to limit developmental activity to producing a less expensive electronic cash register. At the same time, it was NBM's intention to have freestanding equipment sales account for a declining percentage of its overall revenues. The goal communicated to the sales force was to convince current cash register customers to upgrade to electronic cash registers. And, they were told, get our accounting machine customers to upgrade to small computers. To create a positive climate, it was necessary to make sure sales personnel understood what Somerville was trying to accomplish and why it was necessary for the corporation's survival.

A second strategy was for the company to commit itself to developing dedicated systems for the retail and financial markets and not to worry about penetrating other markets. This strategy was intended to take advantage of the extensive network of retail stores and banks that were the best prospects for the company's products. They provided the opportunity for selling large numbers of similar machines to similar customers. This tactic would require the company to make a major investment in maintaining technical and market superiority in the terminals themselves. It would also mean that NBM would have to spend a large amount of money in training the sales force to upgrade its knowledge of systems.

In its third strategic business decision, the company decided to commit itself fully to the general-purpose computer to protect its current customer base and to go after the first-time computer purchaser.

Having decided what the company's goals were and having taken steps to communicate them, Somerville tended next to the task of achieving better organizational integration in NBM. One problem was an unevenness of talent.

The financial function was the least sophisticated staff function in the company, and most of its energies were devoted to the traditional task of gathering financial information and producing reports of the company's recent business activities. If NBM were to fulfill its overall mission, the financial group would have to acquire a stronger capability in financial planning, budgeting and forecasting, and cost analysis.

The other major problem that surfaced in the climate study was a weak performance orientation and a compensation system that was costly but ineffective. Although NBM had originally been built on the capabilities of a superior sales force, the company was now saddled with a group of highly paid, poorly producing, lazy salespersons. Cooper's original straight-sales-commission compensation arrangement still existed in a number of the company's divisions. It made the average salesperson's take-home pay more than that of the typical middle manager in the company, and the highly tenured salesperson's bonus was exorbitant. The top twenty members of the sales force earned, in salary and bonus, more than all but the top three officers of NBM.

Somerville was determined to change this. He hired a consultant to design a management-by-objectives approach to sales compensation and to explain the new program at the company's annual sales meeting. During the meeting over a dozen of the top producers in the company walked out, and within a week forty resigned. As someone who had left half his company of Marines dead on the beach at Iwo Jima, Somerville was impressed but undaunted. Using experienced people recruited from other electronics manufacturers, he managed to increase sales 30 percent within the first year of the new incentive program and decrease cost of sales by 50 percent. People began to feel that they were earning their money, and the sales force became as gung-ho as it had been during the old days when Cooper was riding point.

Besides a new compensation program, the sales force was given intensive training in systems. The training course was conducted at a former boys' vocational school in Hamburg, a small lakeside town sixty miles northwest of Detroit. Somerville began each day's training by leading his sales troops on a five-mile jog (or walk if necessary) around the shores of Strawberry

Lake. Participants were encouraged to minimize their nighttime socializing and to retire by 10:00 P.M. Since reveille was at 5:30 A.M., few of them argued about it. The intent was to create a climate of high achievers dedicated to excellence, to sharpen the company's performance orientation.

The NBM executives knew that the company needed to move from a freestanding business to a systems-oriented business, and they were concerned that the organization lacked the management skills necessary to run a systems-oriented business. Consequently, a management training program was developed that included courses in market planning and accountability management. Lower and middle managers with above-average potential were put through the program. This was not a response to the climate survey's findings about career development opportunities but rather a real concern about lack of management depth.

A major reorganizational need was seen in the research and development department. The company had always relied more on its marketing ability than on the technical superiority of its products to achieve sales. Now it developed mechanisms to be sure that intelligence from both domestic and international marketing groups was fed back to research and development. R&D got a bigger budget, and its director had every member of his department go through accountability management workshops in which one- and three-year goals were developed.

Finally, the officers felt that one of the problems in their company was that too many people reported to the chief executive officer. Somerville's management span was ten, too broad to permit him the time he needed for strategic planning. Through a major reorganization, it was reduced to the following positions: president, international operating groups; president, domestic operating group; executive vice-president and chief administrative officer; and general counsel. Somerville was advised to spend most of his time on board relationships, long-range planning, and management continuity.

NBM's employees felt that the organization's goals were fairly clear but that planning systems in support of these goals were ill defined and incomplete. Somerville had made his vision known to company employees through annual meetings, annual reports, and frequent field trips. What was missing was a formalized accountability management program that would break down this corporate mission into functional, unit, and personal goals.

The organization's vitality was seen as average, hampered by the belief that little job security existed and that the company had not been responsive to the rapid technical changes in its industry. Somerville admitted that the company had been unresponsive to technical changes in electronics equipment, but he was amused by the interpretation that little job security existed. He felt that the company had a reputation for tolerating incompetence and that many executives had "retired" while still on the job.

Management's style was felt to be satisfactory by the top three levels in the organization, but managers at the fourth level and below felt that they had little freedom and were not encouraged to take risks or to offer constructive criticism. Although the company was decentralized, these managers still perceived a strong sense of centralization and felt that most decisions, even those that did not involve major capital outlays, were still made in Detroit. As a result of reorganization and a new management-by-objectives program, limits of authority were increased, decision making was pushed well down within the divisions, and a participatory management style was encouraged.

Decision making, besides being viewed as centralized and systematic, was seen as focused on the short-term goals of increases in earnings per share and in sales volume. Because the financial function was weak, employees also felt that decision making was based on inadequate forecast information.

Like the cobbler's children who had no shoes, the company, despite being in the information systems business, was seen as having a weak systems capability, and its control systems were viewed as reactive rather than anticipatory. The data-processing department was given six months to respond to the criticisms that had been made of it and to meet with major user departments to develop a list of priorities for new systems and programs. A small research and development department was created within data processing so that the company could itself use the more advanced systems it was selling to others.

Because Somerville was a strong, demanding leader, he was determined to instill a performance orientation in the company and to make sure that individual goals were established and, at least at the top levels, end results were clearly defined and measurable. For several years the company had had a management incentive plan, but little attention had been paid to it. The climate survey revealed below-average satisfaction with the company's compensation. Employees expressed displeasure over the internal equity and external competitiveness of the compensation programs.

The climate data, taken in their entirety, suggested that NBM would face a number of challenges as it attempted to implement its overall business strategy. As the company developed from a single-product organization to a company emphasizing the marketing of total systems, the increased complexity and diversification would strain the organization's ability to integrate and meet organizational goals. This capacity for integration and interunit cooperation was especially lacking at the third and fourth levels of management. It was managers at these levels who were also most dissatisfied with the current compensation programs and for whom the need for management development was most critical. The company would be faced with a need for a massive infusion of management talent and needed to find new managers both within the company and outside it. More support systems were going to be needed, including a performance appraisal program based on accountability management, management development programs, and improved systems capabilities, especially in the financial area.

Within five years of Somerville's shakeup of NBM, the company's performance had improved significantly. Its five-year average return on equity was 18 percent, and it had averaged a 24 percent annual increase in earnings per share. Over the same five-year period, its net profit margins were close to the industry average of about 8 percent. Because its basic freestanding business was in a nongrowth sector of the market and it was still investing in its new products, the company's sales growth was not as impressive. It lagged a few points behind the industry average five-year growth in sales, 23 percent. However, its greatly improved profitability had allowed the company to invest heavily in its new products, and it anticipated a marked improvement in sales growth during the 1980s.

Somerville had used the climate data as a compass for himself and as marching orders to his employees, communicating to them his sense of mission. By setting goals, pulling diverse units together, emphasizing performance, and paying for results, he succeeded in getting NBM off the beach and on the offensive.

4

Primary Measures
of Performance

The mark of a company's success is its quantitative performance. To begin a chapter on corporate measures of performance by writing, "No single standard of performance exists for corporations," is both to tell the truth and to lie. Yes, corporations vary greatly in character, and success is measured differently at various times. It is true that for a corpus as complex as business no single tape takes the whole measure of performance. But it is wrong to assert that there is no best quantitative measure of corporate performance—because there is a best measure: It is profit. Profit is the best single indicator that the organization is doing things right.

Profit

The primary measure of the success of an organization, and its primary responsibility to society, is the performance of its mission. Its second responsibility, and the key to the organization's ability to continue to contribute to society, is the economically effective performance of its mission. To make a profit, a company must create more value than it consumes. If it does not make a profit, both the company and society suffer. Because profit is the primary measure of organizational success, it is important that a description of measuring corporate performance begin with an explanation of profit and its role in business.

Definition. Profit is such a misunderstood concept that it seems wise to begin in the most prosaic of ways—by consulting dictionaries. Webster's defines *profit* as "the excess of income over expenditure in a given transaction." The unabridged *Oxford English Dictionary*'s definition is "the surplus product of industry after deducting wages, cost of raw material, rent, and charges."

From these definitions we see that the idea of profit involves finishing with more than you started with. It means adding, creating, and increasing. The concept immediately becomes more complicated as one tries to further refine the definition. Although profit is the best measure of performance, still there is something lacking in all measures of profit. So, although singular definitions are possible, multiple measures are best. In this and later chapters, such measures of profit as return on sales and return on capital will be discussed in detail and illustrations provided of the profitability of various industries.

Although the word *profit* is used in the Old Testament, in context it means progress or advance: "All was vanity and vexation of spirit and there was no profit under the sun" (Ecclesiastes 2:11). The idea of gaining financial profit from doing business to advance one's station in life was a value not widely held before the industrial revolution. It was only with the rise of capitalism that the idea of profit as financial gain was born. In this concept, profit is the natural result of the economical use of money, materials, and labor. A product or service is sold at a price that exceeds the cost of producing it. The resulting additional money is a return on capital, a savings fund. Profit is a fee earned for the use of money or other means of production.

Another explanation of profit is the one Karl Marx put forward in his book *Das Kapital.* The Marxian view is that profit is surplus value. Surplus value is defined as the true value of the labor that goes into a product minus the value paid to the worker in wages. The worker is required by the capitalist, the person providing the investment and the machinery, to work more hours than he is actually paid for. The worker works longer hours than is required for his basic sustenance. This additional labor, in Marx's view, creates the surplus value. Profit is a result of unpaid-for labor, rather than a fee paid for the use of capital.

Role of Profit in Society. The Nobel Prize–winning economist Milton Friedman, in *Free to Choose* (Friedman and Friedman, 1979), writes that the accumulation of capital is essential to economic growth. The maintenance of that capital from one generation to the next is necessary to restrict needless dissipation. If there is no reward for accumulating capital, if it must all be given to the government through taxes for income redistribution, then why save? Why not spend the capital for goods and services today rather than investing that capital for tomorrow?

Peter Drucker also vigorously defends the role of profit in society. In *Management* (1973) he writes that profit serves vital economic functions. It is the premium paid for risk, an insurance cost of staying in business, the fund necessary to help business through unforeseen but inevitable setbacks and losses. Capital is necessary for producing the jobs of tomorrow. Without investment capital the fundamental equation of production—capital, labor, materials—cannot operate. Capital is needed as a source of innovation and growth.

For Drucker, the key to the issue of profit is *needed profit.* Business needs to produce a minimum amount of profit, or surplus value, in order to survive. Profit should be viewed as a minimum phenomenon or as a needed phenomenon, not as a maximum phenomenon. Profit is the result of efficient performance in marketing and production, and profit, along with the product or service provided, is one of the contributions of business to society.

To fail to produce profit is to borrow against the future. Only profit maximization does not matter. Companies that have a strategy of maximum profit are borrowing against their future at their own peril.

The right questions to ask regarding profit are (1) What is the minimum profit acceptable in the conduct of our business? (2) What is the optimum profit acceptable at this time in the life of our business? One interpretation of minimum acceptable profit is based on the cost of capital. The concept is that, at a minimum, the rate of profitability of a business enterprise must exceed the cost of its capital; otherwise the business will eventually devour itself. For example, if the organization is lent capital by its bank at a prime rate of 10 percent, then the organization must achieve a minimum profitability in excess of 10 percent.

Another concept of minimum corporate profitability is based on the return that investors would be able to earn by placing their capital in fixed-income vehicles with minimum risks. For example, if U.S. government treasury bills are returning 10 percent to investors, then the minimum rate of profitability of a business enterprise should be greater than 10 percent. Stockholders have a right to ask: "Why should I place my capital in a venture that has risk? Why not place my capital in a vehicle that has no risk if I can receive an equal return on my investment?" Such questions may seem elementary to some, but they seem to be seldom asked by those who argue that the profits of business are excessive. If a business cannot earn more than a fixed-income investment, there is little monetary incentive for doing that business.

A prime motivator of entrepreneurship is to be able to achieve a higher rate of return on an investment through business activity than through a pure financial vehicle. When the overall rate of return on investment for a business drops below that of fixed-income vehicles, then the minimum rate of profitability for that business enterprise is too low. The only counterargument to this viewpoint is in a planned economy, where rate of return is unimportant. In this instance capital is placed where the planners believe it will do the most good regardless of profitability.

How Much Profit? A common misconception is that most businesses are profitable, and obscenely so. This is not true. The median return on total capital for the years 1976–1981 was only 11.1 percent, according to *Forbes* magazine's annual analysis of the profitability of over 1,000 American businesses. This was up somewhat from the 8.6 percent achieved during the first five years of the 1970s.

There are other statistics that help put the question of profitability in perspective. In a given year only about 60 percent of businesses are profitable. The other 40 percent either break even or operate at a loss. To better understand how negligible profits are in the overall flow of dollars, it is useful to compare profits with the cost of labor. Wages consist of about 40 percent of the gross sales of the average company. Wages and salaries together are approximately 65 percent of the gross national product of the United States. Profits, in contrast, historically have averaged about 5 percent of corporate sales. Therefore, profits are rarely more than 15 percent of wages. The surplus value in the economic equation is an important but small number.

Size and Growth

Beyond profit, the other major measures of corporate performance are size and growth. Like profit, size is a concept, not a statistic. Size can be measured in terms of number of employees, value added, number of markets, and so on. But most often size and growth are measured in terms of revenue, and this is the most appropriate measure.

Companies grow in sales, in people, in capital, and in profitability. Companies that choose to grow at the price of lower profitability, and those that choose higher rates of profit growth at a sacrifice in market position, threaten their long-term survival. Regarding ultimate size, the company must ask itself, "Beyond what limits is further growth harmful? At what point have we exceeded our ability to perform our corporate mission economically with the financial and human resources at our disposal?"

Organizations must grow in order to survive. An old business bromide is that you never stand still—you either go forward or go backward. Like most clichés, it is partially true. Organizations that do not grow will eventually be acquired by other organizations, or they will go out of existence. Organizations need to be dynamic. This dynamism finds expression in increased size and complexity. Growth should be the result of the proficient achievement of the corporate mission. The company should grow because it is doing things right. If it simply attempts to grow for growth's sake, it is wasting its resources.

If growth for its own sake is not virtue, then an organization needs a policy regarding growth. It needs to establish strategies, priorities, and objectives for corporate growth—to decide on the amount of growth it needs to remain vigorous and to provide career opportunities for its people. Growth is usually expressed by corporations in exponential form as a percentage of last year's sales. Exponential growth is difficult to sustain. Traditional numerical indices of corporate growth have been 10 percent in profit and 10 percent in sales. These numbers were typical during the 1950s and 1960s. During the 1970s growth in sales averaged closer to 14 percent.

Most industries do not continue to grow over time at an exponential rate, whether that rate is 5 percent or 25 percent a year. Instead, industries tend to follow traditional patterns of growth. The first phase in an industry is the opening of a market. Opportunities are seen for new products and new markets, and a sense of excitement brings many companies into the business. Everyone does well initially, and this success brings in more organizations. The second phase of industry growth is therefore characterized by many small companies. The third phase is overcrowding. The market begins to become saturated, and less efficient companies experience smaller margins. Price cutting often occurs. The fourth phase is a shakeout, with less efficient organizations either going out of business or being acquired.

The final phase is consolidation; as few as three and no more than about a dozen major companies survive. Moderate-sized organizations may find a special niche in the market. The remaining successful companies tend to be small cottage industries. An example of this kind of industry growth pattern is the automotive industry from 1880 to 1980.

The *Fortune* 500 Ratings

One of the readily available compendiums on corporate performance published each year is the *Fortune* 500. *Fortune* magazine ranks the 500 largest industrial corporations in the United States, along with the 500 next largest, and the 500 largest industrial corporations outside the United States. *Fortune* also ranks the 50 largest commercial banks, diversified financial, retailing, and transportation corporations, and utilities in the United States; the 50 largest industrial corporations in the world; and the 50 largest commercial banking corporations outside the United States.

Size is the basis for these rankings. For industrial corporations, total sales volume is the main criterion. Also recorded are assets, net income, stockholders' equity, number of employees, net income as a percentage of sales, net income as a percentage of stockholders' equity, earnings per share, growth rate, and total return to investors for one year and ten years. Financial institutions and utilities are ranked by assets, retail corporations by sales, and transportation corporations by operating revenues.

It is difficult to translate these ratings into an evaluation of performance for a particular corporation because of the standards used. For example, Exxon, the largest American corporation in 1981 according to sales, was also number one in assets, net income, and stockholders' equity. It was 8th in number of employees but 198th in net income as a percentage of sales, 84th in net income as a percentage of stockholders' equity, 191st in growth rate, and 347th in total return.

Measures of Size and Performance. Fortune acknowledges that its ratings measure size more than performance by also including an evaluation of "Who did best and worst among the 500," ranking the ten highest and five lowest performers, along with the industry medians. An important measure of corporate performance is earnings per share. *Fortune* defines this as a weighted average of the number of common shares and common-stock equivalents outstanding during the year. The growth rate in earnings per share is the average annual growth compounded.

An interesting and rarely used measure of corporate performance is the total return to investors who might have bought the company's stock. It is really a measure of stock-market performance rather than corporate performance. Total return to investors includes both price appreciation and dividend yield.

Fortune presents industry medians for 27 industry codes. The numbers identifying the industry groups are based on categories established by the U.S. Office of Management and Budget and are issued by the federal Office of Statistical Policy and Standards. For 1981 the *Fortune* 500 industrials showed a sales increase of 7.5 percent. Median return on sales was 4.6 percent in 1981, down from 4.8 percent the previous year. Median return on equity dropped from 14.4 percent to 13.8 percent.

A popular measure of corporate performance is return on stockholders' equity (ROE). This figure is net income divided by equity. For 1981 *Fortune* reported a median return on stockholders' equity of 13.8 percent. But the figure is misleading, says *Fortune,* because it contains illusions: deductions for depreciation that are too low and gains on inventory that are too high.

The favorite measure of performance of the stock market, return to investors, is not really a measure of corporate performance. It is a statement about trading activity in the company's stock. Historically there has been only a modest relationship between a company's performance and what the public is willing to pay for its stock. Over the last ten years, the average annual rate of return to a hypothetical investor who bought the stock of the *Fortune* 500 was 8.52 percent. This rate of return does not encourage risk. Aerospace and mining did much better, with a rate of return to investors of over 15 percent.

The value of the *Fortune* 500 to executive management is that it permits a quick look at how one's own organization measures up against others. The corporation can compare its overall size with the 500. It can calculate ratios to contrast its economic performance with that of companies in similar industries. For example, net income as a percentage of sales is easy to calculate and is meaningful. Return on equity—net income as a percentage of stockholders' equity—is also a calculation that is easy to make. For some reason *Fortune* does not provide information on return on total capital invested, probably one of the better summary measures of corporate efficiency. Instead, it devotes considerable space to an analysis of total return to investors, more a measure of stock-market than corporate performance.

Changes in the Fortune *500.* Does corporate performance vary much over the years? Do the standings change? About 7.6 percent of the *Fortune* 500 were displaced from the ranks in 1979. Only five companies, 1 percent, were displaced because their growth failed to keep pace with the other companies. The other organizations dropped out of the 500 because they merged with other companies or were acquired by them.

The *Fortune* list can be analyzed over a long time span. For example, 47.6 percent of the companies that were on the list in 1955 were no longer there in 1980. Only 1 percent of these companies actually went out of business. Another 1 percent decided that the benefits of public ownership were not worth the aggravation, and they reacquired enough of their stock to become privately owned. *Fortune* defines an industrial company as one in which at least 50 percent of revenues come from manufacturing. Three percent of the companies on the list twenty-five years ago no longer meet this criterion. About 6 percent of the original list maintained their independent public stature but failed to grow at the 9.9 percent average annual rate of sales to keep up with the rest. The largest percentage of companies no longer on the list were absorbed by other companies.

Growth. With the *Fortune* premium on growth in sales, consider the fate of the top 100 companies on the first list, the surviving Goliaths of industry. All the top 100 companies on the original list twenty-five years ago are on the current list, but only nine of them are still in the top 100. This supports the argument that exponential growth in sales is difficult to maintain over an extended period of time. It also reflects the changing emphases in American industry. In 1955 the top 100 list was dominated by such industries as food, textiles, autos, rubber, and metal manufacturing. These basic industries, plus oils, accounted for 43 percent of the total sales of the group. In twenty-five years this share had shrunk to 30 percent. The problems of the auto industry and the success of the oil industry are well known. The decline in the importance of food and textiles is due to changing demographics and tastes. Industries that grew rapidly in the last twenty-five years include high-technology companies. Xerox, for example, grew from $17 million in sales to $7 billion. Cosmetic and pharmaceutical companies also made large gains in sales.

Most companies whose sales gains exceeded their industry medians or the median for the entire list were companies that used mergers and acquisitions to increase volume. The company that ranked second in sales growth over this period, Georgia Pacific, made over seventy acquisitions and in the process changed itself from a small lumber company into an integrated manufacturer of paper and pulp. Other companies in the top ten in sales gains made an average of twenty acquisitions each. Signal Companies, for example, acquired two companies that were in the original *Fortune* 500—Mack Truck and the Garrett Corporation. The 500 companies in the core group made approximately 4,500 acquisitions over the twenty-five-year period.

Twenty-Five-Year Profitability. Total profits of the 500 as measured by return on equity grew over the twenty-five years at an average rate of 4 percent per annum. Return on stockholders' equity improved dramatically, from 11.1 percent in 1964 to 16.9 percent in 1979. This increase is largely a function of inflation. *Fortune* calculates return on stockholder equity as profit divided by book value. The denominator, book value, is artificially low because assets acquired many years ago are shown at historical cost minus depreciation.

During the same twenty-five years another measure of profitability actually showed a decline. This measure may be a more realistic indicator of corporate performance. Between 1954 and 1979 the average profit margin, or return on sales, dropped from 6 percent to 5.4 percent. As corporations became larger and acquired smaller corporations, profits often declined.

Marx predicted such a decline in profits and attributed it to increased wages paid to workers, who would still, nevertheless, be exploited. Salary increases, though substantial, are only one reason for the decline in profit margins. The costs of commodities and energy have soared. In the last twenty-five years government has added greatly to the cost of doing business by requiring compliance with regulations purporting to protect the environment, the worker, and the consumer. Corporations that grow through acquisition appear to have a lower overall level of profitability than those that grow internally. Companies that made five or fewer acquisitions over the last twenty-five years showed a 9.4 percent increase in earnings per share, compared with 8.9 percent for companies that made more than thirty acquisitions during the same period.

If an investor had been clever enough to buy the stock of every company that remained in the *Fortune* 500 during the entire quarter century, he would have made a decent return on his investment—9.1 percent. A person who invested $100 in a core *Fortune* 500 stock in 1954 would have had stock worth $886 at the end of 1979. This figure does not look bad when compared with the 4 percent compounded rate of inflation over the same period. It is better than the average rate of return the investor would have made by putting his money in a more secure fixed-income vehicle. That is what capitalism is supposedly about. More risk yields more return.

For executives interested in the longer term, however defined, the numbers to remember for average annual rates over the twenty-five-year period are these: growth in sales, 9.9 percent; earnings per share, 8.1 percent; total return to investors, 9.4 percent.

Forbes's Annual Report on American Industry

Although *Fortune* is the best-known reference on numerical indices of corporate performance, it is not the only reference. For the past thirty-four years *Forbes* magazine has published an annual report on American industry, which has become the other major annual ranking system by which American businesses judge themselves. *Forbes*'s measures are somewhat different from *Fortune*'s. *Forbes* covers the top 1,023 public companies, most of them with sales in excess of $400 million. Like the *Fortune* 500, *Forbes* measures profitability and return on capital. It also provides a measure of return on total capital that it calls the "ultimate" or "basic" measure of an enterprise's profitability. Its industry groups are more extensive than the *Fortune* 500—forty-six for 1981, compared with *Fortune*'s twenty-seven. Its report places less emphasis on size and is more concerned with profitability and growth. *Forbes* concentrates on performance and leaves size to *Fortune*.

The six measures of performance used by *Forbes* are the following:

1. *Debt-to-equity ratio.* There are two major sources of capital for businesses. One is stockholder equity, and the other is debt—bank loans and bonds. The debt-to-equity ratio is the long-term debt divided by total stockholders' equity. The all-industry median of debt to equity is 0.4. Companies with higher ratios than that are using more borrowed funds (leverage) in their attempts to improve profits. Since many financial analysts are enamored of return on stockholder equity, by holding down the use of equity and using more debt, the company can make its ROE figures higher and make a more favorable impression on the stock analyst.

2. *Return on stockholders' equity.* This is the percentage return on the stockholders' portion of the total capital used by the company. *Forbes* expresses earnings per common share as a percentage of stockholders' equity per share. The calculation involves an assumption that all convertible preferred stock is converted at the start of the year. Although return on equity is probably the most popular and frequently used measure of corporate profitability, it is not necessarily the best measure.

3. *Return on total capital.* This is the percentage return on stockholders' equity plus long-term debt. The sum of these two figures is the denominator. The numerator is the sum of net income, minority interest in that income, and esti-

mated after-tax interest paid on long-term debt. Stated another way, it is income before charges that relate to the nonequity portion of capital.

4. *Net profit margin.* The simplest measure of corporate profitability is the percentage of each dollar of revenue available after all expenses have been paid. It is calculated by dividing net profit by sales. When the amount of capital used is not taken into account, then the most profitable businesses are those that bring down to the "bottom line" the greatest percentage of their sales dollars.

5. *Earnings-per-share growth.* Another popular measure of corporate performance is growth in earnings per share, calculated by taking the average earnings per share for the most recent five years and computing the percentage change from the average for the preceding five years. *Forbes* expresses that change in terms of a five-year compounded annual rate of growth.

6. *Sales growth.* This figure is computed by comparing the average sales for the company's most recent five years against the average for the preceding five years and expressing the change in terms of a compounded annual growth rate.

For 1981 a summary of the key measures from *Forbes* was as follows:

1. Debt-to-equity ratio—0.4.
2. Return on stockholders' equity—14.7 percent.
3. Return on total capital—11.1 percent.
4. Net profit margin—4.5 percent.
5. Growth in earnings per share—12.5 percent.
6. Growth in sales—14.0 percent.

In the first five years of the 1970s, *Forbes*'s all-industry median for return on equity was 11.6 percent. Over the last half of the decade, return on equity had increased to 15.8 percent. Return on total capital similarly increased from 8.6 percent over the first half of the decade to 11.1 percent in the latter half. The median debt-to-equity ratio stayed about the same, 0.4. The median net profit margin increased from 3.9 percent to 5 percent.

Forbes's interpretation of these data is that American businesses are doing a better job than ever in economic performance. Their figures and conclusions are somewhat different from those reported by *Fortune* magazine. *Fortune* generally tends to be more sedate, *Forbes* more buoyant. But journalistic style cannot entirely account for the differences in findings and interpretations. Part of the answer may reside in the sample. Another difference between the approaches of the two magazines is that *Forbes* uses the same yardsticks of corporate performance for manufacturing and for financial institutions. There is some question about the advisability of doing this. Finally, because of the time of year when data were gathered, their figures are close but not exactly comparable.

Return on Equity Versus Return on Capital. In 1982 *Forbes* stated that "the most commonly used measure of profitability for a company is return on equity. The ultimate measure is return on total capital—equity plus debt." A highly leveraged company, one with more than 50 cents in debt for every dollar of equity, can show spectacular increases in ROE with modest increases in net income.

Forbes reported that 27 percent of the companies whose growth it analyzed had failed to keep pace with inflation. Of those that did keep up, 45 percent appeared to do so at the cost of earnings growth. They showed greater sales growth than growth in earnings. Maximizing sales appears to reduce profits. The manager must decide on the optimum growth in sales and profits that will sustain the achievement of the corporate mission over time.

It is apparent from examining the major measures of corporate performance—profit, size, and growth—that each business must decide for itself what measures honestly tell management how it is doing. Such decisions should be made independently of any predictions of how the stock market will react to that performance.

One useful feature of the *Forbes* treatment is its brief but telling analysis of selected industries. It allows a manager to compare results with peers and to peek over the fence at the color of his neighbor's grass.

Autos and Trucks. By any standard the auto and truck industry is a second-rate business. With a little less leverage than the average industrial company, over the last five years it has turned in a poor performance on all measures of profitability and growth. Its return on equity is below industry medians, and so are its return on capital, net profit margin, and growth in earnings per share.

The automotive industry is now suffering the consequences of having failed earlier to review and renew its corporate mission. The car companies had an outdated corporate strategy—to produce large cars when their customers wanted economical smaller ones. Because the auto industry directly or indirectly employs one of every five industrial workers in the United States, the problem is important. Peter Drucker says that the first priority of every business is to have a customer. The automotive industry lost contact with its customers, failing to alter its business strategy to meet their changing demands.

Electronics. The electronics industry is a huge success by any measure of corporate performance. Although it is less leveraged than the average company, its returns on equity and on capital are both higher than average, and net profit margins run 6.2 percent, compared with the industry average of 4.5 percent. Growth in sales is also above average, and compounded increases in earnings far outstrip other industries. The business has been characterized by cycles of high demand, overcapacity, and price cutting. Despite the profits of the industry, there is evidence of cautiousness in capital spending.

Capital Equipment. If you asked the average business executive, "How profitable is the capital-equipment business?," chances are he would answer, "Not very." He would be wrong.

Over the last five years, the capital-goods industry has

been living a life of quiet respectability. CEOs have maintained average net profit margins. With slightly less debt than average, they have turned in respectable performances in profitability, both in return on equity and in return on capital. Growth in sales has matched that of other industries, while earnings have steadily improved.

Yet, the industrial and equipment manufacturers are at the heart of the crisis facing American industry. What should be a terrific market for them may turn out to be no market at all. American companies have billions of dollars' worth of obsolete production machinery that they should be replacing. More than two thirds of American machine tools are over ten years old, and more than one third are over twenty years old.

During recessions U.S. industry operates at about three quarters of capacity. Capital investment by companies is low when the cost of capital is high. Lower interest rates and more capital investment are critical if the United States is to continue to compete as a major international industrial power. More lenient depreciation schedules may help the industry, but what is really necessary is a fundamentally strong economy. If growth in real gross national product remains low and cost of capital stays high, then the capital-goods industry may become the unprofitable business that most executives think it is.

Financial Institutions. The financial business is undergoing a transformation more substantial than any it has experienced since the Great Depression. The Depository Institutions Deregulation and Monetary Control Act of 1980, one of the most significant pieces of financial legislation ever passed by Congress, will have a dramatic impact on both banks and savings and loan institutions. At the same time that the basic mission of financial institutions is being reshaped, the historical links between cost of money, earning power of money, and stability in interest rates have been hacked apart. The resulting changes in costs, products, customers, and missions will alter the financial business as we know it. Innovative and aggressive qualities will typify the financial CEOs who see their organizations survive into the next century.

Financial Institutions

The landmark Depository Institutions Deregulation and Monetary Control Act deregulated the banking industry. It gradually lifts the limits on what banks can pay for funds. It permits banks to pay interest on checking accounts, money that previously had been cost-free. Deregulation may result in higher operating costs and declining profit margins and profitability ratios. Another result could be a consolidation by almost half of the country's 14,000 banks. The consolidation will come primarily from mergers and acquisitions rather than from outright bank failures. Interstate banking is expected to further accelerate the consolidation.

Unfortunately, all this is happening at a time when the strength of the banking system itself is questionable. The controller of the currency has warned the public that hundreds of banks in the United States are considered problem banks and that a number of these institutions could fail. The ratio of bank equity to assets has fallen below 4 percent. Every $1 in stockholder equity supports more than $25 in loans and investments. And banks are relying more and more on high-cost purchase money, which can be withdrawn on short notice.

In response to these changes, banks are pushing hard to strengthen their commercial loan business and to have their short-term bank loans replace long-term bonds as the major supplier of capital to business. During the 1970s U.S. companies tried to avoid issuing bonds or taking a bank loan by raising capital through commercial paper and foreign borrowing. In their scramble to redefine their basic mission and their customers, the banks will have to stop short of managing equity placements. The Glass-Steagall Act of 1933 still separates commercial banking from investment banking.

With the same debt-to-equity ratio as the average industrial company, banks have had substantially higher profit margins (6.7 percent, compared with 5.0 percent). But their overall profitability has been only about average for return on capital and a little below average for return on equity. The only big money made in banking over the next ten years may be by the owners of small banks who sell out to the larger acquiring ones.

Savings and Loan Institutions. There was a time when running a savings and loan business was one of the easiest top-management jobs around. A savings and loan, no matter how large, was the least complex of all financial institutions. It had simply to take in savings deposits at relatively low rates and lend them back out at higher rates, making only one kind of loan—a mortgage loan on a single-family dwelling. You could make a good profit doing this, earning above-average returns on capital and an average return on your equity. Growth in sales was great, and compounded growth in earnings per share was acceptable.

Deregulation of the industry blurred the distinctions between savings and loan institutions and commercial banks. The larger savings and loan institutions are really financial holding companies in which the savings and loan business is merely the core.

As with banks, what can be expected in savings and loan associations is the consolidation of the industry, with smaller and medium-sized companies being swallowed by the industry giants. Savings and loans that will survive will be characterized not only by size but by diversity and the ability to devise financial packages that are not destroyed by the ravages of inflation.

Insurance. The insurance business has traditionally been an extremely profitable one. With sweet debt-to-equity ratios and fat profit margins, the business has been scrumptiously profitable. Return on equity has been 18.9 percent for all lines and as high as 22.5 percent in the fire and casualty business. Fire and casualty companies have returned a fantastic 20 percent on capital at times, while insurance as a whole has returned better than the all-industry median. Although five-year growth in sales has dragged a bit, growth in earnings per share has been strong.

All this could be just so much history. Inflation has changed what the customer buys from insurance companies. Whole-life insurance policies were the mainstay of insurance. Through them policyholders insured their lives and built up a savings account through a portion of their premium. But inflation made customers reluctant to buy these types of policies, and they turned to cheaper term insurance, investing the remainder of their money in vehicles paying higher rates.

Life insurance companies have had to change their products to make them more competitive with other investment vehicles. Undoubtedly this will reduce profit margins. They are also trying to sell more group insurance policies. These policies now account for 33 percent of all life insurance policies, up from 25 percent ten years ago.

One reason for the excellent profitability of the property and casualty companies is that their premiums rise as inflation drives up the value of the insured object. The property and casualty industry receives roughly half of the insurance industry's total of $18 billion in annual premiums. Consequently, more and more life insurance companies are attempting to enter the more profitable property and casualty business.

Besides developing new types of insurance coverage and trying to grab a piece of the profitable property and casualty business, the insurance companies are scrambling to find methods to protect their investments from inflation. Traditionally insurance companies derive a substantial—in some cases, a major—portion of their income from the investment of premiums. So they are experimenting with a number of new investment vehicles, which they hope will protect them from the squeeze inflation is putting on their profit margins.

Business Week *and the Banks.* Some industries require their own specialized measures of performance to accurately reflect achievement in that business. One such industry is commercial banking.

Since 1971 *Business Week* magazine has published a *Bank Score Card* in April of each year. Its survey, prepared by the Denver-based Standard & Poor's Compustat Services, Inc., analyzes the performance of the 200 largest banks in the United States. *Large,* in this case, is defined by assets.

In addition to the standard return-on-equity and return-on-capital measures of performance available from other sources, *Business Week* provides several other measures of corporate profitability. These are return on average assets, leverage, and operating income as a percentage of net interest income. Abbreviated and simplified definitions of the *Business Week* bank measures are as follows:

- *Return on average assets.* This figure is the net operating income minus preferred dividends, divided by the bank's average daily assets.
- *Net interest income.* The amount the bank takes in on its earning assets, primarily loans, minus the amount it pays out on its funds, primarily deposits.
- *Operating income as a percentage of net interest income.* Net operating income (adjusted for security gains and losses) divided by net interest income. The larger the figure, the more of a cushion the bank has to cover other operating costs.

The most important single indicator of a commercial bank's performance is its return on average assets. This is a measure of how well the bank is able to generate profits from earning assets (loans and investments) and physical assets (branches and equipment). A bank can raise its return on average assets by raising its net operating income through doing a larger volume of business, increasing its rates, or utilizing its facilities more productively.

Business Week uses the concept of capitalized leverage to examine bank performance. Leverage is defined as average assets divided by common equity. Bank regulatory agencies have guidelines about leverage, and banks are expected to come under increasing pressure as their leverage grows.

In the banking community, a return on average assets of over 1.0 is generally viewed as distinguished performance. The average ROA for the twenty-five largest banks is usually around 0.7. Return on average assets decreases as bank size increases (see Table 6).

In addition to size, a bank must also consider whether it

Table 6. Typical Relations Between Bank Size and Profitability.

Rank	Banks with ROA over 1%
1–50	12% ($N = 6$)
51–100	18% ($N = 9$)
101–150	34% ($N = 17$)
151–200	36% ($N = 18$)

is a money-center bank, such as the large banks located around New York and Chicago, or a regional bank. Regional banks in Texas and Minnesota tend to rank highest in return on average assets. California and Texas banks tend to lead the field in return on equity. Regional banks are more profitable than money-center banks. Return on equity shows a similar pattern, higher for regional banks than for money-center banks.

Business Week's *Bank Score Card* illustrates how the executive may need to consult a number of published data sources to uncover the most useful set of statistics for evaluating and managing organizational performance.

Real Numbers or Imaginary Numbers?

Any of the measures of corporate performance just reviewed can be challenged. The most fundamental of challenges is "Are these real numbers produced by the actions of the corporation, or are they imaginary numbers, the result of inflation?" The answer is as important as the difference between fact and fiction, success and ruin.

The bloat of inflation so distended sales and profits that the Financial Accounting Standards Board required a change in the 1980 annual reports of publicly traded corporations. This affects how revenues, sales, and profits are reported by about 1,350 of the largest publicly owned companies in the United States. The rule is known as FAS No. 33. It requires companies to show shareholders the effect of inflation on earnings. The former chairman of the Securities and Exchange Commission called it "the most important short-term act of the SEC during my term" (quoted in Los Angeles *Times,* January 18, 1981). He said he hoped that the inflation-adjusted figures would shock Congress into passing tax incentives to promote capital investment.

The historical-cost method has been the one used by companies in accounting for the performance described by *Fortune* and *Forbes.* Companies add up their revenues for products, investments, and other income sources and simply subtract from that total all the costs required to produce the product. The difference is the profit. They have been using the profit to pay dividends and to invest in corporate growth.

Over the years, the percentage of profit available as working capital for reinvestment has been declining regularly. For example, General Electric's regular financial statement of 1979 shows that 41 percent of its earnings went for taxes and 26 percent for dividends; the remaining 39 percent was retained earnings for reinvestment and growth. But after adjusting for inflation, the new numbers look much different. Taxes now consumed 51 percent of earnings, dividends were 32 percent, and profit for reinvestment was only 17 percent.

In another example, Bethlehem Steel's 1979 profits shrank from $276 million to $54 million when readjusted for inflation. In its annual report, Bethlehem Steel commented on the variance with patrician placidity: "In particular, the generation of funds during these inflationary times has fallen far short of what is needed to replace and modernize our production facilities." Explaining the effect of inflation on earnings, Bethlehem says, "The primary reason is that depreciation expense, as reported, does not adequately reflect the rapidly increasing cost of replacing capital equipment."

In a survey of 695 companies in thirty-five industry classifications compiled by the accounting firm of Ernst and Whinney, 1979 historical-cost financial figures were sharply lowered when adjusted for inflation. They are 40 percent lower in income and 50 percent lower in return on equity. The average ROE for industrial corporations in 1979, calculated on the basis of historical cost, was approximately 16 percent. This means that the actual inflation-adjusted ROE during that year was 8 percent—which is 20 percent lower than the traditional 10 percent ROE that industry has come to expect from the investment of stockholder equity.

The new FASB rules on inflation require that a company provide information on "purchasing-power gains or losses." Gains are derived from borrowing long-term at fixed interest rates and paying back the money with cheaper dollars. These purchasing-power gains are achieved by passing on to corporate creditors and vendors the liabilities of inflation. In its 1979 annual report Pepsico, Inc., reported that about one third of its net income was due to purchasing-power gain. This is because a 1970 dollar of debt could be repaid with 53 cents in 1979.

Besides showing more realistic sales and profitability figures, an additional value of the new accounting changes is that they show the increased burden of taxes for U.S. corporations. Using a historical-cost method of accounting, the effective tax rate of the 695 companies surveyed was 40 percent. Using inflation-adjusted accounting methods, the actual tax burden is 53 percent. Either number is outrageous. Corporations and individuals alike now tithe into the government poor box 40 cents on every dollar they make, and that dollar diminishes daily in value.

Even the accounting profession is no longer sure how to add 2 + 2 or subtract 4 from 5. Accountants have recommended that companies use two different methods to calculate the effects of inflation. Under the constant-dollar method, companies adjust their earnings based on the change in the Consumer Price Index. The premise is that inflation indiscriminately erodes the purchasing power of the dollar. The other method of calculation is the current-cost method. The premise here is that inflation affects each business in a different way, and each company is allowed to make its own calculations. The difference between the two methods can be enormous. Storage Technology Corporation's earnings, calculated by historical cost, were $39.7 million in 1979. Under the constant-dollar method they were $21.3 million. Using the company's own calculations of current cost, they were $52.2 million.

Managing corporate performance requires the ability to compare yourself against other companies. Businesses can be compared only if the measurements are taken in the same way and if the calculations are done using the same assumptions. It would seem that either the constant-dollar method or the historical-cost method, adjusted by some simple, universally applied inflation factor, will be the best way to allow intercompany comparisons.

5

Supplemental Measures
of Performance

The primary measures of corporate performance are profitability, size, and growth. They are quantitative, are relative, and allow an organization to compare its own achievements over time. Equally important, they permit companies to examine themselves against others so they can know whether their performance is commonplace or special.

Most managers rely heavily, but preferably not exclusively, on corporate measures of performance such as revenues, assets, and the common measures of profit: return on equity, return on capital, and profit margin (return on sales). Their choice of growth measures includes compounded growth in revenues and compounded growth in earnings per share. None of these measures is perfect, but all have utility. Picking some of these measures in advance and establishing annual and long-term levels of achievement will aid the executive in assuring corporate performance.

Although quantitative standards of profit and growth are the most frequently cited and used methods of comparison, they should not be the only measures used for a company's long-term success. It is necessary to go beyond profit and growth to consider measures that are collateral and supplemental. This chapter is about some of these ancillary measures—where to find them and what they mean. There may be times when measures that on an annual basis would be considered supplemental are actually of great use in corporate planning. The case study in this chapter is an example of this kind of instance.

Supplemental measures of corporate performance that are quantitative add detail to what is already known. Their purpose is to lower the risk, to add balance, and to correct any deficiency that may be inherent in relying on a primary measure. They are collateral measures in the sense that they accompany or are related to the primary measures but are usually subordinate to them.

Hay Performance Compensation

Because of its expertise in executive compensation, the Hay Group is frequently asked to assist organizations in positioning their incentive compensation and salaries at the appropriate level based on executives' performance. In response to this need, Hay has designed an analytical tool that it calls "Performance Compensation." This is a statistical modeling procedure that projects the appropriate total cash compensation (salary plus bonus) for degrees of corporate performance achieved.

Regression analysis is first used to determine how the marketplace actually evaluates different kinds of performance. The results show to what extent pay and performance are equated. Next a model is used that selects various performance criteria and projects correlated compensation levels. This customized approach acknowledges that the performance factors used in the regression equation and their subsequent results may not support the company's current strategic mission and corporate plans. The model has the corporation select the performance variable and its weight.

The first decision the company makes is the "comparable corporations" decision. There are about 600 manufacturing companies in the Hay Compensation Comparison from which the organization can choose to make compensation comparisons. The company can choose to make various performance comparisons with the approximately 1,700 companies that are followed in the Value Line Investment Survey. The company chooses its comparison group.

The next step in the model is for the company to decide which of the various performance factors to use. Figure 3 shows eight major measures of corporate performance that can be used. Three of the measures relate to the absolute level of performance, and three relate to improvement. The absolute levels are annualized performance figures. These would typically be used in setting annual goals for the corporation. When performance is tied to compensation, these are the areas of corporate performance for which an organization would pay an annual bonus or incentive. The improvement measures are selected to show sustained achievement over time. These normally are considered in conjunction with long-term incentive plans. There are a total of thirty-two factors measuring absolute and improvement levels of performance. Corporate management is thus forced to think through its short- and longer-term aims and to tie this strategic decision to its compensation plan.

Once a company has decided on the category of performance that it believes is most relevant, it then considers which of the three to five individual measures of performance within that concept are most applicable. For example, assuming profitability is a conceptually valid measure of corporate performance for the organization, which of the five measures should it choose? Most corporations select either return on equity or return on capital, sometimes both. Fewer choose return on assets or return on employees. Return on sales, commonly called profit margin, tends to be in the middle. Sometimes it is a useful measure of profitability, sometimes not.

A discernible trend has developed, particularly among larger organizations, to track performance over time. Many larger corporations pay both short-term incentives (bonuses) and longer-term incentives for sustained achievement over three to five years. Consequently, another decision each corporation must make is the time-frame decision. What is the appropriate period of time over which performance should be tracked? The most favored period is five years.

The measures of performance will vary in importance to

Figure 3. Primary and Supplemental Measures of Performance.

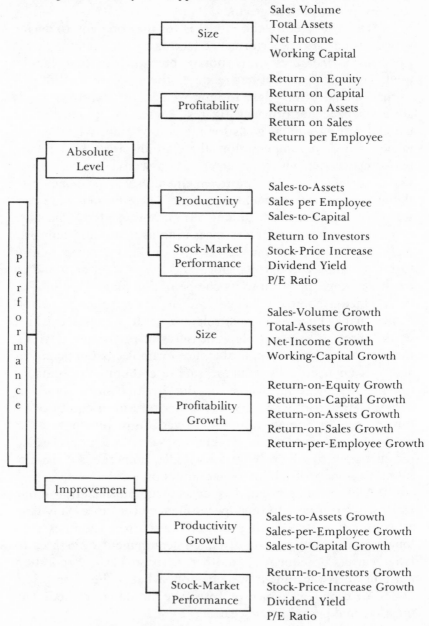

Source: The Hay Group, Philadelphia.

an organization at different times. If a company has historically been profitable but finds its sales beginning to stagnate, an improvement measure such as sales-volume growth might properly be ranked as the performance measure to receive more emphasis. However, to protect the company from unnecessarily buying market share or sacrificing profitability, it should also choose a profitability or profitability-growth measure. Return on sales and return-on-sales growth will help the company achieve renewed vigor and growth without sacrificing economic performance.

Performance compensation as defined by the Hay Group is used occasionally to calculate levels of compensation warranted by corporate performance. But that use is the exception, not the rule. The real value of the list of thirty-two performance variables is that it gives managers a fairly extensive, yet still comprehensible, shopping list of corporate measures from which to choose.

"How do you measure the performance of your company?," the executive will be asked. He usually gives a simple answer. Size is selected, with sales volume chosen as the specific measure, by industrials, and assets by many financials. Return on equity or capital is a good manufacturing measure of profitability, and return on assets is a good measure for financials. But many operating managers also like a return-on-sales figure as a guide or, for financial executives, the margin spread—the difference between the cost of money and their average return on their money. The absolute-level measures are by far the most popular, although others are selected occasionally.

Rather than use the measures as part of a statistical model that calculates bonus payouts, however, what usually happens is that the bonus program is designed so that if sales volume reaches X and return on equity Y, then the bonus earned will be Z percent of salary. An attempt is made to tie compensation to performance, but the knot is loose. As the total remuneration of more CEOs exceeds $1 million annually, we may see increased interest in the use of techniques such as Performance Compensation to demonstrate to shareholders that the salaries and bonuses of management are the result of *sustained* performance improvement. This is especially true if credence is given to those who complain that management should not profit if shareholders suffer. Longer-term indexes of performance, such as growth in return on capital or in earnings per share, could then be expected to become the preferred measures.

The Value Line Data Base

The thirty-two measures of corporate performance in the Performance Compensation model are far from the maximum number of variables that can be used to measure performance. Probably the largest data base currently available to the public is the Value Line Investment Survey, published by Value Line Data Services (New York). The Value Line sheet on General Motors Corporation, for example, contains approximately 550 different statistical measures. The data-base sheet for general industry (Exhibit 2) has field locations for 416 variables.

Value Line includes all the primary quantitative measures of performance, such as gross income, debt to equity, and return on capital. As Exhibit 2 shows, there are some very esoteric variables as well. For example, earnings per share is calculated in six different ways for Investment Survey subscribers. Ultimately all these statistics are reduced to only two numbers. One number ranks stocks by *timeliness,* a measure of investment suitability over the coming twelve-month period. The second number is a *safety* ranking, which is a measure of financial strength. The Value Line system is, in the words of its owner, "simple" (quoted in *Wall Street Journal,* January 14, 1981).

This particular approach to corporate performance analysis, probably the ultimate from a quantitative point of view, is entirely mathematical. All human value judgments have been eliminated. Instead, the company relies on a cross-sectional multiple regression analysis to produce the basic ranking by the computer.

The Value Line survey is the most popular investment advisory survey, with 90,000 subscribers in 1980. Besides its usefulness to equity investors, it represents the most detailed data base available for comparing corporate performance using quantitative measures.

From its beginning in 1935, Value Line has contended that stock values are capable of objective quantification. From a low of two issues in 1936, the survey is now issued weekly to its subscribers. It covers 1,700 stocks in ninety industries. These listings account for about 96 percent of the trading volume on all stock exchanges, making coverage all but complete.

The two main signals provided subscribers, as just mentioned, are timeliness and safety. Timeliness is the probable relative price performance of the stock within the next twelve months. Updates are weekly. Safety is a measure of the stock's future price stability and the company's current financial strength. Full-page updates on all stocks are issued at least every three months, and full-page quarterly reports are issued weekly at the rate of about 130 each week. Since 1965, stocks ranked 1 and 2 for timeliness, as a group, have outperformed those ranked 3, 4, and 5, as groups. Furthermore, in twelve of fourteen years the stock market's performance has followed perfectly, in order, the 1 through 5 rank. The rationale for the service is that by holding a diversified list of stocks ranked 1 (highest) or 2 (above average) for timeliness, the investor will achieve better-than-chance results for the year.

Rank for Timeliness. Timeliness (the prediction of a stock's relative price performance) is based on three criteria, which are all indexes of earnings performance. The rationale is that a stock's performance in the marketplace is a reflection of the profit achievement of the corporation. Executives who wish to manage stock prices are therefore encouraged to manage their company's earnings.

The first timeliness criterion is called the "nonparametric value position." It is a function of the latest relative reported earnings and the relative price against a background of ten years of experience. The higher the earnings relative to the price rank, the more undervalued the stock. The stock analyst also calculates a price momentum factor—the last ten weeks' average price divided by the fifty-two-week average relative price.

Exhibit 2. The Value Line Data-Base Sheet for General Industry.

GENERAL INDUSTRIAL DESCRIPTION

FIELD	
1	Cusip Number
2	Cusip Suffix
3	Ticker Symbol
4	Format Type
5	SIC Classification
416	Industry Code (Value Line)
6	Company Name
7	Data Year
199	Annual Data Availability

ANNUAL INCOME STATEMENT

8	Sales or Revenues
9	Cost of Goods Sold
10	Gross Income
11	Selling, General, Admin. Exp.
12	Operating Expenses
13	Operating Income
14	Depreciation, Depletion, Amort.
15	Total Interest
16	Est'd Interest Paid On Long-Term Debt
17	Interest Charged to Construction
18	Equity in Earnings of Unconsolidated Subsidiaries
19	Other Income
20	Other Expenses
21	Pretax Minority Interest
22	Pretax Income
23	Current Income Taxes
24	Deferred Income Taxes
25	Total Taxes
26	Special Items
27	After-tax Minority Interest
28	Net Income Before Extraordinaries
29	Preferred Dividends Paid and Accumulated
30	Net Income for the Common
31	Extraordinaries

BALANCE SHEET—ASSETS

32	Cash and Equivalents
33	Accounts Receivable
381	Allowance for Doubtful Accts.—Current Receivables
34	Inventories
35	Other Current Assets
36	Current Assets
37	Gross Plant
38	Accumulated Depreciation
39	Net Plant
40	Long-Term Investments
41	Deferred Charge Asset
42	Intangible Assets
43	Other Long-Term Assets
44	Total Reported Assets

BALANCE SHEET—LIABILITIES

45	Notes Payable
46	Current Portion of Long-Term Debt
47	Accounts Payable
48	Taxes Payable
49	Other Current Liabilities
50	Current Liabilities
51	Deferred Tax Liability
52	Minority Interest Liability
53	Long-Term Debt
54	Total Debt
55	Other Long-Term Liabilities
56	Total Reported Liabilities
57	Convertible Debt
58	Convertible Preferred Equity

SOURCES OF FUNDS

59	Beginning Working Capital
60	Cash Flow
61	Cash Flow Plus Def'd Taxes
62	Property Sales
63	Common Financing
64	Preferred Financing
65	Miscellaneous Stock Financing
66	Long-Term Debt Financing
67	Other Sources

USES OF FUNDS

68	Capital Spending
69	Other Investments
70	Common Retired
71	Preferred Retired
72	Debt Retired
73	Common Dividends
74	Preferred Dividends
75	Ending Working Capital

PER SHARE

76	Earnings per share (year-end)
77	Earnings per share (primary)
78	Earnings per share (diluted)
79	Book Value per share (A)
80	Modified Book Value per share (B)
81	Tangible Book Value per share (C)
82	Sales or Revenues per share
83	Cash Flow per share
84	Depreciation, etc. per share
85	Capital Spending per share
86	Dividends Declared per share
87	Working Capital per share
191	"Net" Working Capital per sh.

MARGINS

88	Gross Margin
89	Operating Margin before Depreciation
90	Utility Oper Margin after Depr & Tax
91	Pretax Margin
92	Net Income Margin
93	Net for Common Margin

ANALYTICAL RATIOS %

94	Income Tax Rate
95	% Current Taxes to Pretax Income
96	% Expense Ratio before Depreciation
97	% Utility Exp Ratio after Depr & Tax
98	% Dividend Payout to Net Income
99	% Dividend Payout to Cash Flow
100	% Divds. + Cap'l Spending to Cash Flow + Defd Tax
101	% Cash to Current Assets
102	% Cash to Current Liabilities
103	% Cash to Working Capital
104	% Inventories to Sales
105	% Accounts Payable to Sales
106	% Current Assets to Current Liab
107	% Cash to Sales
108	% Working Capital to Sales
109	% Curr Assets Less Inven to Sales
110	% Sales to Gross Plant
111	% Sales to Net Plant
112	% Sales to Total Assets
113	% Sales to Reported Total Capital (A)
114	% Sales to Modified Total Capital (B)
115	% Sales to Tangible Total Capital (C)
116	% Sales to Reported Total Capital (D)
117	% Sales to Reptd Cap'l incl defd tax + S.T. debt (E)
118	% Debt to Reported Equity (A)
119	% Debt to Modified Equity (B)
120	% Debt to Tangible Equity (C)
121	% Convertible Senior Capital to Total Senior Capital

261	Debt-to-Cap'l Ratio
262	Preferred-to-Cap'l Ratio
263	Common-to-Cap'l Ratio

CAPITAL AND EQUITY

122	Total Reported Capital (A)
123	Total Modified Capital (B)
124	Total Tangible Capital (C)
125	Total Reported Capital incl defd tax
126	Total Reported Capital incl def tax + S.T. debt
127	Reported Net Worth (A)
128	Modified Net Worth (B)
129	Tangible Net Worth (C)
130	Preferred Equity
131	Common Equity (A)
132	Modified Common Equity (B)
133	Tangible Common Equity (C)

RATES OF RETURN/INTANGIBLES

134	% Intangible Assets to Reptd Net Worth (A)
135	% Intangibles + Defd Charges to Reptd Net Worth
136	% Pretax Earned Reptd Total Capital (A)
137	% Pretax Earned Modified Total Capital (B)
138	% Pretax Earned Tangible Total Capital (C)
139	% Earned Reptd Total Capital (A)
140	% Earned Modified Total Capital (B)
141	% Earned Tangible Total Capital (C)
142	% Net Income to Reptd Total Capital (A)
143	% Net for Common to Reptd Total Capital (A)
144	% Earned Reptd Net Worth (A)
145	% Earned Modified Net Worth (B)
146	% Earned Tangible Net Worth (C)
147	% Earned Common (A)
148	% Earned Modified Common Equity (B)
149	% Earned Tangible Common Equity (C)

RATIOS

150	Price/Book Value (A)
151	Price/Modified Book Value (B)
152	Price/Tangible Book Value (C)
153	P/E Ratio (Year-end)
154	P/E Ratio (Primary)
155	P/E Ratio (Diluted)
156	Dividend Yield
157	Average Annual Price

EMPLOYEES—SHARES—FISCAL YR.

158	Number of Employees
159	Cumulative Multiplier (Stk split/Div'd adjust fac)
160	Common Shares Outstanding
161	Comm. Shs. + Conv. Shs. (excl. Warrant, Option Shs.)
162	Date Fiscal Year Ended
163	Accounting Code
164	Equity in Earn'gs of Unconsol. Subs. (Stated Pretax)
165	Equity in Earn'gs of Unconsol. Subs. (Stated Aft Tax)

APBO 30 EARNINGS

166	Unusual Items (APBO 30)	STARTS 1973
167	Discontinued Items (APBO 30)	
168	Special Items (APBO 30)	
169	Extraordinary Items (APBO 30)	
170	Net Before Discontinueds, Specials, Extras (APBO 30)	
171	Net Before Specials & Extras (APBO 30)	
172	Net Before Extras (APBO 30)	
173	Net Income After Extras (APBO 30)	
174	EPS (Primary) Bef Disc Spec + Extras (APBO 30)	
175	EPS (Primary) Before Specials & Extras (APBO 30)	
176	EPS (Diluted) Before Specials & Extras (APBO 30)	
177	EPS (Primary) Before Extras (APBO 30)	
178	EPS (Diluted) Before Extras (APBO 30)	
179	EPS (Primary) After Extras (APBO 30)	

181	Debt Due Next 5 Years	MISC.
182	Capitalized Leases	

TAXES

188	Reported Pretax Income
189	Reported Tax Rate
190	Depreciation Rate
192	U.S. Cash Income Taxes
193	U.S. Non-Cash Income Taxes
196	Investment Tax Credit Taken
197	Non-Income Taxes

FOREIGN

194	Foreign Cash Income Taxes
195	Foreign Non-Cash Income Taxes
264	Foreign Sales
265	Foreign Pretax Profits
266	Foreign Assets
267	Currency Translation Adjustment

LEASES

277	Operating Lease Rentals, 1st year
278	Capital Lease Obligations, 1st year
279	Total Lease Payments, 1st year
280	Present Value of Capital Leases

REPLACEMENT COST ACCT'G 1976 to 1979

373	Replacement Cost of Goods
374	Replacement Depreciation
375	Replacement Pretax Profits
376	Replacement Inventory Value
377	Replacement Gross Plant Value
378	Replacement Accumulated Depreciation Value
379	Replacement Net Plant Value
380	Replacement Stockholders' Equity
	FASB Statement 33 (to be added 1980)

INVENTORY

382	Inventory: Finished Goods
383	Inventory: In Process
384	Inventory: Raw Materials
385	Inventory: Progress Payments & Others
386	Order Backlog

SUPPLEMENTARY INC. STATE.

188	Maintenance & Repair Expense
189	Payroll Tax
190	Other Non-Income Taxes
191	Advertising Cost
192	Research & Development Outlay

PENSION

195	Pension Expense
196	Unfunded Vested Pension Liability
197	Prior Years' Service Costs (to 1979)
	Present Value of Vested & Nonvested Benefits—FASB 36 (from 1980)

PLANT

98	Construction In Progress
99	Gross Plant: Buildings
00	Gross Plant: Equipment
01	Gross Plant: Land

DEBT

02	L.T. Debt Due, 1st year
03	L.T. Debt Due, 2nd year
04	L.T. Debt Due, 3rd year
05	L.T. Debt Due, 4th year
06	L.T. Debt Due, 5th year

EQUITY

11	Reported Preferred Stock
12	Total Reported Common Stock
13	Reported Add'l Paid-In Cap'l
14	Reported Earned Surplus
15	Reported Value of Treasury Stock

SPECIAL FINANCIAL FORMATS ARE AVAILABLE FOR BANKS, S&L's, BROKERS, INSURANCE, and FINANCE COMPANIES

ESTIMATES (Value Line)

228	Est'd Earn'gs per sh. for the 12 mo. period End'g 6 mos. ahead
229	Est'd Div'ds per sh. next 12 mos.
230	Current Est'd P/E Ratio
231	Est'd Dividend Yield

PROJECTIONS (Value Line)

252	Projected 3-5 yr. Sales p. sh.
253	Projected 3-5 yr. "Cash Flow" p. sh.
254	Projected 3-5 yr. Earnings p. share
255	Projected 3-5 yr. Div'ds p. sh.
256	Projected 3-5 yr. Book Val. p. sh.
257	Projected 3-5 yr. Shares Outstanding
234	Projected 3-5 Yr. Hi Price Target
235	Projected 3-5 Yr. Lo Price Target
236	Est'd 3-5 Yr. Hi Appreciation Target (%)
237	Est'd 3-5 Yr. Lo Appreciation Target (%)

GROWTH RATES (HISTORICAL)

362	5-Yr. Sales p sh.	growth rate
363	5-Yr. Cash Flow p sh.	
364	5-Yr. Earn'gs p. sh. as reported	
365	5-Yr. Tangible Book Value p. sh.	
370	5-Yr. Div'd p. sh.	
366	10-Yr. Sales p sh.	
367	10-Yr. Cash Flow p sh.	
368	10-Yr. Earn'gs p sh. as reptd.	
369	10-Yr. Tangible Book Value p sh.	
371	10-Yr. Div'd p. sh.	

BUSINESS SEGMENTS (ANNUAL)

281	Restated Company Sales
282	Restated Company Earnings
283	Type of Income Reported
284	Intracompany Sales
285	Intracompany Income

Division A to J Business Segments

NAME — CODE — SALES — INCOME

A	286	287	288	289
B	290	291	292	293
C	294	295	296	297
D	298	299	300	301
E	302	303	304	305
F	306	307	308	309
G	310	311	312	313
H	314	315	316	317
I	318	319	320	321
J	322	323	324	325

UTILITIES

184	% Residential Utility Sales
185	% Industrial Utility Sales
186	% Commercial Utility Sales
187	% Other Utility Sales

INDUSTRIES

268	Drill, Exploration (Exp.)
269	Number of Stores (Retail)
270	Sales per Store (Retail)
271	Market Share (Auto)
272	Load Factor (Air Transport)
273	Gross Equipment (Air Transport)
274	Cap'l Gains p sh (Real Estate)
275	Gross Property (Real Estate)
276	Computers on Lease (Leasing)

RISK MEASURES (Value Line)

238	BETA (Sensitivity to NYSE Composite)
239	Standard Deviation of % Price Change
248	BETA's r-factor

FINANCIAL RATINGS (Value Line)

249	Company's Financial Strength (A++ to C)

QUARTERLY (from 1963)

200	Quarterly Data Availability
201	Type of Earnings per share (P or D)
202	Quarter Fiscal Year Ended
203	Adjustment Date (mmddyy)

204	1st Fiscal Quarter	SALES OR
205	2nd Fiscal Quarter	REVENUES
206	3rd Fiscal Quarter	
207	4th Fiscal Quarter	
208	Annual Fiscal Sales or Revenues	

209	1st Fiscal Quarter	EARNINGS
210	2nd Fiscal Quarter	PER SHARE
211	3rd Fiscal Quarter	
212	4th Fiscal Quarter	
213	Annual Fiscal Earnings per share	

214	1st Calendar Quarter	DIVIDENDS
215	2nd Calendar Quarter	PER SHARE
216	3rd Calendar Quarter	
217	4th Calendar Quarter	
218	Annual Calendar Div'ds Paid per share	

244	1st Fiscal Quarter	
245	2nd Fiscal Quarter	NET INCOME
246	3rd Fiscal Quarter	
247	4th Fiscal Quarter	

219	1st Calendar Quarter	AVERAGE
220	2nd Calendar Quarter	WEEKLY
221	3rd Calendar Quarter	PRICE
222	4th Calendar Quarter	

223	1st Calendar Quarter	
224	2nd Calendar Quarter	ENDING
225	3rd Calendar Quarter	WEEKLY
226	4th Calendar Quarter	PRICE
227	Recent Price (see field 203 for date)	

MONTHLY PRICES

326	Jan.	HIGH 338	Jan.	LOW
327	Feb.	339	Feb.	
328	March	340	March	
329	April	341	April	
330	May	342	May	
331	June	343	June	
332	July	344	July	
333	Aug.	345	Aug.	
334	Sept.	346	Sept.	
335	Oct.	347	Oct.	
336	Nov.	348	Nov.	
337	Dec.	349	Dec.	

% SHARES TRADED

350	Jan.	356	July
351	Feb.	357	Aug.
352	March	358	Sept.
353	April	359	Oct.
354	May	360	Nov.
355	June	361	Dec.

 VALUE LINE DATA SERVICES, William C. Close, Director
711 THIRD AVENUE, N.Y., N.Y. 10017 Phone: 212-687-3965

The second timeliness criterion is earnings momentum. This is the year-to-year change in the stock's quarterly earnings relative to all other stocks. The most favorable quarterly earnings comparisons are assigned the number 1200, the middle third 800, and the lowest third 400. The analyst can use a "contradiction factor" if he feels the latest quarter's earnings will change markedly for better or worse.

The third timeliness criterion is an earnings surprise factor. Because stock prices tend to move sharply in the direction of unexpected news, up to 400 points are added to or subtracted from timeliness ratings for deviations between expected and actual earnings. Put simply, the executive can expect a positive movement in the price of his company's stock if (1) earnings are better than the current price would suggest, (2) earnings are better than other companies', or (3) earnings forecasts are conservative compared with actual results.

Rank for Safety. The safety rank as computed by Value Line is a measure of the total risk of a stock. As an index of performance, it is a much broader financial measure, going beyond earnings and stock price. The safety rank is a comprehensive analysis of risk derived by averaging two variables: (1) price stability and (2) financial strength.

Price stability refers to the standard deviation of weekly percentage changes in stock price over a five-year period. A stable stock has a lower standard deviation. The financial-strength rating is a relative ranking, based mainly on these variables: equity coverage of debt, equity coverage of intangibles, "quick ratio" accounting methods, variability of return, quality of fixed-charge coverage, stock price stability, and company size.

The executive who cares about the performance of his company's stock will strive for a Value Line safety rating of at least 3 (average). This would be achieved in accordance with strong, consistent earnings, which would give a timeliness rating of 1. Such an executive would, in essence, be a fundamentalist rather than what Wall Street calls a "chartist" or a "random walker." Fundamentalists believe that stock price reflects earnings and other financial data describing the company. Chartists, or technicians, believe that the behavior of the market and the investors mostly determines a stock's price. Random walkers are the cynics of managing either a company or a stock portfolio. Everything is random, they believe, and neither a corporation's financial performance nor the tracks it leaves on a technician's chart can predict the price of a stock. For an executive striving to manage stock price as part of the corporation's performance, it would seem that the only choice is to be a fundamentalist, since only variables like those included in the Value Line approach are within the executive's control.

Subjective Measures of Corporate Performance

No single list of statistical measures of corporate performance is exhaustive. It is always possible to think of another measure of achievement that may be useful to someone at some time. But eventually devising measures becomes futile and succumbs to the law of diminishing returns. For most corporations, the quantitative measures of performance as provided by *Forbes* and *Fortune,* supplemented by specific lists for individual industries such as *Business Week* provides for banks, plus a detailed list applicable to all industries, like Value Line, is all most managers will ever need.

The subjective nonquantitative appraisal of corporate performance, however, is limited in theory only by one's imagination. Although subjective measures are infinite in theory, in practice it is possible to audit most companies using about a dozen constructs developed for this purpose. The American Institute of Management (AIM) has for many years provided a guideline of these softer measurement areas and included a scale in an attempt to quantify them (American Institute of Management, 1970). AIM's ten categories of corporate achievement are economic function, corporate structure, health of earnings, service to stockholders, research and development, directorate effectiveness, fiscal policies, production efficiency, sales vigor, and executive quality.

The rating scale that AIM provides suggests an optimum point total of 10,000 points in evaluating a company. It recommends that 22 percent of these optimum points be awarded for executive quality and 13 percent for sales vigor. Production efficiency, fiscal policies, and economic function should each receive 10 percent of the total points. Two of the variables should be given weights of 8 percent—research and development and directorate effectiveness. The least important variables in the AIM index are service to stockholders (7 percent), health of earnings (6 percent), and corporate structure (5 percent). It would be too easy to take issue with the weightings that AIM suggests for the variables. It is more useful to briefly review the variables themselves. For a detailed discussion the AIM manual is highly recommended.

How Companies Were Selected. The American Institute of Management was founded in 1948. By 1970 it had developed five methods for selecting the 513 companies that would be listed in its manual. The original procedure was used to select the companies that appeared on the first list in 1952. A panel of executives and university professors prepared a list of the most outstanding companies in each of a number of major industrial classifications. A thorough but arm's-length investigation followed nomination, using material available from the public domain. A second procedure was applied to companies that asked AIM to review them for possible listing. Here an analyst also visited the company and conducted interviews as well as reviewing public information. The third procedure involved filling out an extensive management audit questionnaire, and the fourth and fifth procedures involved carrying out full-scale management audits, with variations in the type of audit questionnaire used and who was asked to complete it.

Economic Function. An analyst evaluating the performance of a company needs to consider how well the corporation has defined its basic mission strategy. Does the organization have a firm grasp on the reason for its existence and the value it adds to the economy and to society? This includes a definition of its products and customers. It also includes an analysis of the amount of social responsibility that the company feels it is appropriate to accept.

Economic function is not a statistical measure but rather a public estimate of how useful the company is in the conduct of daily life. It is a matter of reputation, the relative importance of the company's self-assumed economic obligation to society. The American Institute of Management's 301-question audit includes twenty-six questions appraising the company's economic function. The qualities sought are integrity, quality, and durability. Some questions are quite specific and obvious. Has the company ever defaulted on a debt? Has the company ever been convicted of antitrust violations? Some are more subtle. Maximum points are given if the company's business is essential to the conduct of life (food, agriculture). Minimum points are given if the business is potentially health-damaging (alcoholic beverages, cigarettes). Railroads are seen as more important to the economy than airlines. The more integrated companies (banks) are given a higher rating than those with more limited functions (mortgage banking). A department store (integrated) is considered more valuable to society than a shop selling shoes to runners (subfunction of a subfunction).

Other factors go into a positive opinion regarding the company's economic function, including control over critical sources of materials, keeping pace with technical advances in the industry, whether acquisitions were made for paper (good) or cash (bad), ability to expand even in a depressed economy, management continuity, and movement into public office of key corporate executives.

Corporate Structure. That structure follows strategy has now become a business cliché. But the statement is accurate. A subjective appraisal of organizational effectiveness should include the appropriateness of the company's organizational structures to its goals. Does the company meet the test of harmonious strategy and structure? Are lines of communication clear and spans of management manageable? Are like functions clustered under one accountable executive? Is there overlap and duplication in the company, gaps or missing assignments of necessary accountabilities to specific people? Is the corporate structure too tall? Corporate structure should amplify performance, not impede it.

This category of the AIM management audit deals with the system through which management organizes the corporation to achieve its ends. AIM asks these questions: "Does the actual structure enable the enterprise to achieve its ends with reasonable success, ... does the structure in some degree impede maximum progress towards the enterprise's goals?" (1970, p. 83). AIM recognizes that no ideal organizational structure will fit all companies or situations and that the criterion for soundness has to be whether the structure fits the company's needs. Is it logical? Does it work?

The AIM format calls for a qualitative examination of several forms of organization: economic and technical functions, social cooperation, and formal and informal structure. It considers differentiation of line and staff, separation of top management from upper operating management, and forms of divisionalization. The corporate structure is tested against these rules of thumb for efficient organizations:

1. Each person understands his job and how it fits into the whole.
2. Each person knows the limits of his authority.
3. Each person knows whom he supervises, what his tasks are, and what goals he is to achieve.
4. Each person has only one boss who supervises his work and whose standards he must meet.
5. No one has to supervise too many people.
6. No one has to take direction from more than one boss.
7. No one is required to exercise contradictory or inappropriately different skills.
8. Each group has the authority and resources to achieve its goals.
9. Assignments, titles, and authority at the same organizational level are as similar as possible.
10. Between the head of a unit and those carrying out its work, there is the smallest possible number of intermediaries.
11. The *span of control* is appropriate to the positions supervised. The more similar the work being done by subordinates, the more of them one manager can direct.

12.   The *span of contact* (the requirement to consult with, receive information from, and advise) is consonant with the span of control. No one should have such an extensive span-of-contact requirement that he does not have time to meet his primary responsibilities.
13.   The *span of information* (required technical knowledge and skills) is reasonable. Where technical know-how is not personally held by the executive, it is provided to him by internal specialists or consultants.
14.   The *chain of command* is minimal, the guiding principle being that short lines of command are clear lines and that each additional management layer adds to overhead, diffuses authority, increases the chance of misunderstanding, and delays communication.

A sound organizational structure will avoid the more obvious mistakes found in badly organized companies. Common organizational flaws include illogical assignment of duties, splitting a function among several departments, duplication of functions, missing important functions, illogical clustering of functions, assigning too many or too few functions to one executive, responsibility without authority, vagueness in assignments, lack of coordination, inadequate staff support, poor person/job match, lack of standard titles and designations, too many management levels, inadequate staff support, and discrepancy between stated organizational relationships and accountabilities and actual ones.

Finally, a sound corporate structure will contain the four essential components of any business enterprise: administration, finance, production, and sales. Administration is a catch-all category for those functions not included elsewhere and will include personnel, research and development, public relations, management information systems, and the like. Finance will normally include the controller, treasurer, audit, and tax functions. Sales and marketing are usually combined under one executive, but production may be split, with manufacturing reporting to one executive while engineering reports to another. These four major functions, in turn, can be either centralized or decentralized.

To repeat the point made earlier, the AIM audit emphasizes, and properly so, that the essential test of corporate organizational structure is whether it fits the company's needs and
helps it achieve its overall strategy. The executive wants to
structure responsibilities and people so that corporate goals are
achieved. More often than not, the tests of soundness enumerated above are good guides to the best way to structure the
company—but the ultimate test of structure is whether it works.

Health of Earnings. It is useless to talk in terms of maximizing
profits. Instead, the chief executive should ask, "What is the
minimum level of earnings I need to sustain corporate health
and growth?" "How do my earnings compare with those of
other companies in the same business?" "Can I sustain these
profits through contractions in the economic cycle?" "Will the
corporation's earnings performance be such that I can raise capital?" "How am I rated by services such as Standard & Poor's
and Moody's?" High marks from the rating services significantly
affect costs of capital, and a steadily declining rating indicates a
corporation ready for acquisition or liquidation.

Although the AIM management audit gives health of earnings only 6 percent of the total evaluation, AIM regards the
category as one of the most important of the factors. Healthy
earnings are a precondition for successful ratings in many of the
other categories. Determination of health of earnings is a comparative process. The sophisticated manager will ask many questions about corporate earnings. What is the ten-year earnings
history? How have earnings fared in major business cycles? Have
profit margins increased or decreased? What percentage of sales
is from products developed internally? How do the company's
earnings look against competition? Does the corporate financial
structure penalize the earnings potential of common shares? Has
the company overbuilt or otherwise overextended itself? Has
maintenance been deferred to pump up earnings? The score a
company is given by AIM is based on its accomplishments
against a background of opportunity and adversity. If two companies achieved identical results, company A might still be given
higher marks because the institute judged that its management
had a more difficult environment in which to operate.

Research and Development. The percentage of gross revenues or net income that a company invests in research and development is a valuable clue to how much the corporation believes in its own products and future. Single-product corporations may fail when the consumer no longer needs or likes the product. Sustained growth is more difficult when you have only one product. Some types of industries, especially soft-goods manufacturers, are dependent on new-product development and market segmentation for their survival. In addition to actual dollars spent on R&D, the manager should ask, "How do I really feel toward R&D?" "What is my policy about applied versus basic research?" "Do I have R&D employees who can make measurable contributions to corporate development?" R&D efforts may range from tokenism to real commitment.

About 40 percent of the country's total R&D expenditure is government-sponsored—technical research being but one type of research. Market, management, and economic research is also done by some companies at some time in their growth cycle. For a manufacturing company to grow, it needs new products, improved products, or superior production processes that give it a quality or a price edge in the marketplace. As the traditional distinctions between financial institutions blur, even banks, savings and loans, credit unions, and brokerage firms now think of their services as products and seek to research their customers' needs to create new products to meet them.

AIM does not measure the effectiveness of a company's R&D efforts merely in terms of R&D dollars spent as a percentage of total sales. It has concluded that this simple ratio is an inadequate test. Instead, it takes a broader view of the activity. It looks at the department itself to see whether it is well organized. Is there adequate liaison and communication between R&D and other departments? Is the division that does or will use the product kept informed of progress in its development? Does the head of R&D have sufficient visibility and status to indicate that the company takes the function seriously? Is the R&D executive competent?

An R&D department that is properly integrated into the company will respond mainly to the needs of sales and production but also will accept the input of other divisions. Between

R&D and other units there needs to be a delicate balance: independence versus integration, responsiveness versus leadership.

Research expenditures should be primarily for work related to the commercial success of the company. This is not always done, but it is a sensible policy. The ultimate goal of research by private companies must remain the preservation of existing profit or the generation of future profit. Creation of pure knowledge, regardless of its commercial value, is the responsibility of the university researcher.

Some companies prefer to use outside contract research. This may be because they do not wish to have the facilities and salaries of a research department as a fixed cost, or they want to be sure the research they use is conducted independently and objectively. Battelle Memorial Institute, in Pittsburgh, and SRI International, in Palo Alto, California, are two of the better-known research institutes. A few consulting firms have major research capabilities. The biggest and best known are Booz·Allen & Hamilton and Arthur D. Little. If research is contracted out, there are checkpoints that, according to the AIM guidelines, characterize well-managed contracts: (1) the scope and costs are clearly understood in advance, (2) one executive inside the company has responsibility for following the progress of the project and serving as liaison with the contractor, (3) management is well informed about the progress, and (4) the results of completed projects can be translated into useful recommendations for implementation.

There are essentially two kinds of applied research in which companies can engage. One is the development and evaluation of new products and processes. This is the more "basic" kind of applied research and is often carried out in a pilot plant or in a lab. The second kind of research, more allied to production, is process work, the search for improved methods of making current products. The most advanced companies do both kinds of engineering-oriented research, analyzing and testing existing and new products. Some expect research to pay for itself by coming up with a steady stream of products within defined time parameters that meet minimal-rate-of-return objectives.

About research, AIM asks broad questions to ascertain the quality of the organization's R&D efforts. Has the company made any technical discoveries or innovations that are now part of its industries? What equipment or methods has it developed for its own operations as a result of research? What patents does the company have? What portion of current revenues comes from products developed from recent research? Can an improvement in market position be attributed to research?

Finally, AIM makes several recommendations for managing excellent research. Even a medium-sized company should conduct or sponsor research. The best form of organizational structure for a research department is by function or area of scientific inquiry. The head of R&D should be a member of top management reporting to the chief executive officer or the chief operating officer. Research should be a stand-alone department, not part of some other function like engineering or manufacturing. Money allocated to research should be a function of need and opportunity, not merely a percentage of sales or profits. Research facilities should be kept flexible to enable quick response to changing circumstances. Although the search for R&D employee candidates is the function of the personnel department, setting the position qualifications and the final selection of candidates are prerogatives of the R&D department.

Directorate Effectiveness. Like other aspects of American business, the role of the board of directors has changed. There was a time when the board was made up of persons close to the chief executive officer who could be counted on to approve all recommendations brought to their attention. Board members were selected for amiability and personal contacts. Interlocking boards were the rule rather than the exception, and it was not uncommon to have the corporation's commercial banker, investment banker, and outside legal counsel as members of the board. This has changed because of consumer and regulatory pressures. Board members now have significant legal responsibilities that require them to take themselves and their duties seriously.

Proper questions about directorate effectiveness include

"How well is the board discharging its legal responsibilities as the trustees of the owners?" "How well does the board monitor compliance with the various regulatory requirements and restrictions?" "Does the board have representatives of the larger ownership blocks?" "Has the board considered its legal and moral responsibilities to its consumers, and does it have members who can be relied on to speak up for the consumer and other special-interest groups?"

The executive who will successfully manage organizational performance will now manage the board and measure its performance along with other departments and functions of the company. For the chief executive officer especially, it is the board that has the most to say about his own relative success and tenure. Failure to have a good board or to relate to it effectively can mean eventual dismissal for a president or chairman even if, by quantitative measures, corporate performance is an apparent success. A board can disapprove of how the results were achieved or become convinced that the future of the company would be better served by a change in top management even if the CEO's track record to date has been acceptable. Skilled board management has, however, bought time for the executive whose performance, judged solely by the numbers, has not been impressive. Directorate effectiveness is the result of both board composition and action—who are on the board and what they do. AIM assigns an optimum point total of 800 out of 10,000, or 8 percent, to board effectiveness.

What does a board do? Primarily it serves in the role of public trustee. An obvious example of this trusteeship is its governing role over matters of executive compensation. The board wants to attract and retain able top executives. But it also has an obligation to stockholders not to compensate the company's top managers in a manner that is exorbitant or self-serving. Because of this requirement, the compensation committees of many companies' boards use an outside third party, a consultant specializing in these matters, to make recommendations about the reasonableness of the remuneration package.

Functions of the board are derived from its legal status. These may include (1) general safeguarding and controlling of corporate assets, (2) selecting management, (3) approving the corporate strategy and one-year and three-year business plans, (4) reviewing company results on a quarterly and annual basis, and (5) setting and controlling overall corporate policy and direction.

The composition of the board is important in determining what it can do. There is no ideal size for a board (they range from about five to fifty members), but the average board size of an excellently managed manufacturing company is twelve, according to AIM figures. Service companies seem to have larger boards than industrial companies. Health care companies, such as hospitals, may have the biggest boards and closely held corporations the smallest. Research on group-size effectiveness does suggest that the optimum size for real decision making is about eight to fifteen members, and so a board of ten to twelve would be the obvious choice. A balance in the age of directors is wise, the biggest risk being the board in which all members are of advanced age.

The residence of board members can be important. It may be useful or even necessary to have members represent the service area—for example, for a utility company. Statewide representation may be desirable—for a Blue Cross/Blue Shield plan, for instance. In other cases residence may be less important than occupation or even sex and ethnicity. A well-constituted board will be representative as well as competent. The AIM favors multiple board directors and stock ownership for directors.

On the issue of "inside" boards (management-dominated) versus "outside" boards (nonmanagement-dominated), the institute believes that the more effective, better-quality board is one in which the majority of members are outsiders. But outsiders must be of equal caliber to insiders.

Regarding frequency of board meetings, AIM believes that monthly meetings are about right. Board-meeting minutes should be full though not verbatim. Informed members are vital to an effective board meeting. This means agendas, operating reports, and minutes are distributed far enough in advance of the meeting so that they can be studied. The effective manager managing an effective board will keep in personal contact with members, not only to ask for advice and to take an informal census but also to keep them informed. These personal contacts are also useful, of course, for building and maintaining the trust and rapport that the shrewd CEO wants to have with each director. It is the time-consuming nature of these personal contacts that makes a small board easier to manage than a large board.

The effective chairperson of the board will look after (1) regular attendance and participation, (2) focusing board work and assigning functional or project responsibility to individuals or committees where possible, and (3) harmony among directors and the executive team. Committees may be advisory or may exercise authority, and they may be temporary or permanent. The institute sees in the common executive committee the potential for abuse, and its existence in a company automatically triggers a more detailed audit. Other typical committees are those for executive compensation, finance, and audit. A function of these committees is to study matters germane to their areas. Another is to prepare relevant agendas for the board. The institute believes the board should deal with policy, plans, and results and leave operations to management.

The company with a board of active, distinguished directors has an advantage over the competitors who lack such guidance. A measure of corporate performance, though admittedly a subjective one, is: How good is your board, and how good is your relationship with its members? The ideal situation is a strong board that holds its CEO in high esteem.

Fiscal Policies. A corporation is an organization that uses monetary and human resources to provide its customers with products or services. Corporations manage limited resources. Are these resources being used effectively? The executive wanting to manage fiscal policy should review the company's accounting practices. Can it produce reliable forecasts? How does it use debt and equity? Has it articulated minimum performance levels for return on equity and return on capital? Has it decided on the amount of profit that is desirable? Does it understand its capital needs, and has it a plan to meet them? Has it established goals for taxes, dividends, retained earnings? A well-managed company should have guidelines in these areas and should produce results that are close to plan.

The business of business—at least in the private sector—is to make money. Understanding this is the necessary first step in quality fiscal management. The AIM audit of fiscal policies focuses on four areas: (1) capital analysis, (2) financial organization and planning, (3) fiscal policies and operations, and (4) the cumulative effect of fiscal policies.

In capital and balance-sheet analysis, AIM believes that sound management will pursue a half-dozen main objectives. It will promote sufficient fixed and working capital. It will build its investment credit to maintain access to sources of capital. It will maintain the proper balance among all forms of corporate assets. There will be a balance between equity and debt capital. The company will strive to increase its net worth. Stockholder ownership will be protected.

Additionally, AIM gives the following fiscal advice to managers striving for corporate performance. Young companies should generally avoid debt financing. For the ordinary industrial company, the debt component should preferably not exceed half the total capital. Additions to capital should be to finance growth. It is better if equity capital in a new company is private rather than public. Preferred dividends are to be avoided. When growth is assured but dilution of earnings is not desired, finance through convertible debentures. When earnings are on the rise and the company commands a high price/earnings ratio, try to replace debt with convertibles and then convertibles with common stock.

The institute also advises you to avoid what it considers poor fiscal policy. This includes (1) financial reorganization, (2) property writeups, (3) writeoffs of intangibles, (4) use of contingency reserves either to hide earnings (through transfer to the balance sheet) or to stabilize earnings in low-earning years, and (5) use of depreciation funds totally to replace old plants, to retire debt, or to pay dividends.

One of the chief responsibilities of the financial department is to issue operating reports. Competent management will be sure that the company prepares a capital, sales, and operating budget. Have these budgets been accurate? Do the financial reports provide management with information on the profitability of each product, service, and division? Does the company over-rely either on operating reports or on personal consultation with department heads? A little of each is best. Does the chief financial officer report to the chief executive officer (good) or to the chief operating officer (bad)? To whom does the auditor report—to the chief financial officer (bad) or to the CEO (better) or to the board (best)?

The first financial task of the corporate executive is to think through the conceptual relationship between the company's major purpose and the financial means and structure necessary to achieve it. Next, the executive must focus on implementing that financial strategy in the company's daily operations. This normally requires the CEO to ensure that the following are quickly and accurately accomplished: (1) allocation of overhead, (2) analysis of current costs, (3) systems for inventory control and credit, and (4) coordination of manufacturing schedules and sales forecasts.

Managers doing an audit of their own company using AIM guidelines will inquire into the detail of various financial calculations. How are factory burden, administrative, and selling costs allocated by product and division? How are cash-flow sheets (income plus depreciation) prepared? Are they used? Does the company know the profitability of each of its businesses? Does it investigate before it invests? Can the company control its inventories? What is its track record on receivables and writeoffs? How do the company's payroll, material, administrative, and plant costs compare with others in its industry?

Managers striving for financial quality may also look at pertinent historical financial ratios. They would look at the ratio of earnings to fixed debt charges (including sinking-fund requirements); for example, 30 to 1 is high, and 5 to 1 is narrow and, perhaps, cause for concern. Over the years, the ratio of earnings to preferred dividends should progressively rise. AIM believes that, as a general rule, funded debt should not exceed one third of the net tangible assets of an industrial corporation or one quarter of the total invested capital. Quick cash assets should equal at least half of short-term and long-term payables (funded debt plus current liabilities). Finally, cash plus government securities plus receivables should equal or exceed current liabilities plus long-term debt. Few of us are in such excellent shape in our personal finances. AIM admits these guidelines are harsh, but if a company meets them, it will be in a position to acquire other companies on favorable terms. Regarding the ratio of current assets to current liabilities, the institute regards 2 to 1 as typically favorable. However, it recognizes that, according to the five-year averages published by Dunn and Bradstreet, the ratio can be as high as 4 to 1 for retail men's clothing and less than 1.9 to 1 for wine wholesalers.

Management auditors will review the company's income statements for the past fifteen years. They will question revenues derived from sale of assets. The way depreciation is handled must be given careful examination. Aggressive and growing companies tend to retain more of their earnings than more established, slower-growing companies. Nevertheless, the more rapid the growth, the more likely the company is to assume debt despite retaining earnings. The *desirable* rate of dividend payments relative to net cash flow will depend in large part on the growth rate and cash needs of the company. An overaccumulation of cash suggests underemployment of resources.

Managers concerned with corporate performance will ask themselves these broad questions to be sure their financial strategy supports their corporate objectives:

1. Have I invested my capital in ways that will help the company achieve its goals?
2. Have I taken steps to protect my capital from unnecessary risk?
3. Do I know how my investments are doing product by product, business by business?
4. Do I have accurate financial information in time to make informed decisions?

AIM also likens running a company to sailing a ship: "Fiscal policy, in its ultimate significance, is like the selecting and equipping of a ship for a predetermined voyage and the laying down of a set of destinations, sailing directions, and general rules for navigation that will supply all necessary equipment; and then on the one hand, it must *supply guidance* for making every individual decision for researching the next destination, and on the other, permit sufficient flexibility and initiative to enable the crew to deal with all unexpected events. That it deals with money in arithmetical quantities makes it seem far simpler than it is" (American Institute of Management, 1970, p. 216).

Production Efficiency. The ultimate test of corporate performance is the achievement of its basic mission in an economically efficient manner. To do this, the corporation must be able to produce salable products at competitive prices. This requires capital equipment and facilities capable of maintaining quality standards and controlling the cost of goods produced. Important measures of corporate manufacturing efficiency include the quality of plants and equipment, the tenor of labor relations, and control over materials and inventory. If the first priority of a business is to have a customer, the second priority is to provide that customer with a quality product or service.

In the AIM audit, production efficiency is outranked in the scale of corporate values only by executive effectiveness and by sales vigor. This section is applicable not merely to manufacturing companies but even to the operations of a service company. The audit covers the two general divisions of personnel management and material and machinery management. Specifically, there are twelve headings under which the corporate executive can evaluate the operation to ascertain whether it is measuring up:

1. Organization.
2. Technology.
3. Location and layout.
4. Equipment.
5. Planning and control.
6. Purchasing and outside services.

7. Material usage.
8. Maintenance and safety.
9. Cost accounting.
10. Labor/management relations.
11. Personnel policies.
12. Recruitment and training.

The relative importance of the factors will vary with the company and the nature of its industry.

When looking at the organization of the production department, the executive asks whether the structure is effective and permits adequate controls. Efficiency can be measured by actual results against budget: labor costs, spoilage, materials, unscheduled downtime, on-time shipments.

The next production category appraised is technical competence. In a company with stable products (those that seldom change), technical competence can be shown in two ways. The first is to develop machinery that reduces the cost of producing the goods. The second is to make the best possible use of existing equipment. In a company with "stylish" goods (ones that change frequently), competence means making efforts to keep up with change. A technically able management knows how to improve its products and has programs in place or developing to effect those changes. It aggressively seeks ways to improve its products and its manufacturing processes. A company that has invested little or nothing in its plants and machines over the last several years cannot be considered progressive. Major evidence of technical competence is the existence of a long-range plan for capital investment. How good are the company's manufacturing methods, compared with the best in the industry? Does management have a basically progressive technical outlook?

The appraisal of production location and layout considers the efficiency of manufacturing geography and its effect on profits. Measures of location efficiency include satisfactory labor supply, available materials, transportation costs from plant to market, and local government. A production facility with a good layout permits an easy flow of parts and material, is flexible enough to accommodate expansions and alterations, facilitates supervision and communication, and uses available space efficiently. An excellently managed company will often have a plant improvement program.

Judging whether a company is using its equipment well is usually difficult for a manager who is not technically trained. Evidence that the company has considered quality, volume, and cost of labor and materials may be found in production engineering manuals and reports. Beyond this, the next most useful guide can be the manufacturing flow-process chart. Does it stand the challenge of logic and common sense? Have alternatives been explored? Are economies of scale being practiced? For example, does the company subcontract out specialty parts or processes that volume or equipment expense does not justify making internally? Check the age and condition of equipment. Look at the maintenance schedules. The use of automatic machinery requires careful scrutiny. Overinvestment in such equipment can be expensive and can lower manufacturing flexibility. Try comparing the company's ratios of dollar machinery investment to dollar sales and to payroll costs with those of leading companies in the same Standard Industrial Code category.

Production planning and control is a manufacturing services function. The department exists to schedule material, route work, and determine the order of work at the machines. Besides assigning work, production control, in conjunction with process or industrial engineering, develops and enforces work standards. Scheduling and inventory control can vary by company from the simple to the sublime. In some companies the job of production control is held by a clerk; in others it is viewed as a managerial position every bit as difficult as engineering or production itself. Much depends on the mix of product and customer. Good production management requires accurate information and some method of knowing at any moment where in the total production process a particular product can be found. Competent production planners keep in constant touch with sales, manufacturing, and industrial relations.

Good quality control means the regulation of the manufacturing process, not just an inspection system. The activities of a competent quality effort include these control methods:

analysis of specifications, studies of deficits, studies of variances, progressive quality programs, production statistics. And since quality always involves some sort of inspection, look for it at these points: materials, process checks, finished parts, final preshipment, equipment maintenance, salvage, customer complaints, and technical service.

Purchasing is part of manufacturing and is of considerable importance to production efficiency. Sound purchasing practice ensures competitive prices, available resources, controlled inventories, coordination with other departments, protection against bribery and pilferage, and complete and accurate records.

Since cost of materials averages 50 percent of cost of goods produced in many manufacturing companies, AIM believes that the necessity for close scrutiny in the use of material is self-evident. The major sources of material expense are selection, storage and control, retrieval, receiving and inspection, and use. Attention to detail is the key. Small inefficiencies spread over a large number of items over an extended time add up to many lost dollars.

Physical production facilities must be maintained and kept safe. The size and importance of the maintenance effort should be in direct proportion to the cost and complexity of the company's physical resources. Heavy industry may have up to 25 percent of its total work force in maintenance, safety, and construction. Look for equipment and crew adequate to the task and for a disciplined method of scheduling urgent and planned work. "It can definitely be stated that if over 10 percent of work orders are on an urgent, nonscheduled basis, the maintenance work does not rate as excellently managed" (American Institute of Management, 1970, p. 235). Well-managed maintenance also rotates equipment and keeps an adequate supply of replacement parts.

How can safety be measured by an interested management? First, does the company promote safety? What about the lost-time record, equipment checks, OSHA compliance, random plant inspections, safety and first-aid training? A simple test: How does the place look, sound, and smell? Safe environments usually feel safe.

The second major factor in efficient production management is the management of labor. Turnover is a good measure of the quality of labor relations. Sound compensation practices help control turnover. So do good working conditions and participation in management of the company. Historically, personnel has not been a high-status function in industry. But an excellently managed company goes contrary to this tradition and will recognize the importance of the function by having the executive in charge of personnel report directly to the CEO. In the view of AIM, having the function report at a level lower than three (counting the CEO as the first) is not satisfactory. Personnel, as a function, is better when it is centralized, not decentralized. Positive personnel policies include devices intended to improve the working relationship between labor and management. Successful personnel policies all share the common characteristic of respect for the humanity of the individual.

The institute believes that general advertising is the least desirable method of obtaining people and feels that a good company will normally be able to fill many of its positions from a steady flow of walk-in applicants. Hiring is seldom done well, in the view of AIM. In fact, "it is most unfortunately true that the worst-performed management function in all industry is hiring" (American Institute of Management, 1970, p. 247). Psychological testing and counseling are viewed favorably if done well. Similarly, training in human relations is also useful, provided it is kept in perspective and foremen and first-line supervisors do not consider themselves therapists. Regarding training generally, AIM rightly points out that superficial management exposes employees to training, while excellent management makes sure employees have absorbed the material. While promotion from within is a good policy generally, overly strict adherence to this policy can result in parochialism. The institute looks at techniques of recruiting, assigning, training, motivating, promoting, and compensating employees to see whether they help advance the goal of a competent, loyal, stable work force. When separations occur—and in normal times they will, often averaging 20 percent—the company should have policies that retain the maximum in good will from those who leave for whatever reasons.

Sales Vigor. Good quantitative measures of sales performance are usually available for constructing historical trends and for intercompany comparisons. Subjective measures of sales vigor include the corporation's understanding of its products. Included too is the company's knowledge of its customers and its ability to match products with customers. Some industries depend on market research for their survival. These highly market-sensitive industries (for example, tobacco, electronics, and cosmetics) are sometimes also the most profitable of businesses, with the best margins and return on equity.

It is possible to argue that the sales function is the most critical activity in a company. Although the service or product can be created by labor and supported by fiscal management, a company is not a business until it has customers, secured through marketing and sales. Although the sales force is as important to a company as top management, selling is a belittled, low-status profession. This is partly the fault of such writers as Sinclair Lewis (*Babbitt*) and Arthur Miller (*Death of a Salesman*) and partly the fault of executives with technical backgrounds who have never sold for a living and who lack an understanding of how difficult it is to sell. It is only in hard times that the sales rep is truly appreciated.

The AIM audit of sales vigor involves a series of related questions, the sum of the answers to which allows appraisal of the company's excellence:

1. What were the company's original markets?
2. How have these markets changed?
3. What is the fifteen-year history of net revenue as a percentage of sales?
4. Which products generate the most volume?
5. Which products have the largest margins?
6. What percentage of total sales does each product represent?
7. Has the company created new markets for its products?
8. How does the company distribute its product?
9. What is the annual turnover in the past few years of dealers or distributors?
10. What is the average size of an account?

11. How well does the company service its sales?
12. How does sales coordinate its efforts with manufacturing?
13. What is the procedure for dropping and adding products?
14. How is the sales division organized?
15. What do sales reports look like? How well is sales adminis-
     tered?
16. How do cost-of-sales figures compare with industry norms?
17. Who sets prices; who can change them?
18. How is the sales forecast prepared?
19. How many products are unprofitable, and what plans
     exist to do something about them?
20. What is the sales force like in terms of numbers, educa-
     tion, experience?
21. How are sales representatives trained?
22. How are sales representatives paid?
23. Who does market research? How well?
24. What advertising does the company do; what does it spend
     to advertise?
25. What is the company's image with its various publics?
26. How much of the company's business is international;
     how much is government?

The audit includes other questions, but these are the more sali-
ent ones. Of course, there are no absolute right or wrong answers. Instead, the questions are intended as a tool to give
management data on which to make a subjective judgment
about quality. The best products in the world are worthless if
they cannot be sold, and more than a few companies owe their
success not to superior technology but to the distinguished way
they package and distribute their service or product. It is for
this reason that sales vigor is viewed, after executive effectiveness, as the most important single quality of a company, more
critical than either financial or manufacturing strength.

Executive Quality. The American Institute of Management's
quantitative scale for its ten variables places the greatest weight
on executive quality. Here AIM includes executive ability, experience, and integrity. It includes the climate within the organ-

ization and its capacity for management continuity. To succeed, a corporation needs a good product and a sound financial structure. But more than anything it needs people who are capable of consistently achieving the corporation's goals. This area of corporate performance is both the most difficult to measure and the most vital to an organization's success.

Evaluating executive quality involves two major tasks. The first is to appraise the current executive group. The second is to look at the company's plans for management continuity and succession. Most organizations do only a fair job of understanding their current personnel capabilities, and even fewer do an adequate job of personnel planning.

The AIM appraisal of executive effectiveness looks at three main components: ability, integrity, and industry. It also examines major management practices related to management development, compensation, and provisions for retiring and otherwise separating executives.

By *ability* is meant the individual executive's skill, intelligence, and leadership. Although technical or professional skill is just one aspect of ability, many companies overemphasize it. Professional skill means essentially what the person knows about her job. Since most executives are intelligent, it is seldom the ability variable that separates the successful from the mediocre or the failing.

Industry includes diligence, but it also means the ability to apply time to important tasks. Most executives work hard, but not all work efficiently or effectively. Does the executive finish tasks on time? Does he separate the essential from the trivial? The successful executive works on only the highest-priority items and ignores or delegates the rest. Industry also includes initiative, originating one's own tasks. No executive succeeds without it, because the closer you get to the top, the fewer people there are providing you with direction.

The next trait in the AIM appraisal is integrity. It includes responsibility and a sense of honor. Integrity results in a reputation for quality, reliability, and honesty. It means being respected and trusted by the various communities in which the executive operates.

When appraising the CEO specifically, AIM wants to know how that officer arrives at decisions. Does he delegate? Can he motivate? One of the major responsibilities of the CEO is to staff the organization with its principal officers and to assume the smooth succession of personnel within the firm. Has the CEO made plans for his own successor? How well does he represent the company to the public? Can he think? Is he planful?

The next part of the audit of executive effectiveness deals with the company's human resource features. The following are examined:

- Executive selection.
- Executive compensation.
- Executive development.
- Executive succession.

AIM believes that good management and nepotism are rarely compatible. Where nepotism is found, look for other practices of favoritism or rewarding of executives on a basis other than merit and achievement.

The institute assigns almost 25 percent of its total audit points to executive effectiveness. More companies fail to be recognized as excellent in management because of weakness in this category than for any other reason. Good people well managed is the key to managing organizational performance.

Service to Stockholders. The holders of a corporation's equity instruments have a right to expect regular growth in their investment. A number of quantitative measures of return to investors are available, some exceedingly elaborate. The subjective point of view asks, "How does the corporation perceive its stockholders?" "What is the organization's strategy regarding invested equity capital?" "Does it attempt to communicate regularly and clearly with stockholders?" "Does it encourage active stockholder participation?" In summary, to what extent does management regard itself as the instrument of its owners? The thoughtful executive will try to determine how well management recognizes rights of stockholders. Its obligations include these:

- Safeguarding invested principal from unnecessary risks.
- Determining and executing a dividend policy.
- Enhancing earnings and net worth.
- Maintaining marketability of the company's securities.
- Keeping owners fully informed.
- Providing for owner participation in key decisions.

Well-managed companies do not forget that stockholders are the owners of the corporation and officers are employees. The executive working to manage corporate performance will remember that although he is captain, he does not own the ship. Somewhere back on shore are the investors who are paying for the trip, and he owes them both the courtesies and the fidelity that that relationship commands.

CASE STUDY
Supplemental Performance Measures:
Appalachian Power and Light

In this brief case study we have an opportunity to consider a utility company that decided to go beyond the traditional financial measures of performance in plotting its course over several years. The new chief executive officer understood and accepted the fact that his primary responsibility was to improve operating results. But he also believed that over the next five years he needed to work hard to improve corporate performance in five areas that were supplemental to immediate operating results but important to the utility's long-term survival. He believed that an overconcern with short-term operating results was not in the company's or its customers' best interests. He decided to focus on the future and to manage as if tomorrow mattered.

Appalachian Power and Light, headquartered in Roanoke, Virginia, supplies electrical power to the residents of a four-state area. In 1979 revenues were $1.6 billion and profits were $170 million.

Appalachian Power and Light was founded in 1916 by Dr. Billie Joe Poole, a pharmacist from Atlanta. Dr. Poole had summered regularly in Roanoke, occupying a rambling old Victorian house a few miles out of town on the Roanoke River, where he spent his days fly fishing. He was fond of the Allegheny and Blue Ridge Mountains surrounding the city and so sought an opportunity to retire in the area. His chance came when he was able to purchase a small electricity generation and transmission company, the Blue Ridge Mountain Electricity Company. When he moved his family permanently to his country home, he was fifty years old. Poole raised beagles and was active in the Roanoke Country Club. During his spare moments he took a mild interest in AP&L as chairman.

Appalachian Power and Light grew fast over the next twenty years by aggressively acquiring other small power and lighting companies in the intermountain area. It financed its rapid expansion by issuing bonds as well as borrowing heavily from banks. During the Depression a combination of dramatically lower customer usage and foreclosures caused the company to default on its loan obligations. Appalachian Power and Light went bankrupt in 1934. Eighteen months later it emerged from a reorganization with bankers in control and with the family descendants of Dr. Poole reduced to an 8 percent ownership in the new company—and they no longer had a voting member on the board.

The company's history continued uneventfully until the early 1970s, when a shift in demographics, coupled with revitalization of the coal industry, caused a major new demand for power. The board brought in a new president, Taylor ("Tripp") Smith III, from the old Smith family of Richmond, Virginia. When Smith took over the chief executive role at Appalachian Power and Light, the company was a below-average performer in a below-average industry (see Table 7).

Tripp had attended Woodberry Forest Preparatory School and earned a degree in business administration from the University of Virginia. He married Margaret ("Muffy") Bundy, a graduate of the Foxcroft School and the University of Virginia. Smith had started his career with Duke Power as a financial ana-

Table 7. Five-Year Operating Results: U.S. Industry, Electric Utilities, and Applachian Power and Light.

	5-Year Return on Equity	Debt-to-Equity Ratio	5-Year Return on Capital	Net Profit Margin	5-Year Growth in Sales	5-Year Growth in Earnings per Share
All U.S. industry	15.8%	0.4	11.1%	5.0%	14.3%	13.9%
Electric utilities	11.8	0.9	6.3	10.1	15.8	2.2
Appalachian Power and Light	10.0	1.0	6.0	7.0	18.6	−1.5

lyst, rising through the ranks to chief financial officer. He was well liked and well connected.

Industry Background

Smith was worried about the declining profit performance of Appalachian Power over the last several years, particularly in light of his company's recent strong growth in sales and the projected increase in demands that would be made on it during the next several decades. He was convinced that the standard measures of performance in his industry were insufficient to properly plan and direct the course of the company as it moved toward the year 2000. He wanted to focus on the future and sought measures of corporate performance over and beyond the obvious one-year goals of improved profitability and reduced debt. He also wanted to get back to basics and stress quality service and rigorous operating efficiency.

A quick look at the electric utility industry showed it was characterized by rapidly growing demand, significantly higher expenses, and lower profits. Construction costs had become unmanageable, and most companies were heavily burdened with high debt-to-equity ratios. To raise additional capital to fund construction programs, the industry was being forced to borrow long-term money at high interest rates and to raise additional capital by issuing new stock below market value.

Demand for new power had been growing at about 7 percent per year, a rate that would require the average utility to double its capacity every ten years to keep pace. New capacity was much more expensive than existing capacity: Every new kilowatt cost roughly 100 percent more than an existing kilowatt. If a 7 percent compounded increase in demand were forecast for ten years, an electric utility would have to triple its assets in the same ten years in order to meet that demand. However, if growth and demand could be reduced to 3 percent a year, twenty-four years could pass before the utility would have to double its capacity.

Needless to say, one of the major challenges in the business was long-range planning. Long-range, in this instance, meant planning ten to fifteen years in advance, because of the ten-year lag between the inception of a utility construction project and its completion. Most other industries considered five years the outer limit of a business plan. An error in calculating ten years into the future could have enormous consequences. Besides accurately forecasting demand and construction costs, the utility industry was being challenged to find alternative sources of energy: geothermal, wind power, fuel cells, and steam.

To meet these challenges, industry leaders were emphasizing load management and conservation. They could no longer depend on utility commissions to pass the rate increases necessary to recoup rising building costs. According to industry experts, utilities could save 15–20 percent of their consumption by using conservation methods and alternative energy sources. So the electric utility business was one characterized by enormous capital needs, heavy leverage, and generous profit margins, yet poor return on equity, poor return on capital, and declining growth in earnings per share. The crisis at Appalachian Power and Light was a microcosm of the crisis in the whole industry.

Recommended Supplemental Measures

Because of his financial background, Smith felt confident in his personal ability to set a proper course for regaining control of the company's financial structure. But to keep his focus on the truly long term, he told his board that he wanted to develop supplemental measures of performance in four areas: consumer opinion, consumer service, efficiency, and environmental impact. If he could achieve in these areas as well as in profitability, then he would have positioned the company to show real excellence for many years to come.

Consumer Opinion. The state utilities commission under which Appalachian Power and Light operated, like most in the industry, was especially sensitive to public opinion. Smith directed his consumer affairs department to conduct a consumer attitude survey to measure current opinions held about AP&L by its various publics. This would serve as a starting point for setting goals in this area. The positive findings of the survey could, of course, be used in presentations before the commission. The negative findings could be used to develop a corrective action plan before the opinions became widely publicized and damaging. The first goal, therefore, was to design, conduct, and analyze an opinion survey of consumers.

Consumer Service. Consumers usually judge a utility's performance by its ability to hold down their monthly utility bill. Accordingly, one supplemental measure of a utility's performance would be the relative cost of kilowatts to customers and the growth of rates. The most expensive utility in the country at the time produced electricity at a per-kilowatt-hour rate 230 percent as expensive as the cheapest utility. Another measure of consumer service is reliability, expressed as blackout time as a percentage of total hours of service or as the percentage of reserve margin during peak periods. The recommended safety cushion is 20 percent. Finally, a possible measure of a utility's effort to maintain a reliable system is maintenance expense per dollar of fixed assets. Smith directed his executives to develop standards and goals for cost of kilowatts, percentage of black-out time, reserve margins, and maintenance costs. Back to basics: Supply cheap, reliable electricity.

Efficiency. There were at least four ways AP&L could measure efficiency. The company decided to identify its current standards and to develop goals in all of the following areas.

1. *Fuel management.* This is the number of kilowatt hours generated per dollar of fuel expense. Increasing fuel costs and decreasing fuel supplies make fuel management a major concern for utility companies.
2. *Load management.* This is the ratio of the utility's average load to its maximum capacity. It is a measure of the utility's ability to meet peak load requirements and also a measure of the degree of utilization of its fixed assets. Too low a load-management factor means the utility has overcapacity and is expensive to operate because of high fixed costs. Too high a load-management factor means that its customers may be subjected to brownouts and blackouts during periods of extreme demand.
3. *Human resource management.* The most efficient utility is the one that can produce the most kilowatt hours with the fewest employees. Human resource management determines the relative productivity of the company's labor by measuring kilowatt hours produced per employee. The higher the number, the more efficient the company's labor force.
4. *Capital resource management.* This figure is a measure of the efficiency of the company's fixed assets. It is expressed in terms of kilowatt hours produced per dollar of fixed assets.

Taking a lesson from the Japanese, Smith decided he would worry about efficiency more than earnings per share.

Environmental Impact. The impact a utility has on its environment can be measured by actions taken against the company, including number of lawsuits, and potential liability and dollar value of fines levied against the company by the government's Environmental Protection Agency. After considerable internal debate AP&L decided that because they could not prevent anyone from suing, counting lawsuits made no sense. But they would accept a goal of never losing a suit or having to pay a fine. The company was determined to be a good citizen.

Tripp Smith presented to his board measures of performance and levels of achievement for these future-oriented performance measures. These were viewed as the most important areas for performance monitoring over and beyond the conspicuous need to improve profitability. Accountability for achievement of these goals was allocated to line and staff officers within the utility company. Workers were asked to participate, especially in achieving efficiency and reliability goals.

Muffy Smith became active in volunteer work, taking special interest in the Roanoke Art Museum. Each year she chaired an auction to raise funds to restore historic old buildings and to offer scholarships for young local artists. Ten years after her husband took over AP&L, a delegation from the utility industry in Japan came to study the plant as a model of efficient management. They took many pictures.

A Final Comment

It is never easy to sail solo. Traveling in a convoy is always more reassuring. To decide to go beyond the more obvious quantitative measures of performance requires the strength of one's convictions and a willingness to stand apart from the fleet if necessary. It sometimes also results in a surprising though pleasant return to fundamentalist business practices.

This chapter has offered a list of suggestions for the executive who wants to establish corporate, functional, and divisional goals unique to his enterprise and its particular needs at that time in its organizational history. The chapter began with the Hay Group's concept of *Performance Compensation,* a useful way to think about the important relationship between corporate strategy and compensation. Then *Value Line's* highly detailed analysis of the relationship between financial and stock-market performance was reviewed, providing a veritable feast of numbers guaranteed to satiate even the most gluttonous. Finally, the peerless American Institute of Management approach to auditing performance was described at length. From it executives can pick qualitative and subjective guidelines by which they can judge how well their corporation is doing.

Tripp Smith at AP&L chose to emphasize performance areas that relate to the AIM categories of economic function and production efficiency. But more important, he returned to fundamentals, not just numbers but a commitment to the real purpose of the enterprise. He sought to assure AP&L's future by making sure that it was achieving its basic corporate mission: to deliver reliable, cost-effective power to satisfied consumers without damaging the environment. This was more than return on equity, growth in earnings per share, or any other hard measure of performance. It was the reason the company existed.

Sometimes if you have to sail alone, it is because the convoy is going in the wrong direction.

6

Performance in
Nonprofit Organizations:
Government

The nonprofit or, more accurately, the not-for-profit organization is rapidly becoming the most numerous and pervasive type of institution in the United States. If the definition includes, as it should, the federal, state, and local governments, special jurisdictions such as water districts and schools, nonproprietary hospitals and hundreds of other categories of organizations that qualify under the tax codes—then the number of not-for-profit institutions is large. Conservatively, at least 30 percent of all employed people work for institutions of this kind.

There are at least 500 kinds of not-for-profit organizations. This chapter is about one type of nonprofit institution, the government. Except where other sources are cited, the interested reader should turn to the following six articles that appeared in the *Harvard Business Review* for an extension of some of the ideas presented here: Cammann and Nadler (1976); Lynn and Seidl (1977); Selby (1978); Smalter and Ruggles (1966); Spiegel (1975); Trainor (1966).

Background

The first "public sector" organizations in the United States were companies that are now for profit, and vice versa. The earliest chartered "public" companies were banks. By the year 1800 there were seventy-two chartered private highway corporations that eventually gave way to government-subsidized toll-free roads. Around 1800 almost all water supply companies were private, but by 1900 three quarters were public. And the first schools were private (parochial), not public (Walsh, 1978). The growth in the public sector has been so great that it is now a major employer and represents a major management challenge. "American government is in business in a big way. Government enterprise in the United States has been growing for over half a century. . . . In the United States, for the most part government enterprise involves public ownership without public policy" (Walsh, 1978, p. 3).

An original purpose of the public agency was to create an enterprise that could serve the public free from the pressures of politics. But government has always been heavily subsidized, which has exempted it from economic reality and left it free to do what it pleased. Some experts in the field, essentially sympathetic to the difficulty of managing performance in that sector, nevertheless now believe that "public authorities that are supposed to act in the general interest of state, region, or city frequently do not" (Walsh, 1978, p. 6).

Government agencies differ in how they are funded. This chapter deals mainly with those that obtain their revenues from taxes: states, counties, cities, schools. Tax-based agencies probably have more severe management problems than public authorities because the tax-based agency is budget-driven. A public authority more resembles a for-profit organization in that it generates its own revenues by producing a good or service for which the public pays. Although the public agency frequently has a monopoly, still the public can reduce its consumption as a means of control. Public authorities include agencies in charge of water, gas, electric power, bridges, tunnels, dams, ports, airports, and parks. In addition to engaging in activities that produce revenues, they can raise capital from private investors in the form of a tax-advantaged debt instrument or equity.

Unquestionably there are major differences between the private and public sectors, but there are also similarities. One study of 210 public- and 220 private-sector managers concluded that the job content, job characteristics, and knowledges, skills, and accountabilities ("KSAs") were similar on these high-level managerial jobs. Another study had 1,500 managers in the city of New York as its subjects. Managerial tasks in this government agency ranged from the simple and routine to the difficult and unstructured. But except for more variety in the top jobs, "there was great similarity in the work done by managers at all levels" (Allan, 1981, p. 613).

The public sector represents a special management challenge because the bureaucratic setting in which political executives operate discourages a performance orientation (Macy, 1971). Why government does not work or does not work as well as it should cannot be covered adequately in one chapter of a book. However, these are a few of the reasons offered by Walsh (1978) and others: (1) There are no profit or operating-margin figures on which to measure results. (2) Success is measured by the size of the agency's budget. (3) Performance data are seldom collected in a usable form. (4) Low productivity is tolerated by administration as a trade-off against strikes and other high-visibility labor/management crises. (5) Employees often spend their careers in one department of one agency, depriving both themselves and the public of fresh ideas. "The failure of American government to deliver goods and services promised by legislative proposals is one of the basic causes of contemporary cynicism about politics in the United States. This failure and the disillusionment it has caused are traceable in part to unrealistic expectations and in part to ineptitude in managing the public's business" (Walsh, 1978, p. 233).

Through the remainder of the twentieth century and on into the twenty-first, the public sector will face the challenge of a growing demand for accountability and more pressure for cost-effective organizational behavior and structures. It will need to learn to manage its performance (Thayer, 1980). Public agencies will feel pressure to shift their revenue base from taxation to a fee for a product or service. There will be more experimentation with contract services, decentralization, productivity improvement programs (management by objectives, and so on), and incentive compensation.

Perhaps the primary change in management in the public sector will be in planning and appraising performance. Like its private-sector cousins, government will do more of its own version of corporate planning and performance assurance at the departmental and individual levels. Government employees will participate more in goal setting and will become less distrustful of real merit systems in their agencies. Already there is a movement toward greater openness and disclosure brought about by Equal Employment Opportunity legislation. Increasingly, subordinates are becoming participants in the goal-setting process.

As Walsh (1978, p. 246) notes, "Every effective major business corporation engages extensively in planning, but both policy planning and financial planning are strikingly absent from American government." There is little opposition to increased planning in government, perhaps because it is so badly needed, but perhaps also because it does not directly affect anyone's job tenure or compensation and therefore has not met the resistance that performance assurance programs have confronted.

It is not agreed that employees in the public sector would experience more job satisfaction and be more productive if they were held more accountable for their work. For example, Thayer (1981) contends that performance appraisal systems do not and cannot work—at least in civil service. In addition to the civil service system itself, the nature of the work and supervision makes some experts pessimistic about the value of objective performance evaluation in government. Keeley (1977) carried out a performance appraisal study of 106 federal employees in research, support, and administration centers. Subordinate conflict about performance appraisal varied depending on supervisory characteristics. "Results suggest that the continued emphasis on objective factors in performance evaluation may not be warranted; under certain circumstances it might be quite difficult to define and evaluate a job in objective terms" (p. 301).

Objective performance appraisal in the public sector is more difficult than in the private sector because employees find it threatening to their job security and to the parity of salary increases they have come to expect. The public sector, both by definition and by experience, is a highly political environment in which vagueness is often preferable to clarity. To be clear means to run the risk of offending some individual or some special-interest group. It can be preferable to not have things known. Regarding performance, there are advantages to equal treatment for all and disadvantages to recognizing differences in performance. Consequently, although there is an interest in productivity improvement in government, there is a reality-based fear of its consequences, as well as an understandable resistance to a wholesale application of private-sector incentive principles to government.

Ralph (1980) believes that performance appraisal for government works best when the agency defines its objectives, addresses objectives independently, minimizes distortion, and keeps the program simple. Though concurring, I would offer some additional advice. Personnel and administrative managers in the public sector who want to successfully implement a management-by-objectives type of performance appraisal system in their agencies should understand that they are faced with an organizational climate that has tremendous distrust of any attempt to measure and discriminate performance among employees. As a group the unit may truly want to do better, but as individuals they will be vigorously and almost unanimously opposed to "objective" performance appraisal.

When dealing with a suspicious and hostile organization, the only strategy that can possibly work—and even it has a substantial chance of failure—is to use a methodology designed to build trust and minimize threat. The program must be run totally in the open, its advocates being careful to fully explain all assumptions, terms, procedures, forms, and applications. In the first year of a quantitative or management-by-objectives-type performance appraisal program, pay *should not* be tied to results. In fact, to build trust, it may be advisable not even to officially record performance results by individuals. Instead, management should communicate the following ideas: (1) Organizations do better when they plan their goals and measure results than when they do not. (2) People feel better about their jobs when they participate in setting goals for themselves and tracking their performance than when they do not. (3) Management's sole objective is to improve the agency's performance and the employee's job satisfaction.

It is difficult to overstate the amount of suspicion and resistance that public-sector managers can encounter in planning and controlling performance. The climate for such efforts can be improved somewhat if steps are taken to minimize the impact that these management tools can have on job security and individual pay treatment. Although it is possible to measure performance objectively in the public sector, it may not be currently possible or desirable to tie individual compensation to individual performance except for certain jobs or certain types of agencies.

Performance appraisal in government can be made more objective, as was shown in one study of 370 personnel employees in Florida. Cascio and Valenzi (1977) concluded that it is possible to rate performance objectively using behaviorally anchored rating scales and that "neither rater nor ratee characteristics exerted any practically significant effects" (p. 278). Another study of 1,961 state government employees found that making performance-appraisal feedback voluntary led to lower ratings than under a mandatory feedback system. Perhaps under the mandatory system a fear of conflict was involved or a concern about being accused of bias. Blacks and women, both Equal Employment Opportunity–protected classes, received statistically significantly higher performance ratings (Field and Holley, 1977). The U.S. Air Force Academy changed its performance appraisal and development systems (PADS) to make the goal-setting process more collaborative. Taylor and Zawacki (1978) found that this had three positive effects: (1) there was more perceived involvement in the process, (2) attitudes toward the system improved, and (3) ratees felt they were receiving more positive feedback.

Arguing for more objectivity in the public sector, Carr

(1980) feels that process measures of performance are obtrusive and disruptive. Outcome measures are better because they are readily observable and do not infer with doing the job but emphasize its end results. In Carr's evaluation of police training programs, outcome measures of performance included report writing, crisis intervention, and court appearances. "Development of several outcome measures can provide field sergeants with adequate tools for active supervision and can form the basis for objective performance-based personnel evaluations" (p. 165).

One of the more popular and effective methods of measuring performance quantitatively is management by objectives (MBO). After reviewing the literature and case law, Thompson (1981) concluded that MBO is a useful tool for public-sector managers. The Civil Service Reform Act has made performance appraisal an especially sensitive issue in government, and Thompson believes that an MBO system is best able to withstand the challenge of the Reform Act. MBO was used with twelve supervisors and twenty-three counselors in a state human services agency. Another group served as a control. Both the quantity and quality of work improved under MBO, as did satisfaction with supervision. Employees under MBO, however, did not report any more satisfaction with the work itself.

Demonstrating the importance of the right climate, a study involving 2,200 employees of a mass-transit organization showed that MBO was better received by those who trusted their superiors and trusted top management. These successes with MBO in the public sector are not isolated instances. Moore and Stauton (1981) surveyed thirty-one cities using an MBO-type performance planning and control system. The city agencies reported that MBO was useful for increasing goal clarity and employees' certainty about the nature of their jobs. Achievement motivation was enhanced. MBO facilitated organizational communication, and 70 percent of the cities responding thought that productivity under the program had increased. Again, however, employees generally resisted quantitative evaluation of performance, and so most of the cities did not pay individually on the basis of MBO results.

With this descriptive background in place, it is now time to move on to a more detailed analysis of the issues in managing performance in the public sector. Critical differences exist between government and for-profit organizations that increase the difficulty of performance assurance in the not-for-profit organization. These inevitably frustrate even the veteran executive or the organizational behavior specialist and need to be understood by public administration students. Although business planning is more acceptable to public employees than performance appraisal, it is not easy, and one of the sections to follow outlines a planning process first used by Robert McNamara when he was secretary of defense. Since measuring performance is so difficult in budget-driven organizations, the topic is discussed with special emphasis on getting started rather than being perfect. Finally, the chapter concludes with a section on management style. The principles of successful management described tend to be more universal than sector-specific. All corporate mariners could benefit from memorizing these rules of the nautical road.

Differences Between Nonprofit and
Profit-Making Organizations

The definitive difference between not-for-profit organizations and for-profit ones is that not-for-profit organizations exist for reasons other than to make money. They exist to provide a service and usually lose money while doing so.

For-profit companies must generate more income from the goods and services they sell than they spend for labor, materials, and use of capital. This surplus is the profit. If the for-profit organization fails to produce an operating surplus, it must use up some of its reserve capital or go and raise more capital, further encumbering itself and lowering its return on capital because it now owes more of it. This state of affairs cannot continue for long. If the managers of the for-profit institution fail to make a surplus for too long, they will be removed by the owners, or the company will be seized by its creditors and the fixed assets liquidated to repay the borrowed capital, at a loss to both owners and creditors. The sum total of all income over time must exceed the sum total of all expenses by a percentage that represents the acceptable level of profit. Such are the stark economics of private business. Prodigality is not forgiven.

Governments do not suffer from the restriction of having to end up with more than they started with. Government agencies can consume capital they do not have in return for providing common services—administrative, judicial, police, and so forth. They do this by borrowing against the future.

Inherent in the definition of acceptable performance in the not-for-profit institution is a mandate for both efficiency and effectiveness. Since as a citizenry we have only limited resources, it is prudent to demand from government that we receive the optimum service possible for the resources expended. Standards of excellence that are applicable in measuring government include lean organizational structures, focused agency missions, meaningful functional accountabilities, targeted goals and timetables, and a level of compensation that in total is no more than the prevailing rate found in private industry. We are far from this ideal state of affairs.

A characteristic that defines the differences between the nonprofit and profit sectors is the concept of accountability. Not-for-profit organizations are not held so accountable by their constituencies for the achievement of specific end results. Often the primary purpose of the institution has become obscured and its goals misfiled in the labyrinthine archives of its own bureaucracy.

Inside the not-for-profit, one finds a phantasmagoria of regulations and reporting relationships. There are often two or three management structures, not one. In local government there is a board of trustees or a board of supervisors in addition to administration. There is a personnel commission separate and distinct from both administration and the board. There are civil service positions and elected positions. There are employee unions, professional and management associations, advisory groups, and benevolent associations.

So who runs government? The civil servant. Elected and appointed managers come and go, but the civil servant carries on. Supervisors and employees may belong to the same union. Voluntary turnover is low and termination rare.

The civil service creates a special climate in which managers in the public sector must function.

1. Managers must placate demands from a multitude of pressure groups and be more political.
2. They operate in structures that are overlayered, overstaffed, artificially symmetrical, and designed by committees.
3. They must work both with people whose careers are highly transitory (appointed and elected officials) and with those whose careers are highly stable (civil servants).
4. They operate with ambiguous missions, vague functional emphasis, and few specific accountabilities and goals.
5. They are not responsible for generating revenue, only spending it.

Frustrations of Managing Not-for-Profit Institutions

The magnitude of the task of managing the not-for-profit institution is evident from the frustration that task generates. People are complaining more loudly and more often about government bureaucracy, about agencies run for the convenience of their employees rather than for the public, and about a government that takes so much in taxes and gives so little in service. As a result, the government has become the target of righteous anger and revisionist zeal.

Suggestions for improving management systems in the public sector have emphasized more controls or more technology. Technology can work; for example, a new phone system can reduce phone costs. But systems requiring employees' participation will fail if a sense of mission is not installed along with the new system. The impaired ability to perform that characterizes the not-for-profit institution stems from a blurred sense of mission, a budget-based rather than a revenue-based economy, and employees who are motivated more by survival than by achievement.

There are two types of people in government, those who are going to leave and those who are going to stay. The temporary people are the elected officials and the appointed managers, those outside the civil service network. Knowing their posts are temporary, they bring to the job a mixture of time-shortened perspective, fervor for change, and a propensity for becoming ensnared in the net of political opinion. The success of elected or appointed managers is determined during the honeymoon period, the first six months in office, when the press and the loyal opposition promise not to attack new officeholders, and their shortcomings are still hidden from public view. Their enthusiasm is intense, their enemies are few, and it may be possible for them to implement the reforms that were part of their campaign platforms. Most politicians promise reform. They invariably campaign on pledges to dismantle the apparatus of government, to untangle regulations, to increase employment, to lower taxes.

The manager new to government soon finds that there are laws of momentum in government, just as there are in physics. The First Law is the *Law of Perpetuity.* It says that a body of government in existence tends to stay in existence. The Second Law is the *Law of Acceleration.* It says that the budgetary spending of a governmental unit tends to grow geometrically over time. The Third Law is the *Law of Reverse Effect.* It states that, once in office, politicians produce effects opposite to the campaign promises on which they were elected. If they promised to lower inflation, it will rise while they are in office. If a tax cut was promised, the actual percentage of income paid in taxes after their election will be higher, not lower. Given the current structures, motivations, and funding sources of budget-driven enterprises, the temporary managers leave office with unachieved goals and an unshakable conviction that it was not their fault.

Job security may be more important to the civil servant than to the private-sector employee, although the data on this question is mixed. But it seems fair to say that security is important to those who seek a civil service career. They cannot be fired except under the most extreme circumstances. Promotions result from passing examinations. Salary increases are automatic, based on tenure. Most government salary programs have regular step sequences for each salary grade, and the employee, given sufficient time in grade, automatically passes through these steps to the maximum.

The civil service system was initially created with the intention of making government work better. It was designed to protect employees from patronage, nepotism, and arbitrary and partial treatment. Following the natural laws of government, civil service has grown beyond merely protecting employees from management. When the muscle of labor unions was added to the codification of civil service, a colossus was created with enough power to bring cities, states, and countries to their knees.

Even if government managers were to focus their mission and shift their thinking from that appropriate to a budget-driven organization, they would be frustrated in their ability to perform. There is no more legalistic climate than the public sector. Many employees of government are paid to devise, revise, compile, administer, and enforce laws regulating the conduct of their own activities. What an agency can do is limited by the legal and political context in which it functions.

Apologists traditionally offer three reasons for the not-for-profit's inability to perform. The first is that results are hard to measure because government does not have good plans. The second is that the public sector needs better people to perform better. Finally, it is said that the sector needs to get better control over costs.

Business Planning for Government

Managing the government organization means changing it into an enterprise with a strategic business plan. Such plans go by a variety of names. Some think of the plan as a detailed mission statement, a series of declarations about the purpose of the organization and what it intends or does not intend to achieve. A mistake made by the government agency is to assume that the purpose of the organization is self-evident and to fail to develop plans for the delivery of service.

Zero-based budgeting would strengthen the performance of government agencies. The process would begin by presuming that there was no further purpose for the department and that it ought to be dismantled. Department heads would be obliged to prove that the department was still needed. With survival as the starting point for preliminary negotiations, costs would be contained more than under the current practice, which is to start with last year's budget and add an inflation factor.

By starting the planning process with a mission statement, managers in not-for-profits can assure themselves and their boards that they are focusing the limited resources of their organizations on the most pressing needs of their constituency. In life generally, those who achieve most are those who have decided to do a few things well. Service organizations are no exception. Those who will contribute most will identify a few things they believe are needed by their local community and then devote all their resources to providing them. Diversification may help protect the organization, but it dilutes its excellence.

It is best to have organizations dissolve when their reason for existence has ceased to be a need of society. The argument for organizational *seppuku* makes more sense in government than in private industry. The market economy eliminates profit organizations that try to provide obsolete goods and services. But the self-perpetuating nature of the government lacks a similar built-in self-destruct mechanism. Unless one begins with the premise that the service is *not* needed and proceeds from there, there is no provision to prune the deadwood department branch from the bureaucratic tree.

One of the benefits of formalizing the mission of the organization is that the process can be participatory. By helping identify their mission, government employees gain a clearer vision of their job and a sense of ownership in departmental results. Establishing the mission facilitates the setting of functional accountabilities, putting the organization's resources behind the goals that best support its general objectives.

After establishing its mission, the organization should (1) allocate resources, (2) set priorities, (3) set deadlines, and (4) hold people accountable. These are the major steps by which managers in not-for-profits can take action to make their organizations perform.

One of the more successful examples of planning for performance in the public sector was the work done by Secretary of Defense Robert McNamara, who later became head of the World Bank. In the Defense Department in the early 1960s, McNamara instituted a planning/programming/budgeting process that was combined with cost analysis.

This was the planning cycle used by McNamara and the Defense Department:

1. *Strategic planning.* Planning was done by mission statements. Each mission had allocated to it a portion of the department's limited resources. Programs were planned in detail, including a careful projection of costs.
2. *Annual cycles.* Strategic planning was integrated with the department's annual budgeting process.
3. *Participatory planning.* Line and staff groups participated in the planning process. They were required to respond in writing by given dates to formal planning questions.
4. *Needs research.* A formal analysis was made of constituent problems and opportunities.
5. *Operations research.* Statistical analysis was performed to determine the quantitative outcomes of various combinations of resources, people, and conditions.
6. *Systems planning.* Distinct planning steps and logic-sequence network diagrams were used to coordinate long-term projects.

The planning cycle summarized looked like this:

Planning
- Mission statement
- Challenges identified

Programming
- Goals commitment
- Action plan drafted

Budgeting
- Cost plan prepared
- Performance against plan

Analytical tools can augment the management judgment that all planning involves. But no matter how explicitly the parameters of a decision are stated, and no matter how precise the predictive power of the formulas that state the relationships between the variables, management ultimately must use its judgment to choose the correct course of action. The best managers are not those with the most intricate forecasting models. The best managers are those with good judgment and the courage to take action based on their instincts. Any major management decision contains an element of the unknown that requires an educated best guess based on experience. Good managers are prescient and tolerant of uncertainty.

Resource Allocation. In developing its mission statement, the not-for-profit organization needs to ask: (1) What is the field in which we legitimately ought to be working? (2) What particular part of that field should be our area of specialization? (3) What are the particular characteristics of the group of people to be served? (4) Are there other organizations serving this group? If so, how can we avoid duplication and waste? (5) Are our current resources sufficient to serve this population at a high level of quality?

One of management's top priorities is the allocation of resources to achieve the organization's mission. This resource allocation forces management to look at problems as economic choices.

The Budget. The budget is the traditional management tool used to guide the activities of government. It is the one figure that is taken seriously by public administrators. Management by budget is at the root of what is wrong with the public sector. Money is spent that is allocated, not earned, whether or not the expenditure is any longer appropriate.

Budget is the wrong way to manage in the public sector.

Good performance is defined as spending this year's budget and getting a larger budget approved next year. The budget, not end results, becomes the measure of achievement. Just as it is wrong to focus on the budget as the major measure of program size and effectiveness, it is erroneous to equate cost of service with product.

By law, not-for-profits are prohibited from generating much cash in excess of expense requirements, the rationale being that to achieve too large a cash surplus implies an interest in making money (for-profit) as opposed to spending it (not-for-profit). The lack of a profit equivalent for the not-for-profit sector is a serious handicap in evaluating overall organizational performance, especially if "budget" is put aside as shortsighted. One is left with the concept of the service the organization delivers in support of its basic mission. Such services are not readily quantifiable and are therefore hard to measure.

It would be preferable to allow the not-for-profits to earn a "fee" in excess of their operating costs. This would increase the solvency of the institutions and motivate management to go after their "fee" percentage with the same enthusiasm as private industry. For example, nonprofits in the defense-industry network are allowed to earn a fee of 5–6 percent of the contract value. Since these companies are tax-exempt, this means their return on sales is effectively 10–12 percent. This is not especially lucrative in the service industry, where gross margins on revenues might run double that figure. But compared with the 3 percent of sales earned by some aerospace hardware companies serving that same Defense Department, 10 percent is a good return.

So there is a profit to be earned in some of the nonprofits, a fee or surplus over actual costs. The surplus can be used validly for several purposes: research (which is a cost without an attending immediate service), working capital, acquisition of new facilities, and a reserve against future contingencies. The fiscally prudent organization attempts to save something of what it takes in. This savings is a cushion against bad luck or honest mistakes. Once enough of a safety margin has been acquired, the institution begins to think of accumulating additional money as "working capital" for investment purposes or for acquisition of better facilities.

Encouraging not-for-profits to accumulate more capital, to run not only balanced but surplus budgets, and rewarding them for this effort through various financial incentives would do more to improve fiscal integrity than any other single measure. People do what they are paid to do. If not-for-profits were paid incentives not to spend, one can be sure their cost of delivering service would decline. Cash incentives in not-for-profits are still a novelty, although they have been used successfully in private industry for a hundred years. If a bonus were awarded for spending less, there would be an immediate and significant increase in performance in the direction of the desired behavior, generally about a 20 percent improvement. The amount of the incentive need not be large; about 10–15 percent of salary is sufficient.

Measuring Performance. The challenge in government is measuring performance. Lacking the advantage of the market test as the ultimate assay of its effectiveness, the government needs structure, systems, and planned obsolescence if it is to fulfill its mission. Among the principal accountabilities of the government manager are—

1. To develop an enterprise mission.
2. To develop sound programs and ensure that they meet the needs of the agency's constituency.
3. To operate programs efficiently (cost containment) and effectively (goal achievement).
4. To ensure an adequate source of funds properly allocated to achieve organizational goals.
5. To coordinate agency services with other organizations to obtain maximum service and minimum waste.

Measuring means emphasizing. The more the enterprise's staff perceives that an area is measured, the more effort and care they will devote to it. Employees naturally assume that if management measures and tracks a variable, it must be important, and it will be in the employee's best interest to consider it important too.

It is imperative for managers in the not-for-profit, perhaps even more than in for-profit organizations, to improve productivity. But before productivity can be improved, it has to be defined. There are numerous ways to define productivity, all imperfect, all open to criticism.

Consider a postal carrier delivering the mail. A simple measure of productivity is the number of minutes it takes the carrier to deliver the mail. This measure is imprecise. It would be more accurate to measure the number of pieces delivered per unit time, or the number of pieces per unit time corrected for the number of stops receiving mail, or the number of pieces per unit time corrected for the number of stops and for traffic conditions. Even the number of pieces of mail per unit time may not be a valid measure. What if all the mail were delivered to the wrong address? If the carrier is motorized, what about safety? The measurement of efficient mail delivery—or any other measure—can be nitpicked unmercifully. The main point stands. The minutes it takes to deliver the mail is one valid measure of the efficiency of our postal service.

As a college student, I delivered mail on foot along the streets of Detroit during the Christmas season of 1962 to 1965 (the exact year is lost in memory). I found I could leisurely complete my route in three quarters of the time allotted. With moderate effort I could have covered the route twice while still having time to throw a few snowballs at barking dogs.

Any measure is imperfect. As long as the end result—the goal—is clear, however, almost any measure is acceptable. Since the multiple measures of an end result are interconnected, it is not a matter of life or death which particular measure is used.

Managers should expect to be frustrated in trying to get employees to agree on how to measure end results. This exasperation is not limited to government but is merely more frequent and intense in that climate. The reluctance to commit to a quantitative measure is due to a desire to avoid getting stuck with anything that will clearly signal success or failure. It is safer to simply try to do one's best.

In the beginning it may be necessary to use project or program completion as the measure of performance and different timetables as the levels of achievement. For example, the social services department of the county welfare division has a new program, Program A. Minimally, to manage performance, administration and employees should agree that Program A needs to be complete by date Y. This would be acceptable performance and could be called competent. To miss this target date by much would create problems, including loss of credibility for the department, and so completion beyond date Z is marginal performance. Ideally, rather than completing the program by date Y, it would be marvelous if it were all wrapped up by W. It would make it much easier to accomplish other, related tasks, and the department would gain status as a model of efficiency. Date W is defined as distinguished performance. Assuming that W is a desirable but unlikely completion date, date X is still good performance and a desirable goal. Date X is called commendable.

Moving from completion dates as measures to other quantifiable yardsticks is not easy in government, since employees in these sectors are not used to having their activities monitored in this way. This makes the way goals are set especially important if the process is to be successful. The key is a participative process in which the decisions about the performance standards are made by those who will be doing the work.

The sequence for measuring performance in not-for-profit institutions can be broken down into steps. None of these steps can be skipped without weakening the overall process.

1. Define the mission of the organization.
2. Establish clear objectives and goals.
3. Establish priorities.
4. Establish measures of performance.
5. Set levels of achievement for goals.
6. Monitor results.

The nature of the measure is not nearly as important as the fact that a measure is selected, communicated, and monitored. Optimally, the agency should have the latitude to generate its equivalent of a profit, which can be called net income (which it is) or fee-for-service income or operating surplus. This ought minimally to be 10 percent of operating revenues, the equivalent of a 20 percent before-tax return on revenues. Finally, variable cash incentives should be adopted. The additional cost is minimal contrasted with the potential benefits. The catch is to make incentives truly variable and to limit their award to people who are in jobs that make a difference.

Difficult as it is to measure efficiency in the government, measuring effectiveness is even more of a challenge. Effectiveness is the quality and quantity of service actually delivered to the user. To define effectiveness necessitates developing a clearer vision of the organization's mission and a sharper image of its service. The difficulty comes in making judgments about the quality of the service. In some cases this is not a problem. Either the garbage is picked up or it is not. But in other ostensibly mundane service functions, quality *is* an issue. Just go to the post office and buy stamps if you want to experience lack of quality in a simple service.

There are other useful measures of efficiency besides cost-efficiency measures. One is the amount of coordination the organization maintains between itself and other institutions that provide similar or supportive services. There is a surprising amount of overlap between services offered by different agencies, providing opportunities to achieve economies of scale by pooling supplies, services, and even personnel.

The privileges of public service include a high profile, the prerogative of performing before the scrutiny of the community. This visibility is part of the attraction of public service work. It can also be a useful device for making an organization publicly accountable. The media are government's conduit to the public; government uses the media to create and manage an image. The media are also a government watchdog and should be encouraged to report on achievement and malfeasance. Public opinion is a powerful tool, and the media—especially newspapers, which have the time and space to tell a story fully—are able allies in keeping the public sector public.

Management Style for Managing Performance

To better manage the government organization, the executive needs to understand its motivators. There are the usual monetary rewards but also the intangibles of working with the public. The government employee works in a fishbowl, and although this can be a nuisance, it can also be exciting. There is power in serving the public, not so much the pleasure of serving but the power to thwart, to not give the public what it wants. Being obstreperous, especially when you are the sole provider of the service, can make you feel important.

Some employees have purposely chosen to work in a particular type of service organization, picking out the work they want—for example, the Veterans Administration hospital or the county tax collector's department. But the majority of civil servants take whatever is available. Because they have worked carefully to reach their current position and establish territorial equilibrium with their fellow employees, attempts to change these existing arrangements threaten them and make them hostile.

Since managing performance in the government is so formidable a challenge, public agencies must take particular care to husband their resources. Unlike the financial institution, which has money and people to work with, or the manufacturing company, which can manipulate physical resources as well as money and people, the public sector's only hope for improving performance is to improve its people. It is especially important for the government to view people as resources and to manage them with care.

The public-sector managers who are getting the best results are those who are emphasizing personnel motivation. They are not ignoring other tools, such as cost accounting and management information systems, but they are intentionally following a particular style of management designed to get the most out of their people.

The preferred style is participative and supportive rather than hierarchical and punitive. Decision making is pushed down into the organization, so that decisions are made conjointly by the people affected. People are viewed as assets and treated as long-term investments. Characteristic of this style is an especially favorable attitude toward people. Good managers have supportive attitudes and work to build teams. It is a style of management that achieves a higher level of productivity than threats, pressure for production, and one-on-one supervision.

Members of units managed in this manner have a more positive attitude toward their superiors. They see management as friendlier, more interested in them as people, more willing to ask for things for them, and less threatening, critical, and punishing. People in these units perceive their managers as less strict but still setting high performance standards.

The prevailing climate is one of team spirit, group loyalty, and a sense of cooperation between management and employees. Employees have a higher level of confidence in their ability to achieve. Management, because it is trusted more, knows more. Managers are told what people really think, feel, and are doing. Although the participative, less strict units feel less pressure because they set their own work pace, in fact they produce more than groups in which there is pressure to achieve.

In the interaction between employees and management, the individual feels supported and liked. Relations are personally close between people. Managers stay on a friendly, intimate basis with employees; they set expectations of high performance but then refuse to push for results. They also work hard to limit the degree to which they show irritation, issue commands, or insist on doing things their own way because they are the bosses.

This style is hard for some managers to maintain on a day-to-day basis. Work does not go according to plan. People forget, make mistakes, or are apathetic. The natural tendency is for managers to be friendly and supportive when things are going well and to become tense and push when those high expectations are not being met. The best results will be achieved by staying cheerful and supportive, even when what you really want to say is "When the hell are you going to do something about this?"

Supportive managers manage by establishing goals and

objectives for their employees and then leaving their employees free to pursue those goals as they see best. Pressure-oriented managers tend to oversupervise and get involved in the process employees use to carry out objectives. Supportive managers continue to emphasize desired end results, offer suggestions on how to narrow the gap between expected and actual results, communicate to the employee that they are optimistic that goals can be achieved, and generally stay away from direct intervention in the pursuit of those goals.

The successful manager also involves his top subordinates in the overall planning for the department, encouraging broad participation in communal goal setting and problem solving. He himself will focus on a few issues in depth and leave the accomplishment of day-to-day end results to others. At the core of this process is the participatory way in which goals are set. The manager sets the direction but asks the others for their ideas, concerns, suggestions, and support.

Through conjoint decisions the employees vital to the achievement of unit goals feel that their ideas, knowledge, and experience are being considered and used to benefit the group. In experiments contrasting support and pressure management styles, the volume as well as the quality of work has increased under the supportive style and has initially increased but then decreased under the pressure style. Under the supportive style, employees feel more responsible to see that the work gets done. To the manager under stress, nothing is more welcome than to have others shoulder some of the weight of responsibility for the major end results of the department. The manager experiences enormous gratitude and relief when she realizes that there are others she can rely on who care as much as she does about getting results. But it takes a leap of faith to simply agree on goals and then leave people alone to achieve them.

A participatory management style helps a group to accept a high producer. This is the individual who, through energy or talent, routinely exceeds the average output of the unit. In departments that are hierarchically managed, the high producer is viewed as a threat or as management's lackey. In the participatory-style unit, the high producer is seen as someone who can be counted on to contribute more than his share to end results. In the supportive group, high producers make the unit look good. In the pressure group, they make it look bad.

How is turnover affected by management style? The permissive group has less. Participation, approval, and support make people feel they belong, are liked, and are needed. Under the hierarchical style, employees quit when they feel excessive pressure for production. The least turnover occurs in those settings where managers accept employees as they are; managers are willing to accept lower levels of achievement and set expectations but do not push for performance. Under these conditions people rise to the highest level of production of which they are capable and accept the maximum level of pressure they can tolerate. Too much pressure externally generated will cause people to leave. Most employees are quite aware of group norms for productivity, and their sense of self-worth propels them to meet or exceed expectation. When performance exceeds expectation, there is a sense of mastery. When performance is below expectation, there is guilt. Under pressure tactics, exceeding expectation is not satisfying because you feel coerced, and falling below standard makes you angry because you feel shamed.

Employees are investments in time, money, and emotion. To have anyone leave voluntarily is costly and is a message to management that it must renew its efforts to get close to all its people and support them. As in so many things, making do with an imperfect current situation is usually preferable to starting over. Turnover is almost always more costly to the long-term success of an enterprise than is accepting less than exceptional performance. A sense of job security results in a higher level of worker morale and productivity. Self-actualization follows survival.

The best style is an easy style, ambitious but casual. Because hard-nosed pressure to produce gets results through fear, the increases in production do not last. Too much pressure over the long term exhausts the human reserves of the enterprise, which, in government, are its only asset.

It is a delicate balance. Given the security motivation of the government employee, turnover may not be as high as in private industry. But management will be faced with a passive-aggressive work force whose members are indifferent to whether the unit manager achieves his objectives. A hard style in any organization yields lower productivity, higher costs, and higher turnover. Best results occur with supportive managers who set high expectations and let the people manage themselves.

7

~~~~~~

Managing Business-Like Nonprofit Organizations: Hospitals

~~~~~~

Hospitals represent a special case of managing performance in nonprofit organizations. They must generate their own revenue and are not able to rely on the tolls that budget-driven agencies can extract. They are a good example of the challenges facing the CEO in a nongovernment, nonprofit organization. Managing their performance requires special acumen and a particular temperament.

Mission

Hospitals that carefully consider their mission find themselves with a number of alternatives from which to choose (Forsyth and Thomas, 1971). Is it the hospital's mission to provide a place where physicians can work? Are hospitals an extension of medical practice? Physicians loom large in the administrative decisions of a hospital. They can influence the hospital's financial operations by switching their admissions to other institutions. Prudent hospital directors maintain cordial and cooperative relationships with medical staff and, as far as possible, meet their demands for newer equipment, more nurses, and so on.

Another interpretation of the hospital's role is that it is a community health center, an institution that exists to protect and maintain the health of the people in its area. Here the hospital is still an extension of the physician treating patients and ensuring their health. In the community-health-center role model, the hospital has a responsibility to provide care without consideration for ability to pay. City and county hospitals are the epitome of this social-responsibility interpretation of hospitals. They tend to function as large emergency-room treatment centers, with some minimal additional emphasis on dispensing information on preventive health care—family planning, hygiene, and the like.

Some hospitals have defined for themselves a primary mission of being a specialized care center, such as a regional center for burn victims, a teaching institution, or a county cardiac center. These hospitals exist to provide specialized services rather than duplicating more general and readily available services offered by other hospitals. Finally, a few institutions have formulated for themselves a business strategy that calls for them to evolve into a diversified service conglomerate. These hospitals, in addition to providing health care, function as a multihospital coordinator for joint services such as purchasing of materials and supplies. They may form insurance subsidiaries and offer liability coverage for hospitals and for physicians. In general, they are convinced that increasing government regulation will restrict their ability to meet their costs by providing only health care service. Their strategy is to diversify.

Although society is best served by many hospitals having different missions, quality of care is likely to be greatest in institutions that offer a special service and have enough volume in that subspecialty to cover their costs and make a fee contingency cushion.

Difficulties in Hospital Management

Hospitals are interesting examples of managing organizational performance in not-for-profit institutions, first, because of their clear need to establish for themselves a mission, a longer-term business strategy. Second, they are unique in the relationship between the board and administration. Hospital boards are usually larger than boards of directors in the private sector and often are also more powerful than their for-profit, nonhospital counterparts. A hospital administrator, unlike the for-profit chief executive officer, does not sit on the board. He has less influence over the board and fears antagonizing it. Rubber-stamp hospital boards are a rarity. The diversity of opinion inevitable among many people, coupled with the lack of a strong administrator, tends to slow hospital boards in making and implementing consensus decisions.

Hospital management faces a difficult task in planning and forecasting even on an annualized basis. It is difficult to project revenues, to develop staffing tables, and to plan capital expenditures, because of the variance that can occur in the utilization rates of the hospital's services. With their high fixed overhead, hospitals, much like hotels, are most efficient when most of their rooms are full.

Occupancy rate in a hospital is the single statistic that best predicts overall financial performance. Utilization rates, in turn, are determined largely by the admissions of physicians. Doctors' booking preferences therefore make a big difference to the financial performance of a hospital. For example, occupancy can vary as much as 16 percent over the course of a week, with a peak on Tuesday, Wednesday, and Thursday and a low on Saturday. Since the hospital is at its most efficient if it can maintain an occupancy in excess of 90 percent throughout the year, it is a handicap if its utilization rate during the week varies as much as 16 percent. Hospitals may be full (and rooms hard to get) early in the week but only four-fifths full over a weekend.

Fluctuations of another sort affect overall hospital performance. Hospitals carry large amounts of accounts receivable. They collect slowly and have many writeoffs. With receivables averaging forty-five to sixty days, cost of money does not have to be too high for delays in collections to wreck a hospital's net operating income. More and more hospitals are becoming aggressive collectors of receivables. A preventive solution to the receivables problem may be the use of patient counselors who, before treatment, explain to patients their financial obligations and assist them in planning for integration of medical coverage with their own personal liability for reimbursement to the hospital.

Besides scheduling rooms, hospitals also inventory and dispense over 2,000 billable items. These include prescriptions, procedures, tests, and medical supplies distributed in the typical hospital to patients in over thirty units—about ten nursing units and twenty revenue-generating ancillary departments. A department in a hospital is a small, specialized revenue or cost center. Revenue centers can meet costs only if highly utilized throughout the year. The answer to higher productivity is to offer only certain services, to generate additional volume in the most profitable units, and to drop units with low utilization or low margins.

A dollar of revenue in one of the hospital's departments does not necessarily have the same impact on the hospital's net income as a dollar of revenue in another department. A few departments, such as surgical nursing, the pharmacy, the x-ray department, and the medical lab, generate revenues that are used to carry the costs of other departments. Although some of the departments, such as intensive care or maternity, could be dropped, other traditional cost departments, such as the emergency room, cannot be closed.

Decisions to drop departments from the hospital need to be made with care and an eye on the future. In the 1960s many hospitals decided to close their schools of nursing because they were large cost centers. A combination of fewer nursing schools, a reevaluation of the role of the nurse, and more women saying no to a nursing career created a critical shortage of nurses in the 1970s.

Health care is labor-intensive, approximately 65 percent of a hospital's costs being for direct labor. Hospitals are also capital-intensive because of their needs for expensive equipment used in diagnosis and treatment. The medical staff wants the latest paraphernalia, and the public prefers to stay in new or refurbished hospitals rather than in older ones. Hospitals are constantly faced with the need to raise large amounts of capital and to make decisions about the best depreciation schedules for their fixed assets. Other heavy costs are the contract relations the hospital has with certain hospital-based physicians, particularly pathologists and radiologists. These highly paid specialists receive a percentage of their department's operating margins. Another costly requirement is the hospital's need to operate twenty-four hours a day, seven days a week. Three shifts of employees require approximately 4.6 full-time persons per position per day.

Changing patterns of medical care have brought fewer patients to the hospital capable of paying for private rooms and extra services. The average patient stays more briefly than in the past and is covered by a form of insurance, such as Medicare, that limits the fees reimbursed. Hospitals must carefully consider their overall rate structure to generate enough revenue to cover their costs. The question of rates and costs is complicated by Medicare reimbursement. Medicare pays only the lower of costs or customary charges for the departments of a hospital. Many hospitals have historically run some of their departments at a loss. Customary charges for those departments are lower than actual cost. Therefore, reimbursement is either at break-even or at a loss. Obviously, a hospital cannot operate this way for long, let alone generate the desirable 10 percent net income necessary for working capital, equipment purchases, reserves, and the like. One option for hospitals is to make enough profit on private patients to offset the loss incurred on Medicare patients. The better solution is to revise the rate structure so that customary charges are approximately equal to cost and every department breaks even.

Incentive Compensation

In the case study that follows, we examine a management tool that has been found useful in industry for assuring corporate performance, incentive compensation. The research on climate showed that compensation was an important dimension that distinguished profitable from unprofitable companies. A performance orientation was almost statistically significant in the reported research, and the relation between performance orientation and impressive achievement may be more subtle than a simple, direct positive one.

Studies of the impact of incentive compensation go back at least as far as the so-called Hawthorne studies in the 1930s. In these experiments, researchers determined that workers paid an incentive for piecework produced more. The effect diminished after a time, and some scientists have argued that the "Hawthorne effect" really means that when you pay attention to something, it will temporarily improve.

Although almost 75 percent of major manufacturing companies have bonus plans, other industries have taken longer to see the value of making a direct connection between the goals a company sets and the way it pays its people. In the early 1970s only about one third of full-service banks in this country had bonus plans. By 1980 the proportion had risen to two thirds. In the not-for-profit sector bonus plans are almost nonexistent. Of over 100 hospitals that I surveyed in 1981, five had bonus plans. Four of the five were totally subjective, and the fifth hospital retained me to revise its quantitative bonus plan.

There is a modest textbook literature on pay compensation, some of the better-known and more widely used books being those by Belcher (1974), Henderson (1979), and Patten (1977). Incentive-pay plans have been found effective in increasing motivation, especially when they take into consideration the needs and wants of the individual. Incentives have motivational value but only so long as they do not become stale and habitual. The hoped for effect in giving people incentives is that production will rise and the employees will feel better about their jobs. Usually these results do occur.

Assessing performance in a not-for-profit is never easy. There can be difficulty even in identifying the benchmark quantitative measures that, like volume and profit in proprietary organizations, will be obvious and acceptable to all. The inclination is to begin the search for performance guidelines among supplemental measures: the value of the organization to the community, service to patients, quality of care, research in diagnostics and treatment. In health care, quality and service are, rightly, the predominant concerns. Although these things can be measured and can even be the basis of incentive plans, it is the finances of a hospital that normally preoccupy its board. Are we solvent? Can we support more debt? Is our occupancy rate high enough, and are our operating costs under control? Do we have enough doctors? Are we getting new ones while heading off defections? How much will we have to raise salaries next year?

The finest health care facility in the area will not long survive without a solid financial base from which to work. This means consistently earning a surplus from which it can replace outmoded depreciated assets and which it can use as rainy-day money to cover the operational dips and flutters, the occasional unplanned expenses that are inevitable in any organization with 2,000 billable parts and thirty business units.

Incentive compensation in a not-for-profit has to be tied, in part, to achieving fiscal soundness—not because the primary mission of the organization is to make a surplus but because without one its ability to perform its mission and even to survive is in jeopardy. If an acceptable profit must be the bellwether leading commercial corporations, then an acceptable surplus over and above a balanced budget is the prudent pick to lead our not-for-profit flock. The case study that follows illustrates how generating a surplus can be assured in a hospital.

CASE STUDY
Incentive Compensation for Hospitals:
San Miguel Hospital

The San Miguel case gives us an opportunity to watch two enemies, Alec Locke and Stan Bukowski, work together to accomplish the unusual. Together with a consultant, they design and implement one of the country's few true incentive plans for a hospital. The study takes the reader through the questions all bonus plans must answer: (1) What are the organization's goals? (2) What behavior should we incite? (3) Who should be eligible for the program? (4) How big should bonuses be? Incentive compensation is an ideal device for knotting together corporate goals and individual performance. When done correctly, it is a very effective management tool for managing performance.

San Miguel Hospital is a 1,250-bed community hospital in San Diego, California. Despite its name, San Miguel is a non-denominational hospital, founded in 1879 through the efforts of one Michael O'Riley. O'Riley had accumulated a fortune in the merchant sailing business, and when clipper ships began to lose out to the more competitive steamships of the day, he retired and devoted his efforts to starting a hospital.

Although there were a number of orders of sisters on whom he could have called for management of the hospital, O'Riley, being of a somewhat antireligious bent, preferred to hire a retired ship's captain to be the first administrator of the then 120-bed facility. San Miguel's first patients were a mix of seamen, the families of local business proprietors, and a few indigent natives.

By 1979 San Miguel was recognized as one of the best-managed hospitals in California. Because of its administrator, Alec Locke, it had acquired a reputation for fiscal soundness, creative diversification, and professional administration. The hospital served as a regional health center for San Diego County. It was respected for its cardiac care unit and especially for the Neurological Institute of the Pacific, which conducted research in neurological diseases and offered extensive diagnostic and therapeutic services.

Alec Locke had been at San Miguel for over twenty years. He had attended Columbia, studying chemistry on a naval ROTC scholarship, and then gone to sea as a line officer. Conservative by nature, he had put in his twenty years in order to obtain his full retirement benefits and then spent two years at the University of Michigan acquiring a master's degree in public health administration.

Locke had retained his interest in chemistry and late in life developed an interest in mineralogy, the subspecialty of geology having to do with the crystalline and chemical composition of rocks. Locke lived alone in a Victorian house on Mission Bay. He had a lab built in the attic, placing his workbench in front of three small windows that looked out over the Pacific. So, in a room like a captain's cabin, gazing out at the sea, he spent most of his time in the study of landforms, rocks, and minerals.

Not only did Locke study mineralogy, he published on the subject. His *Guide to the Rocks and Minerals of Southern California* became the definitive manual in its field. Locke spent most of his free time either in the field, in the lab, or working on his second book, but despite his avocation, San Miguel was an exceptionally well-managed institution.

The success of Locke's part-time management efforts especially irritated Chairman of the Board Stanislaus Bukowski, a sixty-two-year-old immigrant from Galicia, in eastern Poland. Bukowski had survived the Second World War as a cook in the Polish army and, through the black market, had managed to accumulate a small amount of capital. He made his way to Frankfurt and from there to Chicago, where he learned English and dreamed about California. Finally in 1955, on the advice of friends, he headed for San Diego. "Stan," they said, "Go to San Diego. That's as far away from Poland as you can get without leaving America."

Looking around for a business, he hit on the incongruous idea of a Mexican restaurant. He was impressed by the cheap cost of the basic ingredients in Mexican food and by its popularity among Anglos. Ten years later Bukowski had acquired a net worth of $15 million and a chain of twelve Mexican restaurants he called The Cortez.

Bukowski's restaurant chain had experienced above-average turnover, even for the volatile food business, as he pressed to increase volume while maintaining his profit margins. His store managers would stay long enough to learn the trade and then leave for another chain with a more low-key approach to work. Or they would open their own restaurants and reap the direct benefits of their long hours. Finally, Bukowski found a managerial style that seemed to work. He kicked himself upstairs. He promoted one of his long-term managers to president of The Cortez and promoted himself to chairman and chief executive officer. The new president was less driving than Bukowski. When he visited the restaurants, he would sit around, drink Dos Equis, and talk sports. Bukowski's style had been to audit the books, count the inventory, inspect the kitchen, and remind the manager of next month's volume goal. His performance orientation had been too intense for the lackadaisical Californians.

Fortunately, it was at this time that Bukowski, like Locke, developed a passion for something outside work. In Bukowski's case it was fishing. At least twice a month he would disappear for three or four days and return sunburned, placid, and stinking of fish.

Bukowski loved fishing as much as he hated Alec Locke. He admired Locke's achievements as hospital administrator and knew that, without Locke, San Miguel would never have achieved the degree of renown that it enjoyed. But he resented Locke's intelligence, his prep school manners, and his ability to get by without trying hard. Locke was not a member of the board of directors, but nevertheless he was powerful. Bukowski was determined that the board should control Locke and saw his first real opportunity to bring this about as chairman of the compensation committee of San Miguel.

Bukowski had installed an incentive compensation program for the store managers of The Cortez. The incentive plan, which offered managers the opportunity to earn up to 50 percent of their salary in bonsuses, helped stabilize turnover and made it less advantageous for managers to open their own restaurants. The Cortez's plan was a simple arrangement. The bonus opportunity was divided into three equal parts—one part for volume, one part for profit, and the final part a subjective appraisal by the president of the individual's performance. After some initial haggling during the first six months about the best way to measure profit, the plan had worked smoothly for several years. The Cortez was highly profitable, and its managers were handsomely paid. Bukowski believed that paying his managers a profit based on restaurant profits was one of the smartest things he had done. Everyone made money.

San Miguel had been performing comfortably in the black over the past ten years, averaging about 4 percent as a percentage of total budget. Although Bukowski was satisfied with the hospital's performance, he was convinced, on the basis of his experience in his own business, that incentive compensation could improve the performance even of San Miguel. He believed that the best way to get things done was to pay people to do them. And he didn't care if the management of San Miguel was the best paid in the country, as long as the hospital was one of the best run.

Bukowski knew that bonuses had been used for a long time in private industry, but there was confusion about IRS rulings on bonus plans in not-for-profit institutions. He discovered a few large, prestigious hospitals that had bonus plans, but these were not of much value in developing a program for San Miguel. Both San Miguel and the health care field had too many unique characteristics that required tailoring incentive compensation concepts specifically to fit a not-for-profit hospital environment. Bukowski strongly believed in incentive compensation and hired a compensation consultant to help the hospital design a plan.

The most obvious difficulty was going to be deciding on the criteria for overall hospital performance. In contrast to the private sector, there was no universal measure of hospital performance. The laws governing hospitals and the differing natures of their corporate missions would make it hard to agree on a single measure even if some measures could be identified.

First the board and administration met and agreed on an overall compensation philosophy for the hospital. San Miguel's total compensation package would be among the best in the country. The reasons were multifold. Hospitals operating on the West and East coasts of the United States paid higher salaries than those in between. Large hospitals paid their employees more than smaller hospitals. San Miguel was a large, West Coast hospital, and so it made good sense for it to pay well.

The reputation of San Miguel Hospital was another factor that argued for high salaries, good benefits, and now a bonus plan. An institution with an excellent reputation may need to offer only average salaries in order to attract the best people. More often, however, the most prestigious institutions are prestigious because they offer excellent compensation, which permits them to get the best people. San Miguel Hospital was in a class occupied by only a handful of high-stature health care institutions. These other institutions were also large regional centers offering specialized diagnostic and therapeutic services, and they were affiliated with educational centers.

Compensation in an organization ought to reflect its performance. One performance factor should be the excellence of the organization's management. Organizations with a reputation for sound administration will perpetuate that soundness if they offer attractive compensation. Another factor influencing compensation philosophy is the organization's financial condition, its ability to pay. A not-for-profit institution that is operating at a loss is a less legitimate candidate for above-average compensation than one that is comfortably pushing the maximum net income permitted by law or considered reasonable by the rate-review authorities.

Imitation is the second most sincere form of flattery. The sincerest form is theft. Other hospitals consistently tried to recruit San Miguel's executive staff over the years. Locke managed to keep executive turnover low by recruiting from only a few schools of public health administration, in particular from the University of Michigan, his alma mater. This fostered a feeling of *esprit de corps.* The group shared a quiet smugness and an elitist self-image. Despite his dominating personality, Locke had a participatory management style that contrasted curiously with his autocratic personal manner. His management team believed rightly that they were the best hospital managers in the country. Locke analyzed people like rocks and was skilled at finding ways to keep his managers from leaving him.

The joint decision of the board and administration was to pay salaries in the top 10 percent nationally. A competitive program of noncash benefits and perquisites was approved. The cost of benefits had risen rapidly during the last few years, so that it now came to about 30 percent of total remuneration dollars expended, but noncash compensation tended to have low motivational value. In fact, a survey showed that San Miguel executives wanted to put only about 10 percent of their total compensation opportunity in benefits programs, significantly below the 30 percent actually spent. The same executives would invest 20 percent of their compensation dollars in bonus opportunities and would pay the remainder in straight salary.

The parameters of the incentive plan were considered next. Bukowski, Locke, and the consultant decided it should be a management incentive plan restricted to those managers in the institution whose positions truly enabled them to make a contribution to the overall organization. Out of an employee population of 5,500, there were nine management positions that had enough freedom to act, magnitude, and direct impact to significantly affect hospital operating results. Then Locke had second thoughts and insisted that two more positions, which were borderline in eligibility, be added to the list—the controller and the director of financial planning.

Bonus as a percentage of salary was considered next. Little information on bonus size could be found in a review of the health care literature, except that a bonus ought not to be less than 10 percent of salary or more than 100 percent. An executive bonus of less than 10 percent was not worth giving, and the not-for-profit nature of the hospital and the potential reaction of the community at large mitigated against a large incentive award. The consultant recommended a bonus opportunity maximum of 50 percent of salary and an expected actual payout of 30 percent. Because of the groundbreaking nature of the undertaking and the concerns about possible adverse public reaction, the board scaled back the bonus maximum opportunity from 50 to 30 percent for the majority of the incentive-eligible positions. Four jobs that were more staff in nature were given a recommended bonus maximum of 20 percent of salary.

Having resolved the issue of eligibility and bonus size, the board turned next to the question of funding the bonus pool. All agreed that a minimum level of organizational performance had to be achieved before any bonus would be paid.

Hospital administration wanted the bonus plan to be related to and driven by the hospital's retirement plan. That retirement plan was unique within the health care industry and had been subjected to a prolonged and intensive review by the Internal Revenue Service. The hospital had eventually received a favorable ruling on the retirement plan and had had excellent success with it over many years. The plan did not have a predetermined retirement benefit but did provide for a defined contribution each year. The unique feature of the contribution plan, and the one the IRS had disputed, was that this contribution was based on operating results as well as investment results. If the hospital achieved a certain level of operating efficiency (always under the 10 percent net as a percentage of gross income allowable by law), then at least 2 percent of the participants' salary earnings went into the retirement plan. The IRS ruling was that the hospital could set aside a percentage of money out of its operating revenues without violating the essential nature of a not-for-profit organization.

Administration wanted to have an incentive plan whose funding was tied directly to the retirement plan. This would have the benefit of increasing management's certainty about the expected payout under the incentive plan. The administration's proposal was considered in detail. One of the values of the retirement plan was that it had developed measures of hospital performance and a decade's history of actual operating results that could be used to compare current results and project future performance. The formulas used in the retirement plan emphasized partial (controllable) expenses and contrasted them with partial (controllable) revenues.

Partial expenses within the control of the hospital included three major categories: payroll, supplies, and services. Payroll was for full-time equivalents and did not include part-time or temporary employees. Supplies included medical and surgical supplies but not such items as utilities. Services included outside contractual services for pathologists and radiologists and miscellaneous services, such as consulting.

The hospital was using a partial gross-revenue measure of performance that was calculated by taking the total revenue dollars or accounts receivable owed to the hospital and subtracting from that figure a number of what were considered to be uncontrollable factors. The subtractions from gross revenue included professional fees, uncollectibles, and allowances. Although Medicare fees had at one time been included in the gross revenues, in recent years they had been excluded. Opinion was split over whether Medicare fees should be in or out of the incentive calculations.

In analyzing the intricate retirement-funding formula, it eventually became clear that the formula could be reduced to a simple ratio without losing much. This ratio was the net income earned by the hospital divided by its total expenses. Over a decade the ratio of net income to expense had been running about 4 percent. By law in California the maximum net income as a percentage of expense that was permitted was 10 percent.

This net-income-to-expense ratio is informally called the "bottom line" among hospital administrators. For example, in the state of Arizona, which does not have laws limiting the amount of net income that a not-for-profit institution may generate as a percentage of its operating budget, 4–6 percent net income as a percentage of expense is the unofficial line that is considered acceptable by rate-review committees, which examine the expenses and income of the state's hospitals.

The hospital administrators understandably did not want to consider utility costs relevant because they viewed them as outside their direct control. Yet, these expenses were a significant entry in the hospital operating statement and were expected to rise over the next several years. There is a trend in the private sector to consider controllable those expenses formerly thought to be fixed. If utility expenses were included in the overall incentive compensation calculation, then the hospital would look for ways to lower utility costs. There was a similar rationale for including Medicare reimbursement in the calculation. It was understood that Medicare was not likely to fully reimburse the claims that the hospital had submitted to it. Yet, to exclude Medicare reimbursement from the hospital's calculations because it could not be predicted with exactness was to ignore a significant variable that influenced the hospital's overall financial performance.

After exhaustive debate the board and administration agreed that the formula used to define overall hospital performance would be the ratio of net income to total expenses.

The next task was to define the levels of performance. The distinguished level of performance was set at 7½ percent and competent or threshold performance at 4 percent. No bonus would be paid if the hospital did not return at least 4 percent net income as a percentage of expense. Bonus payout would be at 10 percent bonus if 5 percent net income were reached and would go up to the maximum of 30 percent bonus if 9 percent net income were achieved.

Because of the experimental nature of the program and the emphasis that Locke placed on team performance, he was given the option of reducing the individual incentive payout for any executive whose individual performance he felt did not warrant a full bonus. But for the first year of the plan no formal mechanism was established to measure individual performance. The consultant protested this weakness, but Locke insisted on a group bonus approach, and the board went along.

The plan had the intended effect. The year it became operational, net income as a percentage of expense rose from 4 to 7 percent. True, income did increase somewhat because of slightly higher room utilization and the addition of a second and third shift to operate the hospital's CAT scan. But it was reduced costs that brought about most of the 75 percent improvement in surplus. The second year, after only six months into the plan, the chief financial officer reported to the board that on an annualized basis net was now 9 percent and they would probably finish the year at that level. Further improvement was both unwise and unnecessary. Some members of the board were not tactful in their opinions that there must have been some sandbagging in the past, but eventually they were mollified. Quality of service appeared to remain excellent, and the doctors were pleased that new-equipment suggestions were heard with more sincere interest than in the past.

Over the next several years, San Miguel Hospital routinely hit the 9 percent net target and paid the maximum bonus under the plan. With Locke's granitelike hand on the tiller and Bukowski's fishy eye on the horizon, the hospital sailed smoothly into the future.

8

Performance of Divisions
and Departments Within
Organizations

There are three types of performance that the executive must manage in her organization—corporate performance, functional performance, and individual performance. This chapter is concerned with functional performance. The discussion that follows is illustrative rather than exhaustive; the idea is to create cameos rather than to paint in all the details. A few key functional specialties have been selected for treatment so that the manager can see the purpose, accountabilities, and potential measures of performance for each of those specialty areas. Enough material is presented so that the concepts can be generalized to other functions and other organizations.

One way to categorize the various functions in an organization is under the simple headings of *line* and *staff*. *Line* and *staff* originally were military terms to assist generals in organizing the human resources of war. The line meant those military formations that were directly engaged in combat. The term also referred to the main chain of command for decision making within that functional unit. Now *line departments* generally refers to those functions that are central to, and representative of, the main elements of the business. They are the departments accountable for the profitability of the organization. The industrial company's line departments are those departments clearly associated with its principal business objectives, such as manufacturing and marketing. In service organizations line units are those directly involved in providing the business's service to the customer. Line units bring money into the organization.

Staff functions are specialists who support the primary activities of the organization. They are ancillary and advisory in nature. Their purpose is to develop policy and procedure, to collect and interpret data, to advise and counsel. Staff departments have historically been viewed as support departments and cost-of-doing-business centers. A specialized staff unit or subunit is formed when a recurring need related to some basic aspect of the company's business appears to require the retention of in-house expertise in that area. Staff units consume money; they are cost centers.

Measuring Performance of Line Units

A fundamental characteristic of line functional units is that they are relatively easy to measure using objective standards. Staff units are relatively difficult to measure using subjective standards. Measuring staff units requires the executive to use such constructs as quality, timeliness, accuracy, and usefulness. Line units are concerned with the achievement of quantifiable levels of performance directly related to corporate goals. Staff units are concerned with the manner and the extent of the service provided to line departments (Glover and Simon, 1976).

Group or Divisional President. Measuring performance at the group-president or divisional-president level is relatively easy. These are top line positions, and quantitative measures applicable for determining corporate performance are also appropriate at the group or divisional level. Group presidents, for example, can be measured on the overall size of their operation, its sales volume. They can be measured on the profitability of their businesses in terms of sales margins and return on investment. They can be measured by growth—the compounded increases in sales.

There is a danger, though a minor one, of mixing up division-level accountabilities with those of the chief executive. This problem can be easily avoided by emphasizing the principal abilities of the chief executive officer for strategy formulation, relations with the board, management continuity, and the profitability and growth of the total enterprise. The divisional president, while contributing to and supporting the role of the chief executive officer, devotes his energies to the achievement of division-specific goals. He has to remain close to his staff, products, and market to achieve his desired operating results.

Group or divisional presidents' accountabilities are clustered around the achievement of sales and profit goals established at the beginning of the business planning cycle. The group or divisional president is accountable for keeping the CEO informed in writing as well as orally about the current status and near-term prospects of his division. Field and customer visits to monitor performance and gather firsthand information usually consume a portion of his time. Finally, there are the traditional general management accountabilities for planning, staff development, and administrative detail.

The Marketing Function. Because the accountabilities of the marketing function are so integral to setting corporate goals, measuring this function is relatively easy. Size of the business, and growth in size, is the best single index of successful management of the marketing unit. If only one measure of the marketing department could be used, the absolute dollar volume of the business would be best. The marketing executive pursues size and growth. She is accountable for implementation and management of the company's marketing strategy. This includes final determination of the product line, establishment of prices for those products, and distribution of the products to customers at targeted volume levels. She must determine the best marketing mix for the company; this task involves the application of product, price, and distribution decisions to various customers in different geographical regions. She must manage the market research subfunction, which supplies information and makes recommendations that support the basic sales effort. "Marketing objectives generally grow out of market research. . . .

Marketing objectives also, of course, are derivative from higher overall company objectives" (Steiner, 1969, p. 541). The marketing executive has an accountability for maintaining sales margins, for ratios of sales dollars to sales representatives, for retention of market share, and for key accounts. But in the final analysis, the marketing executive is the spearhead of the primary purpose of the business enterprise. It is her unit that must create customers and keep them buying the company's products at a profitable price.

The Manufacturing Function. The primary role of manufacturing is to produce the company's products on time, within cost, and at an acceptable level of quality. Along with marketing, the production unit is the other major line department and function of an industrial corporation. Although the accountabilities of the manufacturing department may be easy to list, their measurement can become as complex as the technology of the manufacturing process.

Global measures of manufacturing include production costs, material costs, and labor costs. The challenge to manufacturing is to maintain quality while finding ways to lower costs. Margins are increased either by raising the sales price of the basic unit or by lowering the cost of producing it. Broad measures of manufacturing performance include return on capital, return on assets, and ratio of total sales to total assets. Each particular industry and its plants will have individual measures of productivity. These can include efficiency ratios, such as cost of goods produced as a percentage of sales, and other measures of output. One such gauge of output is units produced per hour of labor, per dollar of investment. Manufacturing efficiency standards can include percentage of scrappage, machinery downtime, and number of rejects. Other criteria of manufacturing are subjective. Is the organization lean? For example, one model of manufacturing organizational spareness proposes that no manufacturing operation needs more than one supervisor for every thirty hourly workers, one manager for every ten supervisors, one director for every six managers, and one chief manufacturing officer for every six directors.

Measuring Performance of Staff Units

Because marketing and manufacturing are line units and are the intrinsic reason for the existence of the corporation, measures for these units are the most straightforward of all. The decision required of the chief executive is to select, from an abundance of available measures, those that are most useful in monitoring progress and making comparisons. The question is not what but which.

Once these decisions are made and marketing and manufacturing functions are set aside, the executive must look at the performance of staff units. Here the task is difficult because the measures are subjective.

For any staff unit, the CEO must herself become directly involved in at least four activities. She must review and approve the department's goals and its budget. She must review and approve the organizational structure. She must choose the executive to lead the department, and she must monitor the department's accomplishments. It is this last responsibility that is most often neglected.

Research and Development. The difficulty of measuring and managing performance in a functional unit can be illustrated by considering the research and development unit of an industrial corporation. The main purpose of this unit in conducting both basic and applied research is to develop the company's future products and improve its existing products. The investigation of new resources and improved technologies is a part of its mandate. Always, it must strike the proper balance between today (product improvement and cost reduction) and tomorrow (product creation and market expansion). Depending on the size of the corporation, research and development may be separate from engineering design. The accountability for improving existing products may be a function of research and development or of engineering, or it may reside elsewhere. There must be some functional unit in the organization whose task it is to make the company's existing products cheaper, more reliable, more durable, with more features, and with broader applications.

There is no single major measure of performance for research and development. Rather, one looks for an affirmative answer to the question "Does the department know where it is going?" or "Does it have clear goals and objectives?" The R&D executive needs to have the technical know-how characteristic of the industry. He requires a hard-to-find combination of an enthusiasm for science and an admiration for profit. Like his other functional counterparts, the head of research and development has a generalized managerial accountability for allocating resources and controlling expenses, deploying people, and reporting on end results.

Tangible signs of meaningful activity in research and development are not plentiful, but they can be found. They include ratios such as the R&D budget as a percentage of sales, the sales of products developed within the last five years as a percentage of total sales, and reduction in cost of goods through new technologies. The number of patents and the number of books and articles produced by the department can be tallied. Professional honors such as election to academies and societies suggest the excellence of the staff. The time and costs required to develop new products can be monitored, even over a period of years if necessary, to determine true research and development performance. Although the determination requires indirect measures, research and development eventually either does or does not contribute to organizational vitality and growth.

An MBO approach can work well for research and development personnel. A study of 271 R&D employees found increased work satisfaction under a program that emphasized goal clarity and planning, subordinate freedom, feedback and evaluation, and participation in the goal-setting process (Mossholder and Dewhirst, 1980).

Engineering. The engineering department is a mix of line and staff. With one foot in each camp, it can create more conflict than any other major support unit. Engineering can displease everyone. Marketing believes that the company's products are not engineered to sell. Manufacturing knows that engineering's tolerances are unrealistic and its production methods wasteful. The engineers themselves suffer from the occupational weaknesses of overengineering their product and being disdainful of products and processes that were not first developed within their own company.

The role of the engineering department is to provide support service to both manufacturing and marketing. Engineering is responsible for the modification of existing product lines. This can involve either extensions or upgradings of existing products. Depending on the organization of the corporation, the department may also be responsible for maintenance of products, for technical service, and for repair. The primary accountabilities of the engineering department include the development of designs, specifications, and production methods for the organization's products. Well-run engineering departments coordinate effectively with marketing to gather information from the company's customers on the product and its applications. They also coordinate their efforts with manufacturing to produce quality products within acceptable cost limits. Goals frequently developed for engineering departments include reducing the cost of the product, standardizing the product's design, improving its features, and protecting the company from the product's liabilities.

Measures of engineering performance include cost of goods produced, percentage increases in the engineering budget compared with percentage increases in sales and profit, sales dollars per engineer, and engineering hours per unit produced. It is ironic that the chief executive will find measures of performance the most difficult to quantify in the functional department that is the most measurement-oriented of all her units. The engineers themselves are no help: They do not believe it is possible to measure their performance.

Finance. The first staff units in organized society were run by accountants. Examples of numerical records can be found in most ancient societies. Egyptian priests, advisers to the pharaohs, kept secret records on the cyclical flooding of the Nile, which gave them the ability to forecast production yields from the pharaoh's crops. This ability to predict, together with the calculated illusion of magic, gave the priests power.

The role of the financial function is to keep concise records, issue timely and accurate reports, and forecast the future on the basis of the past. The principal accountabilities of the financial department of most industrial corporations are at least nine in number:

1. Maintain financial records.
2. Analyze actual in comparison with planned results, and determine the factors responsible for variances.
3. Contribute to corporate profitability through financial decisions about taxes, depreciation, and so on.
4. Recommend to management the cost-effectiveness of its major make/buy alternatives.
5. File timely and accurate reports with regulatory agencies.
6. Recommend to management the advantages and disadvantages of potential mergers and acquisitions.
7. Recommend opportunities for reducing cost of goods produced and improving profit margins.
8. Manage the corporation's financial structure.
9. Raise and manage cash and capital.

These principal accountabilities can be used by the chief executive officer and the chief financial officer to establish specific goals for the finance department. For example, a goal might be to improve the corporation's financial reporting systems. Improvement could be defined as clarifying and documenting each report produced, avoiding duplicating, focusing data to make them more useful, and increasing the speed of information retrieval. Quantitative measures of achievement include the cost in dollars and hours of labor required to produce financial information. The average time required to produce data and the number of errors in the reports could be counted. The usefulness of the data is a subjective measure, based on the opinions of line managers.

The Audit Function. A department that has increased in importance to the chief executive officer over the past years is auditing. The role of the department is the official examination and verification of the records, especially the financial records of a corporation. Audit's primary purpose is to assure management control over the business. The department monitors compliance with important company policy and procedure, it ascertains that authorization was received for important actions, and, where necessary, it carries out special investigations.

Among the accountabilities of the audit function is verification of the accuracy of the basic numbers of the business. The department has an obligation to report its findings in a timely, accurate, and usable manner and to recommend corrective action. It coordinates the investigations of the corporation's outside auditors. A major responsibility of the chief audit executive is to assure the chief executive officer, the stockholders, the board of directors, and the government that the corporation's financial statements are correct.

Goals and measures of performance can be established in the different areas that the audit department investigates. Financial audits and operations audits are common in all large corporations. Factory audits include cost accounting and property surveys. Field-operation audits may cover warehouse and retail reviews. The corporation's subsidiaries and its suppliers under contract may also be subject to internal audit.

The Legal Function. Compliance with the law has become a full-time accountability of the legal departments of major U.S. corporations. The corporation must follow the federal antitrust laws. It must be in compliance with Federal Trade Commission acts. Many industries have acts specific to them that must be obeyed. Compliance with other generic business acts is required. Representative of these acts are national environmental policy, clean air, water pollution control, equal employment opportunity, occupational safety and health, federal energy, consumer product safety, and pension reform. State laws require their own compliance: fair employment, land use, and environmental quality. Beyond compliance, the accountabilities of the legal department include advising management on the legal-ity of the corporation's plans, policies, and actions. The general counsel should be sure that someone in his department is monitoring all legislative bills that may affect the company. From time to time the legal department may determine that taking an advocacy position is in the best interest of the corporation. Counsel should advise management about the procedural steps that must precede a significant corporate action.

The most important accountability of the legal department is the satisfactory management of litigation involving the corporation. This may involve retaining outside counsel, doing courtroom work, and negotiating settlements. The company's officers and directors may be the targets of potential litigation— suits or claims, actual or threatened. At least one in fourteen large industrial corporations reports these types of claims. Of the claims filed, 42 percent are for failure to comply, 30 percent for alleged mismanagement, 15 percent for conflict of interest, and 13 percent for inadequate procedure.

Litigation being such an important part of the accountabilities of the legal department, a high priority might be a goal to satisfactorily negotiate settlements against the corporation. Measures of performance for negotiating settlements might include documentation, use of outside counsel, progress reports, time spent on the projects, fees incurred, and actual settlement compared with potential liability.

CASE STUDY
Pitkin Manufacturing Company

In the case study of Pitkin Manufacturing Company we have an example of too little, too late. The consultant was brought in to assist the management of what had once been a vigorous business with excellent profit margins and an enviable return on capital. The consulting assignment, in broad terms, was to design an incentive compensation plan for the president and those who reported to him. In specific terms, the president wanted the consultant to develop an extensive list of measures for each of the officers. This was done, but the engagement was a failure. The chairman, who owned 90 percent of the stock and did not want any bonus plan that was tied to results agreed on before the fact, rejected the initial recommendations and several successive revisions.

The main points in the Pitkin case are the illustrations of measures of performance at the divisional and functional levels. But there are other points to consider. Managing organizational performance requires that the right compounds in the right amounts be poured through the performance funnel. In the Pitkin consulting assignment, appropriate and useful functional and divisional measures were in fact developed—but to no avail, because so many other components of a successful mix were missing. Good measures do not compensate for a poor strategy or no strategy. Although strategy usually follows structure, it is said, in the Pitkin case the organizational structure was inappropriate, a bad fit for a bad strategy. Further, a climate characterized by paternalism and mistrust hamstrings the achievement of good goals well measured. Because ownership would not share with management either operating results or forecasts, functional and divisional managers could not understand how their goals supported the corporate effort. The officers reporting to the president rightly felt handicapped by being blind to the overall picture. Managing performance is more difficult when you keep secret what it is you are trying to do.

Developing measures for some functions appears simple because of the nature of the activity but can actually be subtle if they are thought about carefully. For example, instead of a simple goal of increasing sales by so many percentage points, the senior vice-president for mine hoists took a tactical approach and focused the year's efforts on trying to change the customer mix.

One final point: A competent incumbent can make a difficult measuring job easy. The vice-president for administration at Pitkin handed the consultant a list of suggested measures, most of them excellent. And a less competent executive (here, in engineering) can make a difficult measuring job almost impossible.

The case is presented to introduce the reader to goals and measures that were developed for the major functional units of a manufacturing company. But even had these been accepted and used as the basis for a management incentive plan, it would not have saved Pitkin and its ownership from their ultimate fate. The company suffered from several problems more pressing than compensation, each of which had the potential to be fatal. First, it lacked a corporate strategy that could save it from a line of business characterized by declining sales and profit margins. That profit was earned through replacement parts, and there was no adequate strategy to produce growth and diversification. Second, the company was improperly structured. No one but the president was accountable for profit. Ownership so distrusted professional management that management was not even privy to total-sales-volume information. The company still had a functional structure although its product lines made divisionalization a natural choice. Finally, management was spotty, with good strength and depth in marketing and administration, acceptable competence in manufacturing, but weaknesses in engineering and in both the president and the chairman, the former inexperienced and the latter arbitrary and autocratic. It took almost 100 years from its formation, but the company was finally liquidated for its assets, and only the name Pitkin remained as a product line.

The Pitkin Manufacturing Company, headquartered in Denver, Colorado, was a privately owned manufacturer of specialty mining equipment. In 1980 it had approximately $150 million in sales and four major product lines: rock crushers, conveyer belts, hoists, and sluice boxes. But margins had dropped to 4 percent, and return on capital was an insipid 6 percent. Still, it was debt-free and totally owned by the founding family.

The company had been formed in the late 1880s by two Irish brothers, the MacKays. After taking approximately $1 million from their silver mine near Leadville in Pitkin County, they decided to come down out of that 10,000-foot city to the less rarefied atmosphere of Denver and set up a mining equipment company. One of the MacKay brothers, James, never married. He dissipated his fortune drinking whisky and betting on horse races. The other brother, William, wisely left the management of the business to his wife, Mary. She hired professionals to look after manufacturing and marketing and elected herself the company's president and treasurer. Alternatively charming and iron-willed, she kept total control of the company in her own hands.

Despite her wealth, Mary walked to church every Sunday with her three daughters and two sons to remind herself of her humble Dublin origins. Kneeling before the altar, she would pray fervently, "Help me keep the old fool out of the saloons and gambling halls, and I'll give you one daughter for a nun and a million dollars to the church for a new hospital." Her prayers were answered. William died at home in his own bed at age sixty-two, sober and with his fortune intact. Mary kept her vow. To God she gave her daughter Bridget, and to the diocese of Denver she gave an endowment of $1 million. When she herself passed on, Pitkin Manufacturing had a book value of $35 million, and Mary was getting 30 percent a year on her capital.

By 1975 the heirs of Mary and William MacKay, mainly Kevin MacKay, an arrogant octogenarian, and his family, still owned Pitkin, but the business they controlled was dying. Product lines all had small markets, high capital requirements, and thin profit margins. Sales had plateaued and return on capital was declining. The president, Dan O'Grady, believed the organization's compensation program was contributing to poor performance, and he wanted to design a new management incentive plan. His consultant advised him that the best approach was to review each functional unit and to work with the manager in charge to establish measures of performance in that area. The consultant set to work to develop goals and measures for the managers who reported directly to O'Grady.

Senior Vice-President for Engineering

For a capital-equipment manufacturer, the company's products were inordinately customized, and the engineering department was constantly quarreling with marketing over extensions of the company's product lines. Although there were only four major product groups, different features and specifications insisted on by marketing had resulted in over 100 separate product categories.

The measures of performance in engineering were reached after an exasperating struggle with the department's vice-president. Eventually, two measures of performance were accepted, reduction in costs of goods manufactured and reduction in product warranty costs. The consultant recommended two supplemental measures—product reliability, as measured by nonbillable field-service calls, and new-product introduction rate, measured by the time required to complete all engineering drawings, specifications, and manufacturing procedures for new-product categories. Both were rejected by engineering management as too inaccurate to be good measures.

Vice-President for Administration

The administrative vice-president's accountabilities included finance, personnel, and data processing. A number of measures of performance were rapidly developed for his area.

There were three measures for the industrial relations department within the administration group: reduction of worker's compensation claims paid as a percentage of payroll, reduction of hours of production time lost because of accidents, and reduction of employee turnover. For data processing the primary measures of performance were reduction of overall data-processing costs and reduction of MIS reports issued past the promised due date. Within the financial function, quantitative measures of performance were percentage reduction of total insurance claims, reduction of credit writeoffs, and reduction of aging in accounts receivable.

Senior Vice-President for Manufacturing

Measures of performance for the company's centralized manufacturing facility were percentage of finished goods delivered to customers on or before promised delivery date, control of scrappage rate as a percentage of total value of goods manufactured, reduction of goods returned as a result of manufacturing deficiencies, increase in productivity measured by units produced per unit time, and total value of cost of goods produced per labor hour per dollar of capital.

Senior Vice-President for Mine Hoists

Each of the company's four major products was managed by a senior vice-president who was accountable for sales volume for that particular line. Because accountability for profit resided only with the president, the measures of performance for the senior vice-president emphasized sales volume. The primary measure of performance for the group was targeted levels of gross sales set at competent, commendable, excellent, and distinguished levels. Another goal was to increase the average sales for each of the company's hoists distributors. The company's sales performance tended to follow the 80/20 rule: 80 percent of mine-hoists sales were achieved by 20 percent of the company's distributors. The final primary goal of mine-hoist sales performance was to reduce the percentage of the company's sales to its six key accounts from 60 percent of total sales to 40 percent.

Reception of the Recommendations

Recommended measures of performance and a bonus plan were presented to the corporation's chairman and chief executive officer, Kevin MacKay, the aging grandson of Mary MacKay. Mr. Kevin MacKay had dismissed the last in a series of professional managers, taking for himself the job of chief executive officer. He had named as president his son-in-law, Daniel O'Grady, but had given him little authority. MacKay did not like the recommendation of the consultants hired by O'Grady to tie executive bonuses to the measures of performance for each functional group. In the past he had paid bonuses based on his subjective appraisal of the contribution of each executive to his company. Because the corporation was still closely held, he was not obliged to make public the organization's profit figures. And he didn't like being pinned down to any before-the-fact bonus plan.

After careful review of the recommendations, MacKay rejected them in favor of continuing his past bonus practices. Profit margins on the company's product lines continued to erode, and no new products were introduced to take their place. Within two years, MacKay sold his company to an English heavy-equipment manufacturer attracted by Pitkin's low debt structure and brand name. MacKay retired to Palm Beach, Florida, where he died less than six months later. His son-in-law, Dan O'Grady, on being dismissed by the new owners, also moved to

Palm Beach, where he mismanaged his wife's inheritance. The English liquidated the company but kept the Pitkin brand name. When the news was reported in the *Denver Post,* the bishop there was said to have remarked that Mary MacKay, God rest her, turned over in her grave.

9

Individual Performance

Managing organizational performance means assuring the achievement of organizational, functional, and individual excellence. It is individual achievement that the next chapters of the book are about.

Establishing a Performance Appraisal Program

Instituting a results-oriented performance appraisal program in a company that has not previously had one requires care to ensure the success of the program. Because evaluating people is such a sensitive issue, it is easy to make mistakes in the initial stages. An orderly, systematic approach can minimize these potential problems.

First, the company must decide whether it really wants to extend its goal-setting and monitoring efforts down to the level of the individual employee. The decision requires a major administrative commitment—detailed documentation, standardized forms, and so on. The burden of appraisal must be considered, not just the expected benefits.

Once a company decides to appraise people, it must determine what it wants to accomplish in the first year or two—whether to use appraisal for short-term purposes such as awarding salary increases, for obtaining information for promotion, for reviewing and clarifying job requirements, or just generally for encouraging better performance.

Usually the personnel department works out the design of the program, with managers providing a critique. Most competent managers already know how to informally establish objectives and appraise staff's performance. Therefore, any formal appraisal program should build on managers' experience by incorporating their ideas. The participation of line managers is necessary to design something that will work.

Management needs training in performance appraisal procedures. The first part of the training should review salary administration with the goal of making supervisors able to explain the factors, apart from performance, that affect an individual's pay. The second part of the program can use examples of specific jobs to show how the company ties pay and performance together, teaching managers how to make salary recommendations based on performance and the company's policies.

Training has little value if managers involved in individual appraisal do not commit themselves to making it work for the organization. This commitment requires—

1. *Acceptance of purposes.* Managers who perform individual appraisal have to believe in the value of doing it. They must agree that employees do their best when they are told how they are doing.
2. *Acceptance of methods.* Managers who are responsible for individual appraisal must find it helpful to them in running their departments. Managers should help to pilot-test appraisal methods and feed back to personnel suggestions for modifying forms and procedures.
3. *Skill in appraisal.* People doing appraisals will acquire skill if provided with coaching and technical assistance.
4. *Maintenance.* An administrative network is needed to maintain an individual performance appraisal system. Files and forms are required, and someone has to be given the responsibility for system maintenance.

In implementing an individual appraisal program, there are six considerations: timing, preparation, approval, discussion with employees, relation to pay changes, and retention of the appraisal form. The particular approach the company chooses depends on its appraisal orientation.

Timing. Annual performance ratings of individuals are sufficient for the administrative needs of most companies and represent an acceptable minimum appraisal effort. If the appraisal is tied to an incentive program, then quarterly reviews are best. When ratings are used for administrative purposes, they are usually made at year end or on some other fixed date within the planning cycle, such as the employee's anniversary date. The advantages of having all appraisals done simultaneously are that managers compare their people at the same time, ensuring greater consistency, and the task is finished until the same time next year. An alternative that is gaining in popularity is to evaluate employees on their job-anniversary dates, thus spreading the task throughout the year.

Where performance appraisal is part of controlling unit operations, then it should be part of the normal business planning cycle. It is most effective if it follows preparation of the one-year and three- to five-year plans. If the company does not have a general planning process, performance planning should normally be done once a year, at the beginning of the fiscal or calendar year or the natural business year. Individual appraisal that emphasizes employee development is a continual process. Processes designed for management succession and career development should be reviewed at least once every three years.

Preparation. When the main purpose of individual appraisal is administrative, the supervisor can prepare the analysis alone because its main purpose is communication about the employee from the manager to the company. Operational individual appraisal, communication between the manager and the employee about the job, can be prepared by either the manager or the employee or both, depending on the situation. In top-down planning organizations, performance appraisals are statements of results against plans. When the main purpose of the appraisal is development, the employee carries out his own performance analysis for himself, and to communicate the company's point of view, management and personnel comment on the analysis.

Approval. To control biases and inconsistencies, the individual appraisal requires approval by the manager's superior and by a central control such as the personnel department. Developmental performance appraisals must be approved by all parties— personnel, management, and the employee.

Discussion with the Employee. An administrative appraisal can be discussed with the employee at the manager's option. An operational appraisal must be discussed between the manager and the employee to have any meaning. The same is true of a developmental appraisal.

Relation to Pay Changes. The classic advice given in books such as this is to keep pay increases separate from performance appraisal. The rationale—and it is a good one—is that the primary purpose of performance appraisal is communication between management and employee regarding the employee's performance. The issue of salary shifts the focus from a developmental experience to an administrative one. However good this advice, in practice it is hard to separate in the employee's mind performance appraisal from merit increases.

If the company is using performance appraisal mainly for administrative purposes, then it is better if the appraisal and the salary adjustment are made at the same time. Where operational use is being made of individual appraisals, the appraisal should be tied directly to bonus pay. If an operational appraisal is to be related to salary, the salary change based on past performance should be made within thirty days after the performance appraisal. Developmental appraisal should be totally separate from specific pay changes. The purpose of developmental appraisal is to plan for future improvement, not to reward or punish past behavior.

Retention of the Appraisal. Rules for retaining personnel forms will vary with individual companies and the states in which they operate, but the following are general guidelines for retention of the appraisal document. Copies of the appraisal for the current period should be available to both the manager and the employee. An administrative appraisal should be retained for three years. After that it is no longer relevant. Annual appraisals have only moderate predictive value after two or three years. There is a tendency for low-rated employees to improve and high-rated employees to decline in performance. The reasons for this regression toward average performance are complex. It may be more a result of the psychology of performance appraisal than of real changes in individuals.

Performance Appraisal Techniques

Although executives have always informally evaluated their subordinates, systematic appraisal techniques first appeared in the early part of the twentieth century. Since then, a number of techniques have been developed and the purposes of appraisal have changed.

Without a doubt, structured appraisal systems are used extensively throughout American business. In 1976 Research for Management, a part of the Hay Group, surveyed 850 American organizations, including the fields of banking, insurance, manufacturing, transportation, utilities, public administration, and the retail trade. Nineteen percent of this group had under 150 employees, and 15 percent had over 10,000. Only 8 percent of the firms in the middle did not use formal appraisal procedures, mainly the smaller ones, which tended to rely on frequent contacts between managers and employees. Banking and insurance firms used formal appraisal systems more than other companies did. Manufacturing and utilities did a lot of individual appraisal, while the transportation industry did the least.

Research for Management found that individual appraisal was used most often to make decisions related to salary changes, promotions, and employee development. The larger firms also relied on appraisal as a planning tool for exempt employees. Two thirds of the larger companies had a formal performance appraisal system, but only one third of the smaller firms did.

Nearly 80 percent of the 850 companies predicted an increase in such systems in the future. Checklist appraisals are typical for lower-level employees; evaluation of those at higher levels emphasizes meeting established goals and objectives. Almost three quarters of the evaluated personnel are always notified of the outcome, and the remainder are notified sometimes. Rarely are employees never notified of appraisal results. Clearly, the primary vehicle for individual performance planning and assurance in American business is performance appraisal.

An earlier survey in 1968 by *Fortune* magazine of its 500 largest corporations yielded similar results. Of the 316 firms that responded, about 80 percent used formal appraisal for counseling, training, promoting, and motivating employees and for deciding whom to keep. Campbell and others (1970) believe that about 60 percent of all business firms have a formal performance appraisal system.

Motivational and developmental uses of appraisal are relatively recent. Originally, formal appraisal systems were used for personnel decisions such as salary increases, promotions, and transfers. Evaluations were made by the employee's manager on the assumption that he was best qualified to judge his subordinates. Appraisal methods were all trait-oriented, attempting to measure individual characteristics such as cooperation, loyalty, sociability, and punctuality.

Since 1950 the trend has been to evaluate the achievement of specific goals, with the employee integrally involved in the formulation of these goals and in the evaluation process. Results are appraised instead of traits. Several historical developments account for this change. The percentage of white-collar workers in the total work force has increased dramatically. Where earlier appraisal methods rated blue-collar employees on traits, such appraisals have been replaced by an emphasis on seniority and bargained pay. Evaluation of executive and technical personnel requires different techniques, an appraisal of how well they achieve objectives that support the company's corporate plan.

Five trends have emerged in appraisal recently: (1) involvement of employees as part of the appraisal process; (2) use of appraisal as much for corporate planning as for controlling performance, (3) more appraisal of management employees than of nonmanagement employees, (4) more-complex appraisal techniques, and (5) litigation involving issues of performance.

Doing performance appraisal correctly is more important than ever because the possibility now exists that organizations can be assessed for damages for making errors in the process (Cascio and Bernardin, 1981). It would be reassuring if using one particular method of appraisal would clearly indemnify the employer; unfortunately, although some systems are better than others, none is foolproof. Massey, Mullins, and Earles (1978) conducted an experiment using three kinds of rating statements—task-oriented, work-oriented, and trait-oriented. Those appraised were 120 noncommissioned Air Force officers. Although some methods correlated better than others with certain external criteria, in the researchers' judgment, none of the three was obviously superior. However, supervisors whose emphasis in managing and appraising is on tasks rather than on human relations get better performance from their people. Human-relations-oriented managers get lower turnover (Furukawa, 1979). When subordinates rate the performance of their bosses, those with both a task and a people orientation are usually viewed more positively than those with an exclusive orientation either to people or to task. Rated lowest of all are managers who seem to emphasize neither task nor people (Misumi, Sugiman, and Kubota, 1979).

Employee Evaluation Techniques

Employees can be rated according to their individual traits and characteristics, according to comparisons with coworkers, and according to descriptions of actual work activities. Trait evaluation has been criticized for confusing employees' characteristics with their achievements. Yet, some correlation does exist between personality traits and job performance. The problem with trait evaluation is not so much the assumptions behind it as the difficulty of developing techniques to evaluate traits.

Person-Oriented Techniques. Three techniques can be used to evaluate traits according to a scale: rating scales, graphic scales, and adjectival scales. Rating scales allow the evaluator a choice between two or more possible ratings of a trait. For example, employees' ability to complete assignments on time could be checked yes or no, or their accuracy could be checked satisfactory or unsatisfactory. Most discrete scales offer several choices, such as poor, fair, satisfactory, good, excellent. The main difficulty with this method is that terms are not well defined and the divisions between them are left to the evaluator's subjective interpretation.

Graphic scales correct these problems by using a series of continuous values and by explaining variations of degree. Although used more widely than the discrete scales, they are still imperfect. The descriptive terms are abstractions, and differentiation is left up to the evaluator. The adjectival scale follows the listing of traits with adjectival statements meant to provide the same kind of continuum as the graphic scale while providing objective descriptions that cannot be interpreted differently by individuals. In actual practice, appropriate phrases may not exist for each level, and the adjectives may be no more discrete than the graphic scale.

Performance comparison appraisal procedures fall into four categories: simple ranking, group ranking, paired comparison, and forced distribution. In simple rankings, the manager ranks a group of employees from the lowest to the highest on several traits. Paired comparisons list each employee with every other employee in the unit. The evaluator checks the better of the two and then tabulates check marks. The employee with the most check marks is ranked highest, and so on downward. Forced distribution requires that a certain percentage of employees in each operating unit be rated according to a predetermined distribution. The method tries to control the tendency of managers to be lenient evaluators and to evaluate most individuals as above average. Performance comparison methods are tedious. They give the illusion of accuracy but do not actually define performance levels of achievement.

Performance description techniques exist in three forms: free-response reports, performance checklists, and forced-choice forms. Free-response reports were among the earliest performance appraisal techniques and even today are still used frequently. The evaluator is asked to discuss, in narrative form, an employee's strengths, weaknesses, and needed improvements. The method suffers from several defects. It is time-consuming, it requires writing skills, it leaves the evaluator free to choose the points emphasized, and it resists summarization and comparison.

Performance checklists contain a series of scaled statements, and the evaluator checks those he considers relevant. The final rating is the average of the scale values of all items checked. The strength of the method is its reduction of perceptual bias. It is effective for employee comparison and employee/manager discussions because all items are job-related. However, the checklists are difficult to construct, complete, and score.

Forced-choice forms, an improvement over performance checklists, require the evaluator to decide which of several descriptive (not evaluative) statements best describes or least describes the employee's job performance. Choices are made on the basis of concrete rather than general impressions. The result is a numerical index. Because the rater does not know the significance of the alternative descriptions, subjectivity and bias are minimized. The outcome is more standardized and objective, and therefore more valid, than that of other methods. The limitation of forced-choice forms, in addition to being time-consuming to fill out and difficult to construct, is that supervisors tend to resist the form because they feel they cannot control the judgments being made.

Person-oriented evaluation techniques, though useful, share several general weaknesses. The evaluations tend to be subjective, and the rating categories are often irrelevant to the actual job. To solve these problems, appraisers have turned to the evaluation of results rather than people.

Results-Oriented Techniques. Results evaluation appraises, through various indices, the performance of the employee rather than the employee himself. The methods include quantitative performance measures, narrative performance evaluations, and consultative evaluation procedures. *Quantitative performance measures* are of three types: output data, efficiency indexes, and financial results. Output-data measures tabulate concrete results such as sales made or items produced and evaluate them against an expected standard. Efficiency indices rate such items as number of absences, grievances, accidents, or errors. Financial results consider budget or profit performance.

Narrative performance evaluation, which uses factual information to support qualitative measures, is of two types: the field-review method and the critical-incident method. In field review, a member of the personnel staff visits a unit and rates all employees after interviewing the supervisor about each employee under him. These interviews are in two stages; the first elicits opinions of performance, and the second discusses future plans for the employee. Each stage is controlled by a fixed set of questions. At the end of the process, suggestions for staffing, transfers, promotions, and so on are made. The critical-incident method analyzes jobs into observable incidents essential to successful performance, to morale, to personnel decisions, and to coaching sessions with the employee.

In *consultative performance evaluation* procedures, the employee participates in setting criteria, helps plan improvements, and discusses the situation openly with his supervisor. These procedures fall into two types: the performance-standards method and the management-by-objectives method.

The performance-standards method, through discussions between the employee and his supervisor, develops a precise description of what the employee must accomplish. The description is then used to evaluate how well a job is being done.

Although, because of semantic confusion, the term *management by objectives* has different meanings in industry, the MBO procedure consists of four basic steps: establishing organizational goals, establishing unit goals, securing individual commitment to these goals, and reviewing actual performance.

MBO seems to work best in organizations with an achievement ethic. Units with a need-for-power climate fare poorest with MBO, and those where the need for affiliation is strongest are intermediate (Srinivas and Long, 1975–76). Ivancevich, Szilagyi, and Wallace (1977) installed a management-by-objectives program at Tenneco, a large Houston-based oil company, and got good results. The system they used had five basic components: diagnosis, commitment, meaningful goals, feedback, and counseling. It was tied to a performance-planning and evaluation model. The authors concluded that if goal setting is properly planned, carefully implemented, and reliably evaluated, it can improve employee attitudes.

Despite some success with MBO, it is far from being universally accepted. Some managers still consider it a fad. Others appear reluctant to involve employees in goal setting because they feel they are letting the employees make decisions that should be made by management (Rosen and Jerdee, 1978). For every ten companies that have tried MBO, as many as five may drop its use. Some do so because the administrative procedures they have set up to support it become burdensome. Others become bored. But the majority discontinue its use because they become frustrated with trying to set goals at the correct degree of difficulty. They may set goals too high and experience failure. Or goals may be correctly set the first year but then are left at that level in subsequent years rather than being thought through each year.

One of the major decisions in using an MBO program is how hard to make the goals. First it needs to be acknowledged that more difficult goals do lead to higher performance and that the very act of goal setting itself generally improves results (Yukl and Latham, 1978). There is an internal, natural inclination among top managers to set goals high, since high achievers, it has been found, tend to set higher goals (McClelland, 1961). Goal theory postulates, and research has confirmed, that harder goals lead to higher performance than easier goals (Matsui, Okada, and Mizuguchi, 1981).

In setting objectives it is important to be sure that they are the right goals and are harmonious with those of the corporation. "If managers are rewarded according to the goals they accomplish, then the organization must make certain that the goals represent desired behavior" (Campbell and others, 1970, p. 374). Goal setting, as opposed to simply trying to do one's best, helps transfer intent into accomplishment. While the individual may be more motivated with clear goals, the important point is that energy is now channeled in a specific direction. Given two individuals with an equal desire to expend effort, the one with the greater specific knowledge of the relation between corporation goals and individual goals is more likely to perform at a high level (McGregor, 1960).

The MBO process is a natural outgrowth of a desire for increased productivity, of the urge to get things done more clearly, quickly, and systematically. It is easy to find evidence that setting goals does indeed increase productivity (Latham and Kinne, 1974), and setting hard, specific goals results in better performance than setting easy or vague goals (Locke and Bryan, 1969). Setting objectives seems to activate behavior, to induce higher levels of performance, and to focus the individual's efforts on the task to be accomplished. Even though it is a good idea to set hard goals, it is also wise to set them realistically. Satisfaction is greatest when there is congruence between goal expectation and performance outcome (Locke, 1967). It is possible to achieve at an admirable level and still feel failure because the results fell short of the objective. In the cultures of many companies, in fact, the only acceptable behavior is to achieve the plan; to do less is to fail, no matter what the absolute level of accomplishment. Given the intense affect associated with meeting the budget or plan as well as the practical consequences of failing to do so, it is imperative that the executive set difficult but realistic goals.

Although it is not always possible, it is helpful if the individual who must achieve the objective has a say in setting the level of performance difficulty. There is some evidence suggesting that if you really want to achieve a goal, you should consciously set a level of performance for yourself and communicate it to others (Bryan and Locke, 1967a). Although it is poor management not to provide feedback about results achieved against goals set, knowing how you are doing may not matter to how much you achieve (Locke, Cartledge, and Koeppel, 1968). Managers who value secrecy for its own sake or who believe that the continual communication of operating results creates a too numbers-oriented climate may take some comfort from this finding.

According to Wholking and others (1972), management by objectives has a number of advantages as an individual planning and appraisal process. It can provide a nice mixture of a structural as well as human approach to getting the work of the organization done. Management is encouraged to focus on both shorter- and longer-term goals. MBO can eliminate uncertainties and clarify the manager's role. But Wholking sees problems with MBO when there is inadequate follow-up and review after the program has been developed and implemented. A second difficulty he sees, one that occupies a central place in this book, is that it is difficult to translate corporate goals into personal goals for the average employee. Finally, there is the problem of the reward system. Should people be paid for performance, for achieving goals? The answer to this question is not necessarily the obvious one—yes. In the chapters on government and (to a lesser extent) on hospitals, large segments of the working world were identified where merit-pay programs have historically not been popular. Despite these and other obstacles, management by objectives has become a deservedly popular tool to help the executive manage corporate performance (Mobley, 1974).

When done well, management by objectives has many advantages. It gives the organization and employees a common purpose. It requires management to plan goals, review them frequently, and inform each unit of its responsibilities. It sets accountabilities for each employee and shows employees how they relate to their unit and the company. Morale is improved and the desire to achieve increases.

To be successful, an MBO program should have these characteristics: (1) the desired results stated in concrete terms, (2) a timetable for the achievement of results, and (3) identified degrees of excellence (Murray, 1973). Management by objectives can fail because of management's inability to define its mission, excessive complexity, inadequate training, or cynicism when objectives are forced from above. The main advantages of results-oriented evaluation techniques are that they can clearly inform the employee what is expected of him and how he can meet standards. By providing definite goals to be measured, they avoid subjective evaluation and remove the judgmental burden from supervisors. The current trend in performance appraisal is to use MBO-type techniques. Because they stress end results, not people's traits, they take some of the sting out of being evaluated—an experience that both appraisers and appraisees can find distasteful.

Problems of Performance Appraisal

The fundamental problem in appraising the individual is psychological. People regard appraisal as a threat. They know appraisals can have negative effects on salary increases and promotions. A poor rating can injure self-esteem and discourage subsequent performance. Everyone wants to be evaluated as performing above average. People hunger for feedback but want to hear only good news. They want to be complimented, not criticized.

Those who must conduct the appraisal dislike the procedure because of its potential for conflict. Managers dislike reproving subordinates and having to defend a negative evaluation. They have found that the conflict generated by differences of opinion about performance sours employees' attitudes. Managers do not want the responsibility of judging another person's worth and having to communicate that judgment to the person. It is not the act of judging that is unpleasant; it is communicating the judgment. Any negative content, no matter how minor or how carefully phrased, can cause resentment. It is this pressure that causes lenience in evaluations, placing the average employee to the right of center on the scale. Consultants commonly see client performance appraisal systems in which 60 percent of the employees are rated above average and 30 percent average. The remainder are seen as either terrific or terrible.

No matter how valid and reliable the appraisal technique, its effectiveness is blunted if results are not capably communicated to the person rated. Most managers lack the skill necessary

to provide ongoing counsel. Training is helpful, but even training cannot eliminate the conflict that is part of appraisal.

To complicate matters, the manager may be worried
about being evaluated as an evaluator. The appraiser knows that
his report itself will be judged and that reactions to it might affect perceptions of his ability to manage.

Construction of the appraisal instrument itself is also a
matter of concern: How does one identify criteria that actually
measure what is being done on the job? There are a number of
reasons that valid criteria are difficult to specify:

1. Lack of clear measures of performance for the positions.
2. Doubt that the traditional indicator, management judgment, really measures performance.
3. Uncertainty over what scales to use to measure performance.
4. Concern that the measures chosen are subjective or irrelevant.
5. Variation in the measures over time.
6. Uncertainty over the validity of combining individual ratings into an overall index.

Good individual appraisal must begin at the top. The success of an organization depends on the leadership of its executive group. If this leadership is inadequate, the evaluation of
lower-level employees is futile because the goals and standards
they are being measured against are faulty to begin with. A
company with effective executive evaluations can function
without evaluation of other employees, but optimally performance evaluation is done at all levels of the organization, both
for personnel development and for communication of performance expectations that enhance overall corporate performance.

Executive appraisal raises special problems. Although
executives' performance can be measured by the financial results of their units or of the company as a whole, these measures have to be viewed against the other accomplishments of
their leadership and the nature of the organizational climate
they have created in their unit.

Individuals with the ability to lead, plan, organize, control, and make decisions are in great demand. The most successful managers are those who, through concern for and commitment to those under them, receive the respect and trust of their subordinates. The dedication of these managers to organizational goals motivates others. They are self-disciplined and possess personal integrity. They can handle frustration and can work under pressure.

Early approaches to executive appraisal were lists of traits thought to be important to the successful executive, such as leadership, initiative, dependability, and judgment. These techniques produced evaluations of the individual rather than of what he accomplished. The quantitative measures of performance that replaced the trait evaluations are preferable because they provide more objectivity.

General managerial skills must be reviewed along with the quantitative results an individual achieves. General skills include the ability to organize current operations, to delegate, to follow up, and to develop subordinates. The appraiser should function as a coach, offering specific suggestions for improvement and compliments on what is being done well.

An appraisal of an executive should be reviewed by a higher level of management. This review assures the chief executive officer that the appraisals are taken seriously by having each executive check the performance of the managers under him and following up on developmental goals. The reviews are also an important source of information for the chief executive. Through them the actual operation of individual units becomes clear and the strengths and weaknesses of each manager, as well as those under him, emerge.

Most evaluations of executives are still subjective because of time constraints, lack of objective measures, indifference, or a desire to avoid conflict. What is needed is an objective approach based on a description of a manager's responsibilities, her goals, and her level of achievement. This focus on results, not abilities or expectations, must be the individual appraisal approach taken by the executive in managing corporate performance. After a discussion of the psychology of goal setting and performance, the remainder of the book deals with the final few knots in our corporate mariner's rope—how to tie together all the pieces: corporate, unit, and individual.

CASE STUDY
Panel Discussion:
The CEO Appraises the Individual
Newport Yacht Club
Newport, Rhode Island

Four company presidents have been brought together in panel by a consultant who is a management psychologist. Other presidents in the audience are observers. The discussion is quite general and free-wheeling, and in their conversation the executives are frequently candid and opinionated—a luxury they cannot always permit themselves when not dealing with peers. The case allows us to listen in on their talk and to hear what they really think about the business of appraising individual performance.

Participants

Robert Woodward
President, Universal Products, Inc.
Seven divisions, $1.5 billion in sales
Transportation products and parts

Richard Vaughn
President, Northwest Paper
Eight divisions, $800 million in sales
Paper products

Bernice Ivory
President, Ivory Cosmetics
Five divisions, $300 million in sales
Cosmetics

Howard Rogers
President, Home Foods
Ten divisions, $400 million in sales
Consumer food products

Dr. Amy Johnson
Management psychologist

To explore special problems and issues in performance appraisal, a president's roundtable was held at the Newport Yacht Club in Newport, Rhode Island, in May 1978. The following is an edited and abridged version of a taped transcript of the panel discussion.

Each chief executive on the panel managed a decentralized company composed of a number of divisions with a general manager in charge of each division.

Dr. Johnson: You're inferring, then, right here at the beginning, that a general manager's performance should be objectively measured, by the numbers. Mr. Vaughn, do you agree with that?

Mr. Vaughn: Yes, I do, very definitely, but you have to be careful. All too often we direct our attention to what has taken place in the past or what's taking place now, rather than trying to turn the process toward what the person should be doing in the future. More attention should be paid to where the division itself is going and how it is to be managed, and this same attitude should be reflected in the appraisal process. Besides results, you have to consider plans, climate, and the development of people.

Dr. Johnson: Mr. Rogers, I understand that you feel that not only should a company evaluate its employees' performance, but it has an obligation to do so. Would you elaborate on that for us?

Mr. Rogers: This obligation stems from the fact that without effective appraisal the company runs the risk of perpetuating a bad man/job fit to the point where, by the time the company and the manager finally realize he's not going anywhere, it's too late for him to switch careers. Under such a circumstance both the company and the individual suffer.

There's something that works against having an appraisal process that is objective enough to discover where an employee stands early in his career. I'm referring to the fact that effective appraisal is, at best, a difficult process; at worst, it can be extremely tough on the appraiser, especially if he has to tell the employee that he isn't going anywhere. But, really, this is the kindest thing that you can do for the person—let him know, kindly but objectively, where he stands while there is still time for him to pursue a career in which he has a greater chance of success.

Dr. Johnson: Mr. Woodward, I believe you know of a real-life example of where the results of appraisal had been delayed far too long?

Mr. Woodward: Yes. It illustrates what Howard was saying, and it was indeed unfortunate. A young product manager of ours went to work some years ago for a medium-sized division. He had everything going for him: an excellent educational background, good physical appearance, bright, well spoken, energetic, and so on. In other words, as far as traits were concerned, he had everything. And since that division's personnel evaluation system was itself trait-oriented, the two of them—he and the division—got along handsomely for several years. Both grew rapidly, the division in size, and the man to the point where, while still in his early forties, he was made general manager in charge of a $100 million pump division.

Unfortunately for him, after about two years in that job, a new executive vice-president was brought in from the outside to head the group. Several months later our friend was called into the new EVP's office to learn that not only was he not performing well, but there was no place at all for him in the organization. It was the EVP's opinion that, based on his numbers and his division team, this man hadn't done the job. You can imagine how this hit a man who, until then, seemingly had done nothing wrong and whose progress, to the contrary, indicated that he was doing well.

This incident might never have happened if somewhere along the line someone had had a serious talk with this fellow and had counseled him. If this division had had a performance evaluation system that was based on accountabilities, objectives, and levels of performance, he might not have gone beyond the product-manager position. Or, as Howard says, he at least would have been told ten or fifteen years earlier that he really didn't have the ability, rather than having the rug pulled out from under him as a general manager.

Ms. Ivory: Frankly, Bob, I find your story a little hard to believe. How could that happen? I can't imagine a general manager getting by for years on his looks. Let me tell you a story of my own. It took place in a division that had switched over to an objective system of performance measurement and involved a regional sales manager. Our employee, compared with the person Bob told us about, was "Mr. Average" as far as traits and physical appearance were concerned—average looks, average education—a guy who really hadn't attracted any special attention. Yet his performance in each of the categories for which objectives were set was consistently outstanding. He beat each of his negotiated goals at a time when his fellow sales managers were having their problems. Market share, business actually sold, product mix, servicing of his accounts—he did everything well. By the time the year had ended, this fellow was far ahead of the other sales managers.

It was one of those cases of almost too good to be true. We really checked him out, but he was clean. Based on his record, he was promoted to VP of marketing in another division earlier than any of us would have anticipated. This case, by the way, developed a lot of firm believers in goal setting in that particular division.

Dr. Johnson: We continue to hear about the resistance that individual appraisal sometimes encounters, particularly for staff positions. Dick Vaughn, do you have any comments on that subject?

Mr. Vaughn: Well, resistance is relative. It varies from person to person. There may be a couple of reasons for more resistance in the staff areas. The first is the offhand observation that the line functions of the business are easier to evaluate. For instance, my plant people have had certain standards of performance for a long time now. In the sales area, results are obvious—either you are moving the products or you are not. The personnel area, by contrast, has always seemed vague to me because the division's performance is several steps removed from the performance of the personnel manager.

The other reason stems from my feeling—and, Amy, you can interpret this however you like—that staff people let themselves be dominated by policy decisions handed down from above; they are relegated to following rules that they had no role in forming. The staff person is so tied up in what he can or can't do that there are few ways you can tell if he is doing a good job. Fortunately, I think that in the last several years we've made progress in giving staff their heads in letting them determine the functional policies under which they'll operate. Now at least we can evaluate them on how well they set policy.

Dr. Johnson: That's great. It seems to me that what we've really been talking about so far is, why even have a formal process of performance evaluation? Two of the reasons we've mentioned are the company's obligation to let the individual know where he stands and, second, to be sure that the real performers are recognized and motivated to continue to perform well.

A few years ago I wrote an article that made some of these same points. I called it the "Employee's Bill of Rights." It said people have a right to know four basic things:

First, I think we all have a right to know "What is my job?" I am continually amazed at the number of companies in which employees either do not have a job description or, if they have one, have never sat down with their boss and really talked it over.

Second is the right to know "What does it pay?" We find so many places where people kid themselves into thinking that salaries are a top secret and that revealing a salary range is not a motivating experience.

Third is the right to know "How am I doing?" Most people know intuitively how they are doing on the job, but too few of them are actually told much by their managers.

Fourth, we have the right to know "What do I have to do to improve?" It is one thing to know how you are doing but another to know what you need to do to be doing better.

You may or may not agree with these "rights" as such, but you might, nevertheless, use them as a checklist to see how your company stacks up.

Ms. Ivory: Amy, I see the direction you're heading in, and I agree. But I think at some point I have to stop you and tell you that performance appraisal can be dangerous unless it is handled properly. . . .

My point is that, while I recognize the benefits to both the company and the individual of good appraisal, while I recognize our obligation to appraise, while I recognize that appraisal is needed, I don't think an appraisal system is just something you jump into with both feet . . . . You can really mess up by splashing around and telling people what you think. A company may have to work an awful long time to undo the harm done by a few "tell it like it is" managers.

What I'm trying to say, and I feel strongly about this, is that while performance appraisal might appear on the surface to be a fairly simple part of a manager's job, it is very hard to do it well, and if you don't do it well, you'd be better off not doing it at all.

Dr. Johnson: Bernice, I agree. Sometimes it seems to me that there are more scrapped appraisal programs than there are live ones.

What you've also done, Bernice, is to pose the question "Should I really have an evaluation program?"

Mr. Woodward: It is literally impossible to come up with a good system overnight. You had better be thinking in terms of years and not in terms of months, before your system is doing what you really want it to do. And you have to know where you want to take the company, what you want it to be. From here you can develop companywide goals, and these can be boiled down to divisional goals, department goals, and so on down to individual goals.

In our own company, for instance, we've been at this sort of thing for about four years, and we are still not quite finished. I will say, though, that each stage has been exceedingly helpful in itself.

Even a simple concept like "developing objectives" can become extremely complex. Think about the objectives of a plant manager, for example. Plant managers are supposed to make quality products, right? Fine—but how do you measure that? Well, quality rejects is certainly one way. But you can't use rejects as a statistic on which to hang a person based on only one quarter's experience. A man's rejects have to be weighed against what kind of production schedule he is running, how difficult his delivery dates are, did his suppliers hamstring him, are we having troubles with the union, and so on.

Even after all that, you still have to temper your arm's-length objectivity with common sense and judgment. All these things—and some I probably haven't even thought of—have to be considered in determining how well a plant manager has met his objective of marketing quality products.

I think it's fine to try to be as precise and objective as possible. But you'll go nuts if you try to reduce evaluation to a mathematical formula.

Mr. Vaughn: As you were talking, Dick, I was sitting here imagining myself the general manager of, say, a $50 million division who was faced with implementing an appraisal system. My overriding impression is that I would be scared to death. Each of the attributes that make up a division's character is different: size, complexity, local versus regional, and so on. I agree that we sometimes tend to take for granted that appraisal is a pretty simple concept. A good management-by-objectives results-oriented system is tough to do. It takes a long time; it takes money; and it takes commitment.

Mr. Woodward: Before we get too excited about the superiority of results-oriented systems, let me raise one point where some compromising might be necessary. . . . I think that somewhere, even in the most objective, results-oriented system, you have to recognize and assign some degree of significance to a trait like cynicism. If an employee's "cynicism" is great enough to be a handicap in his career, somewhere along the line he has to be told this. He deserves to have it said. It is part of that obligation we were talking about earlier.

Mr. Vaughn: As a practical matter, Russ, can any company ever really get away completely from some degree of trait evaluation, even in a rigorous, results-oriented system?

Dr. Johnson: My personal answer would be no. I think any organization should expect to hire and keep people who are loyal, hardworking, and honest. And certainly your assessment of these attributes will enter the picture when you attempt to measure how a certain person is performing. But I do see a danger if undue reliance is placed on traits. That young fellow in Charlie's example, for instance, might well have gone unrecognized if the division hadn't had the common sense to look at results.

Ms. Ivory: In our company we do not exclude traits; in fact, they are currently being used more at the upper end of the management scale than at the lower end of the scale.

For our lower-level managers, we have what we feel is a results-oriented system. We're pleased with it, even though we're still working to improve it. We've now broken down the measurement of performance into four large areas.

For account managers, for example, the first area is the performance of the saleswoman in her calling efforts—the old shoe-leather approach. How many calls did she make? To sell, you have to see a lot of people, and you have to see them often. Each woman has a certain number of accounts and prospects assigned, and we want to know if she can organize herself well enough to accomplish the goals in this area. Some women are better at this than others, and when the woman and her sales manager discuss the goals, this is taken into consideration.

The second category is her actual business development record. What are the actual dollars she successfully produced on her own? How much makeup, lipstick, perfume, and so on has she actually sold? Surprisingly, we found it difficult to monitor performance in this area. We all agreed pretty fast that to merely look at the beginning balance of an account and then skip over to the ending balance is no measure at all. We feel that what has happened in between is important, and what we've finally come up with is a system based on a three-month average.

The third and fourth categories have to do with her continuing management of the account—her servicing it, keeping them happy, getting our share of shelf space, getting them to try our new products.

Now, as we get up to vice-president and above, many more qualitative aspects begin to enter in, such as how well a woman trains her subordinates, her overall leadership in the division, and so on.

Dr. Johnson: Someone in the audience has asked a question of Howard. The question is "How early in a man's career can you realistically evaluate his long-range potential?"

Mr. Rogers: I'd say quite soon, although I realize that that is a general statement and that it depends on the nature of the company's training system and, specifically, how long it takes for training *per se* to stop and on-line performance to begin. And until a man has an opportunity to be on-line—to turn from being a full-time learner to at least a part-time doer—it perhaps doesn't make too much sense to talk about setting objectives and measuring his performance against them.

In short, your question of "how early" cannot be answered categorically. You can spot the extremes right away—the hiring mistakes and the future stars. But for the majority of people an accurate assessment of long-range potential is dependent on how quickly the company is willing to give them an opportunity to succeed or fail.

Dr. Johnson: Let's take another tack for a moment. Things are usually done better when you know why you're doing them. Have any of us ever stopped to wonder *why* we are evaluating performance? What's the reason for it; why go through the motions?

Let me ask the question another way: Is a simple appraisal bad? Do you have to have a complicated program to have a good program? Not at all. Repeated studies have shown a high degree of correlation in the rating of individuals on a simple 5-point rating scale such as "marginal, fair, competent, commendable, distinguished" and the ratings derived by the assessment of actual performance data. If this is true, why go through the whole business of goal setting, measurement standards, and so forth?

Mr. Vaughn: Because one of the by-products of a results-oriented system is that it gives you a look at what you have in inventory in terms of future management.

Ms. Ivory: Another reason, Amy, is that a good MBO or results system helps the manager to get some idea of how to coach a person. Many of us see ourselves differently than the world sees us. And every company, I'm sure, has cases where a person felt his calling was definitely in one area but circumstances proved it wasn't so. Yet, some of these people, early in the game, appeared to have all the right traits. If you don't look at them in a quantitative way, if you continued to look only at these presumably desirable personality traits, you might not find out until it's too late that they need to be oriented in a different direction. Maybe there is some other area of the company that doesn't have quite the emphasis on, say, conflict management. Or perhaps they shouldn't be kept in a line position, but put in a job that would allow them to capitalize fully on the strengths they have. This is what I mean when I refer to coaching.

Dr. Johnson: You could also call this the diagnostic function of good appraisal. In a trait system—or even, for that matter, in a system based on end results—there's always a danger of limiting yourself to measuring performance after the fact. What you should really be aiming for is to predict performance and behavior before the fact and then use the insight to try to influence the end results.

It's like coaching sports. Professional football coaches are some of the best managers in the world today. The reason they pore over those films on Monday morning is not to figure out whether to give the quarterback a raise at the end of the season. They are trying to win the next ball game coming up; they are being diagnostic. They have to predict behavior before it happens with some degree of certainty. This, then, I think, is another reason that an effective appraisal system is worth the effort it takes to set it up.

Turning to another subject, a question has come from the audience to Bernice Ivory asking, "What does your company do with the employee whose performance is rated as poor?"

Ms. Ivory: We have enough faith in our system, even though we're still developing it, that some women have actually been let go. Of course, what with government regulations and all, you have to be careful to document your reasons, lay a paper trail, and so on.

Probably our first reaction in the face of poor performance is to ask "Why?" Perhaps there were unique circumstances that were transitory but affected the person's ability to do her job. She might, for instance, have been overworked, or had health problems, or problems at home. In this case, something less drastic than letting the woman go would appear to be in order.

But what we do specifically about poor performance is less important than the fact that I feel much more comfortable now than under the earlier system in explaining the situation to a person who has been rated as a poor performer. We base our conversation on facts, on predetermined standards and objectives, rather than talking about the employee's shortcomings as a person. Our system enables me to sit down and talk confidently without beating around the bush. People know in which categories they must improve the next time around. This is infinitely better than those sessions we have all been in where you're limited to the old "You've got to try harder" approach, and the person says, "How?," and you can't quite put it in words.

Dr. Johnson: Another question from the floor. This one says, "Please discuss the value of self-evaluation, performed independent of the evaluation made by the manager. Do these two evaluations usually agree or not?"

Mr. Woodward: I think there is a greater chance of agreement if you're using some kind of results-oriented system in which both the senior manager and the employee are concerned with the same set of mutually agreed-on objectives and the degree to which they have or have not been achieved. Under a trait system, by contrast . . . well, we can always remember Robert Burns's lines, "Oh wad some power the giftie gie us / To see oursels as others see us."

Ms. Ivory: Jesus, Bob, don't start that stuff again.

Mr. Woodward: [Ignoring her] At any rate, I tried this with two managers who had reported to me for several years. I did it, frankly, as a double check on whether I was really communicating with them as well as I thought I was.

In one case the man's evaluation of himself was almost precisely the same as mine—an indication that at least this man and I understood each other. The other man's evaluation of himself was at least one notch higher than mine in some fairly important areas. This also was an indication of something—either I was being too indirect or he didn't want to hear me. But we sat down, shared our feelings, talked about it, and the whole process was useful. I think it makes you a little uneasy when you're doing it, though. You're always afraid that you're playing around with people's egos and they're going to get upset with you. But it does seem worthwhile. At least you feel you're treating others as you would like to be treated. You've told them the truth.

Mr. Vaughn: Amy, would you give us your opinion as a professional on this matter of participation? Is it essential, or just an interesting diversion, something nice to try?

Dr. Johnson: I feel participation is important. I feel strongly about it. One of the reasons that management-by-objectives appraisal systems fail sometimes is lack of participation on the part of the people who are going to have to live with them. With the development of measures, the setting of goals, the evaluation process itself, it becomes increasingly critical that there be self-evaluation. If there isn't, it's just another burden you guys impose on people from on high.

Participation takes the manager off his pedestal and brings him down to the same level as the person who is getting an assessment, supposedly for constructive purposes. You're clued in right away as to any breakdown in the communication process, any misunderstandings. It is also, of course, an excellent double check.

Ms. Ivory: [Impatiently] I wonder if I might get a show of hands on something? How many of the people in this audience have never had a good performance review themselves? Come on, show 'em! Not the kind where the boss says, "You've done a good job," or "I'd like you to try harder." That's not an effective appraisal. But a real good review of where you've been and where you're going.

Dr. Johnson: [Trying to keep control] Bernice, it looks like a little less than half of the audience is in that category. Now let me ask one: How many of you out there don't have a formal appraisal program in your company at this present time? Well, again, it looks like half the audience.

Well, ladies and gentlemen, we can draw our own conclusions from this straw poll. At the very least, it would indicate that what we've been discussing here today, the chief executive officer appraising the individual, is an area in which there's still a lot of room for improvement.

10

The Psychology of Goal Setting and Performance Appraisal

To do an effective job of appraising individual performance, you need good content and good technique. Part of the technique is at least a rudimentary understanding of the psychology of performance appraisal. That is what this chapter is about. The chapter describes the effect of both the rater and the ratee on the performance appraisal process and outcome. Rather than an exhaustive description, the chapter provides a backdrop painted with quick, broad strokes, intended to make the reader more sophisticated about individual performance appraisal and consequently more adept at doing it.

One of the fundamentals of performance psychology is that setting goals activates behavior. It increases performance by focusing the person's efforts on specific goals. Many research studies have shown that setting hard goals results in better overall performance than setting easy goals or no goals at all (Atkinson and Feather, 1966; Korman, 1976).

In addition to this generalization about goal setting, a number of more specific things are known. For example, Ivancevich and McMahon (1977) found that, for individuals entering a technical program, the more educated the technician, the more related challenging goals were to actual performance. For the less educated, performance was related more significantly to goal clarity and goal feedback. The more sophisticated people are, the more they can be motivated simply by setting goals. The less sophisticated they are, the more important it is to make those goals clear and to provide them with feedback on their performance.

This finding suggests that if corporations intend to extend goal setting and performance appraisal down within the management ranks, they should be careful to provide formal and detailed educational programs for the employees who will be expected to perform under the program. For upper-level managers, briefer and more general training in goal setting is sufficient. Perhaps educated employees are better able to fill in for themselves the details of the goal-setting process. For the less educated or the less intelligent, these details need to be made concrete.

Variation in Need to Achieve

Goal setting does not work equally well in all companies or even with different people in the same company. A study conducted with a food processor and a manufacturer of capital goods (Fineman, 1975) found that managerial performance was significantly related to two factors. First was the individual employee's overall need to achieve. The more the individual felt a need to be successful, the more he succeeded. The other important finding was that the manager's performance was positively and significantly related to his perception of the environment in which he worked. So the best kind of environment for a high-achieving manager is one which he perceives to be populated by like-minded individuals with high needs to achieve and where achievement is both possible and encouraged.

For managers with high self-confidence, maturity, and experience, there is a statistically significant relationship of performance to the degree of difficulty of the goals set and to their priorities. In other words, seasoned, self-confident executives do best with tough goals for which they have a sense of priority (Carroll and Tosi, 1970). An interesting corollary finding in this research is that the subordinate's influence on the manager's achievement of goals is not an important determinant of success. Goal-achieving managers achieve success even when they need to rely on others to get there.

Successful executives have a high need to achieve. Other things being equal, an individual's achievement motivation is the greatest when the uncertainty of success is the greatest. This does not mean that there is little chance of success; it means that success and failure are equally likely. The odds of succeeding are about 50/50. Motivated, confident individuals, those with a high need to achieve and a low fear of failure, especially tend to prefer challenges of intermediate difficulty (McClelland, 1961).

Less confident executives, who are motivated in larger part by their fear of failure and their need to avoid failure, tend to prefer either very-low-risk tasks or very-high-risk tasks, because they are better able to predict the outcome. In low-risk tasks the chances of failure are small, and the individual can realistically predict a successful outcome. In exceptionally high-risk tasks the probability of success is small, and it is easier to rationalize failure. Failure can be attributed to the difficulty of the undertaking, and the individual feels justified in accepting less personal responsibility. The most successful people combine a high need to achieve with a low fear of failure. These are the people who are most likely to set goals with an intermediate degree of difficulty and a moderate probability of success.

Goal Difficulty

A problem universally encountered in helping organizations implement goal-setting and performance appraisal programs is differences in the degree of difficulty of the goals wanted by top management and by the rest of management. The problem is that top management usually wants more difficult goals than middle and lower management does. The psychological reasons for top management's preference are understandable. Executives in the higher levels of the organization are, by definition, successful. They are also highly likely to have at least average levels of confidence. They are under competitive pressure to meet or exceed the performance of other organizations in their industry. Most of them are also dependent on the organization's performance as a determinant of their own level of compensation. All these factors would lead them to set higher goals.

Middle-level managers want to be successful, and so they naturally want to achieve their goals. Consequently, they will try to set goals of moderate to low risk, where they have the least probability of failure with the maximum appearance of success.

The result is a tension that can damage the entire goal-setting process. Top management is seen as insisting on setting goals that are impossible to achieve. Because they are so unrealistic, they are viewed as demoralizing by the rest of the management team. Middle management argues that although it is a good idea to set hard goals, it is also necessary to be realistic. Middle managers are expressing intuitively what has been demonstrated through experimentation. Feeling satisfied in goal setting and goal outcome is dependent on congruence between expectation and end result. People feel best about their efforts when the outcome is about what they expected. Under these circumstances stress and uncertainty are minimized because goals are viewed as realistic.

So who is right in the conflict between the higher goals set by top management and those preferred by the rest of the management structure? In psychological terms, top management is more correct. Campbell and others (1970) review the literature on goal setting and corporate achievement and state categorically: "Specific difficult goals are better than specific easy goals" (p. 375). If corporate performance is the ultimate judge of who is right, then it is better for corporate goals to be a little too hard than a little too easy. The excessively hard goals will result in better performance.

Successful organizations are those that set hard goals and then do not pressure people to achieve them. Instead, they are highly supportive and encouraging within a participatory management framework.

Time and Goal Difficulty. The difficulty of a goal depends partly on how much time is allotted to achieve the task. For example, if a 30 percent increase in sales is set as a distinguished level of performance, the first question one might properly ask is "Over how long a time period?" *Fortune* magazine reports that the average sales increase over the twenty-five-year period between 1954 and 1979 for its 500 largest manufacturing companies was 10 percent. By this standard, then, a 30 percent increase in sales appears difficult. If, however, a company were beginning from a small base, 30 percent growth over a one-year period might be only a commendable achievement or perhaps even only competent. Using time alone as the independent variable, 30 percent growth in sales in one year is easier than 30 percent over five years, which is far easier than a 30 percent compounded increase in sales over twenty-five years.

Parkinson's famous law states that "the volume of work expands to fill the time available to do it." This aphorism has been proved experimentally (Bryan and Locke, 1967b). Organizations can improve their overall performance by shortening the time frames they give themselves for accomplishing their goals. This truncating process significantly increases the profitability of achieving objectives within the stated time. When goals are set without time limits, the work drifts and picks up unnecessary volume as the velocity slows down.

Supervision and Goal Difficulty. Besides the time limits and degree of difficulty at which goals are set, interactions between supervisors and employees affect goal attainment. If supervisors provide information on how actual achievement compares with plan, performance will improve (Burke, 1970; Kim and Hamner, 1976). Employees are most satisfied with performance appraisal when they feel that their superiors are honest with them about performance and that they, in turn, can be open with their superiors. Goal setting coupled with adequate supervision has been found experimentally to be correlated with higher productivity (Umstot and others, 1976). And goal setting without effective supervision has been found to be correlated with employee turnover (Ronan, 1973).

Participation in Performance Appraisal

Part of effective supervision is encouraging employees to participate in the performance appraisal process (Greller, 1975). The review of actual performance is as important as the initial goal setting. Those who have tried it have liked it. Self-review performance appraisal has been found preferable by a majority of managers (Basset and Meyer, 1968). It results in less defensive behavior by the employee. Subsequent on-the-job performance is significantly less likely to be rated by the manager as falling below expectations. Low-rated employees are especially likely to show improvement in performance after a self-review discussion. It is this mutual problem-solving style of performance appraisal that is superior to the other two common styles—(1) tell and listen and (2) tell and sell. The best way to conduct a performance review appears to be to let the employee prepare his own performance rating (Basset and Meyer, 1968). Everyone is happier under this approach, and subsequent performance improves the most. Simply communicating to the employee that he has a voice in how he is appraised is predictive of his satisfaction, even if later he does not actually participate. It is apparently the elements of openness and trust that cause this sense of employee satisfaction.

Won't employees be more liberal in evaluating themselves than management will be? Won't they be more inclined to give themselves the benefit of the doubt and rate themselves above average? A University of Wisconsin study of 102 managers found just the opposite (Heneman, 1974). Managers' self-ratings of their own performance were less lenient, had a wider range of scores, and showed more halo errors (consistent bias) than ratings by superiors. The results make us wonder: How would the managers have felt if the same ratings that they had assigned themselves had been assigned to them by their superiors without discussion or participation? Probably angry and resentful.

It is an irony of human nature that we can stand in front of a mirror and tell ourselves that we are becoming gray, fat, and so on but resent bitterly anyone else's pointing out these things to us. It is for this reason that the wisest managers never criticize their employees for anything. A far more effective technique is to let employees be self-critical and then to carefully agree partly with a more lenient interpretation of that self-criticism. People are much more sensitive to criticism than most managers realize. There is no such thing as constructive negative feedback.

Reliability of Ratings

Merit ratings over time are not very reliable (Bass, 1962). When performance appraisals are conducted six months apart, the correlation between merit ratings is about .62, but after forty-two months the correlation drops to .29, a correlation not found significant. This means that your superior's current opinion of you is likely to change, given enough time. Individuals who are initially rated as high performers tend to be viewed as less able the longer they stay in the company. Those who are initially viewed as poor performers will later be seen as better—provided they survive about three and a half years. In contrast, some executives tend to change companies every two to three years, perhaps because of an intuitive hunch that after a few years of good reviews it is best to move on before things start to sour.

Positive performance reviews are likely to decline given enough time, and after two to three years people can expect that their stars will start to fall in the corporate firmament. The good news is that employees who are initially rated by their boss as performing below expectations may have some justification in deciding to stick it out. Chances are that after several years their boss, if she has not fired them, will think they are doing better. The bad news is that competent people, no matter how good they are, will eventually make mistakes and that familiarity in any relationship does breed contempt.

Why is performance appraisal less than reliable? Perhaps

because it is done by managers who are themselves in jobs that do not tend to create environments that facilitate accuracy and consistency. "The research of people such as Kotter, Kurke, McCall, Mintzberg, Pascale, Peters, Sayles, and Stewart is beginning to converge on a set of conclusions suggesting that actual managerial work is fragmented, exposed, varied, primarily oral, nonreflective (mindless), frequently interrupted, reactive, inconstant, improvised, synonymous with symbol management, perceived inaccurately by those who do it, oblivious to the chain of command, informed only intermittently by diffuse agendas, overdetermined, difficult to delegate, and nomadic" (Weick, 1982, p. 198). The manager, humbled by such an excerpt, might now supplicate, "Can I learn how to do an effective performance appraisal?" Glasgow, Simkins, and Guerrieri (1981) say it can be learned, either with an instructor or on your own. Having an instructor was found to be more fun.

The characteristics of a good performance appraisal system, according to Yager (1981), are these:

1. The information provided is accurate and needed by both the organization and the employee.
2. Appraisal is done more often than annually.
3. The emphasis is on feedback and building a relationship between manager and subordinate.
4. Ratings of performance are separated from ratings of potential, promotability, and pay.

Managers who have access to selection criteria used in initial hiring or promotion decisions should be careful about using them to predict performance. Do not assume that because the employee scored especially well on some device supposedly predictive of superior performance, he should be performing well. Over a decade ago, Campbell and others (1970) suggested that there may be little relation between intellectual capacity or achievement and a supervisor's assessment of performance. The situation has since improved somewhat, but it is still wise to start fresh each time performance is appraised and to use fairly brief blocks of time as the behavior sample.

Validity of Ratings

One goal of this chapter is to make managers careful when they sit down to evaluate performance. This care ideally will be stimulated by their knowledge that although, as the evaluators, they are in a position of power, this power is easily abused because a significant potential exists for evaluator bias and error. Not only are performance appraisal systems imperfect, even the best of them are capable of being knocked off caliber by extraneous inputs from appraiser and appraisee.

In a study at Temple University, Kipnis and others (1981) looked at the relation between leadership style (democratic, authoritarian, laessez faire) and actual production performance (making paper airplanes). There was no significant relation between actual performance and the leader's evaluation of that performance. But there were relations between the evaluator's management style and her perceptions about performance. Democratic leaders saw employees as more internally motivated to work. The more the leader saw the employee as internally motivated, the more likely she was to evaluate performance positively. Another rater bias, documented by Holzbach (1979), is the existence of a strong halo effect in performance appraisal, the rating on one item influencing the ratings on other items.

To achieve objectivity in rating performance, it may be helpful occasionally to get the opinion of the appraisee's peers, although in a civilian business setting this must usually be done indirectly. But Gilbert and Downey (1978) found that in Army Ranger Training peer ratings had a stronger relation than any other measure to predict performance in the Ranger course. Another advisable precaution if you are concerned about the fairness of your performance appraisals is to use a participatory approach. Distortions in appraisal occur more when goals are imposed than when they are mutually set (Dossett and Greenberg, 1981).

Employee Perceptions

Besides acknowledging their own capacity for bias, raters should realize that there is a good likelihood that the ratee will not share the same perception about the actual performance rating. Certainly this lack of perceptual congruence can be a source of job dissatisfaction. The work of Smircich and Chesser (1981) and others has helped managers become sensitive to the disagreement between superior and subordinate about the subordinate's performance and the boss's failure to understand the subordinate's perspective. This lack of understanding and the separate cognitive sets of each are a more important source of conflict over job performance than the performance itself. It is not always the subordinate whose outlook is skewed.

The more frequent the appraisal (within reason), usually the less distortion you will experience. Most managers formally appraise performance annually. Ilgen (1981) believes annual reviews lead to polite but ineffectual meetings. Boss and subordinate will agree that the meeting was "pleasant" and "objective," but they will not agree on the level of performance. Perhaps both parties have held their opinions so long that changing them becomes impossible.

Frequency of evaluation is associated with perceptions of fairness and accuracy. So are being specific about what needs to be done to eliminate weakness and having firsthand knowledge of the subordinate's job duties and his performance against them (Landy, Barnes, and Murphy, 1978). Employees have positive feelings about the appraisal system and the meeting when (1) they have a chance to state their side of the issues, (2) the factors on which they were evaluated are job-relevant, and (3) objectives and plan are discussed with them (Dipboye and de Pontbriand, 1981).

Employee Traits

Some researchers and personnel practitioners argue that employees who leave their organizations are better employees than those who stay. But at least one study (Martin, Price, and Mueller, 1981) found that those who left a company were not significantly better performers than those who stayed on. So the impact of employee competence on appraisal and tenure still seems open for analysis. Other employee traits have been tested against actual performance, yielding statistical significance in some instances but not in others. Intelligence is one such variable. In a study of the appraisals of 130 Coast Guard officers, Potter and Fielder (1981) found that if you are intelligent, you had better be sure to get along with your boss. Officers who were not getting along with their superiors were more likely to get a negative performance rating if they were smart. If there was harmony between the two, then intelligence was unrelated to the performance rating.

Good performance may not be as easy to make objective as we would like, and in fact ability may be situation-specific. A good or a poor performer in one environment may not necessarily be that way in another. People who are highly anxious produce significantly less than those with low anxiety (Srivastava and Krishna, 1980). And even looks can make a difference. The more physically attractive you are, the more likely you are to get a good performance rating (Ross and Ferris, 1981). But having attitudes and a social background similar to the rater's will not necessarily get you a higher rating.

High performers are likely to be judged competent regardless of their age, but if you are a poor performer, the older you get, the more likely you are to be subjected to pressure to retire. This is true regardless of the type of performance appraisal format used: trait scales, behaviorally anchored rating scales, or management by objectives (Rosen, Jerdee, and Lynn, 1981). Of more concern is the finding of Cleveland and Landy (1981) that the older you are, the more likely your performance is to be rated as poor—suggesting rater bias against the older employee. Being in a job too long can lead to a specific kind of performance problem called job burnout, which is most prevalent in service providers. The symptoms include reduced energy, reduced resistance to illness, lower job performance, increased dissatisfaction and pessimism, and more absenteeism (Veninga and Spradley, 1981).

Changing Behavior

Implicit in the conduct of a performance appraisal is the assumption that the rater wishes to change the ratee's behavior where improvement is needed. Pritchard, Montagno, and Moore

(1978) found a 26 percent increase in quantity and a 27 percent decrease in errors in the processing of purchase requisitions when appraisal feedback to the employee was individualized, impersonal, and highly specific. It did not matter whether this feedback was given in public or in private. The lesson to be learned here is: To effect behavioral change, be concrete and nonaffective. Communicate as exactly as possible the role model to be emulated.

When talking with the employee about her performance, it is best to relay negative information first, followed by positive information. This creates the climate most favorable for change (Field and Ridenheur, 1975). Good performance is a management problem only occasionally (Will I have to give her more money? Will she expect to be promoted?), but poor performance is always a problem. It is a natural reaction (Mitchell and Wood, 1980) to want to punish poor performance when the cause is believed to be within the person (internal attribution) or when the consequences of the performance are serious. Although the inclination to punish may be understandable, an extensive literature in the psychology of learning would suggest strongly that negative reinforcement (punishment) is not the most effective means of extinguishing unwanted performance and replacing it with competence. The correct thing to do with employees who are your poorest performers is to reward the desired behavior when it occurs (Crawford, Thomas, and Fink, 1980). If this fails to bring about the desired results, terminate the employee.

11

Establishing an Integrated Performance Management System

The previous chapters have provided executives with a kind of chemistry of managing corporate performance—initially qualitative and then increasingly quantitative. Corporate image and climate were the "color" and "form" chapters, the substance of business viewed broadly and from afar. Quantitative measures of corporate performance, measures of line and staff—these sections were the identifying characteristics, a look at corporate performance's component parts. These were the compounds of corporate life. At last, in the chapters on individual appraisal, the perspective became atomistic. We looked at achievement with a psychologist's partiality for the basic elements of business, the individual employees. Now what is needed is a system for ensuring the integration or linkage of the corporate mission at all three levels—corporate, unit, and individual.

It is time to step back again and to reassemble the elements and compounds back into a whole. The chapters that follow provide the executive with a system for measuring and managing the entire enterprise. The system is called "participatory performance management" (PPM). It is a device the executive can use to be sure that corporate performance is managed throughout the enterprise.

The Concept of Participatory Performance Management

Participatory performance management is a planning and control process. Wiped clean of jargon, it is merely a common-sense way of establishing and communicating performance expectations and appraising results against those expectations. The concept is built on a few fundamentals of human psychology. To get performance, you have to get *understanding* and *commitment.* This, in turn, is achieved through *participation.*

- People work more effectively if they know *what* they are expected to produce and can determine *how well* they have produced it.
- People are more likely to produce more if they participate in establishing strategies, goals, and quotas.
- People achieve more when they understand how their performance is being measured and participate themselves in determining how well they are doing.
- People are more motivated to produce more at higher levels of quality when what they are being asked to do is important and possible.
- Corporate performance is most assured when everyone understands what it is that top managers are trying to achieve and wants to help them do it.

Participatory performance management is an ongoing management *process,* requiring periodic review and revision. It is not a *program* to be implemented and forgotten. As strategies and goals change, the executive will need to change unit and individual objectives.

Any management system takes time to develop. It may take three to five years to integrate performance management. But setting goals and reviewing results will improve performance. The first year is difficult, but the second year will be better than the first, and the third year better than the second.

If PPM is left unattended, if top management stops involving units and individuals in the effort to manage corporate performance, the positive effects can soon dissipate.

With PPM, overall corporate objectives are translated into division goals and individual goals. Only by tying individual performance planning to the corporate planning process can a company be sure that individual performance goals are integrated and consistent with one another.

Overview

The purpose of this chapter is to provide the executive with the tools for meeting three objectives that are part of any manager's job:

- Establishing the goals for his own performance (individual performance planning).
- Establishing goals for the performance of his subordinates.
- Improving both quality and productivity.

Specifically, it should help to—

- Identify levels of achievement.
- Determine priorities.
- Plan steps and timetables for goal achievement.
- Delegate particular goals to particular subordinates.
- Evaluate performance against goal achievement.
- Improve quality.
- Boost productivity.

Management needs to be sure that corporate goals are being translated into individual goals at various levels. If all individual goals are achieved, then the corporation will achieve its goals. It's like a play pattern in football. If everyone executes his assignment perfectly, the team will score on every play. Admittedly, there are no perfect plays. The CEO throws an interception, a group VP is dropped for a loss, the controller misses a block. But if everyone understands his role, with a bit of luck and consistent execution, you eventually score.

As summarized in Figure 4, corporate goals "cascade" down through the chain of command in this way:

Figure 4. Participatory Performance Management Flow Chart.

1. The process begins at the top with a clear vision by the CEO of the mission of the corporation. She has a vision; she forms the corporation's image. This is often written up as the corporate plan.
2. This, in turn, leads to establishing more short-range (annual) performance objectives for the entire organization.
3. Each major function or business derives its objectives from those of the corporation.
4. Objectives are established for each unit in each department.
5. The process continues on down to the lowest level in the organization, usually the first level of supervision.
6. Each individual establishes his own goals.

Managing performance from the top down and from the bottom up can, for the sake of understanding, be broken down into seven basic elements. They apply to performance at all three levels: corporate, unit, and personal.

| Specific Accountabilities (1) |

- *Specific accountabilities* are major end results. They differ from goals in that they are timeless and general, rather than time-specific and targeted, performance levels. Accountabilities generally do not change from year to year. When clearly worded, they imply how performance can be measured.

| Measures (2) |

- *Measures* are the means of quantifying position accountabilities. They are the units of performance.

| Performance Standards (3) |

- *Performance standards* are established levels of performance against which goal setting and achievement can be compared. Though reflecting current internal capabilities, they are set at expected future levels of performance.

  A standard for many goals will be the past year's or several years' performance. Where standards exist, they provide a useful tool for ensuring that goals have been established at appropriate levels.

| Goals (4) |

- Goals are specific levels of measured performance expected for a given time period, set in relation to a standard. Goals flow from accountabilities and require action plans for achieving them.

| Action Plans (5) |

- Action plans are the steps required to achieve goals. In detailing action plans, the assumptions (business conditions, costs, and so on) and the support required from others are documented. Good action plans outline clearly the milestones and dates by which goals should be complete. In this manner, performance can be monitored.

| Progress Review (6) |

- Progress review normally occurs at scheduled intervals (usually quarterly) and provides an opportunity to review progress toward goals and alter action plans as needed.

| Performance Appraisal (7) |

- Performance appraisal normally occurs at the end of a performance period (at least annually) and is the process by which actual performance is compared against goals set for the period.

In its purest form, the process may be pictured as follows:

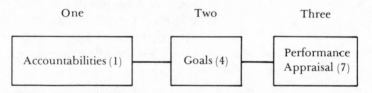

The remaining elements (measures, standards, action plans, and progress review) are devices to support the basic process. The model shown in Figure 5 may clarify the notion of *major* and *supporting* elements in the process.

Accountabilities

The accountabilities are the specific major end results expected for a company, unit, or person. Taken together, accountabilities define why a business entity exists—that is, expected ongoing

Figure 5. The Participatory Performance Management Process.

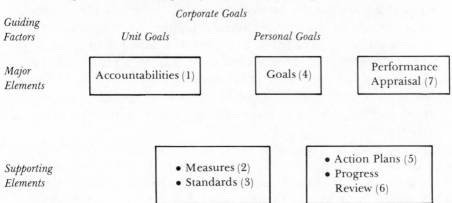

results. Typically, major end results can be expressed in four to eight specific accountability statements. Accountability statements define *what* is to be achieved, not *how* or *how much*. They are not descriptions of activities but descriptions of the results of those activities. In the hectic pace of business, involvement in day-to-day activities can cause managers to lose sight of the overall end results. An accountability orientation helps keep the focus on the end product.

Accountabilities are—

- The major end results for which a company, function, business unit, or position is answerable.
- The ongoing results that must be achieved.
- Anchor points for the day-to-day activities needed to produce important end results.
- Accurately worded to reflect the true impact the unit has on the end result.
- Stated in ways that suggest objective, quantifiable measures of performance.
- Timeless and ongoing.

Accountability statements describe continuous results to be achieved. Accountabilities do not change unless the basic structure of the business, unit, or job changes. Goals, the level of performance in an accountability area expected for a given time period, do change, but accountabilities do not. Accountabilities should be worded so that they will almost automatically lead to thoughts of how achievement can be measured. They should suggest means of quantification. For management the focus of accountabilities is on the elements of managing (organizing, staffing, planning, reviewing), as well as on the functional end results.

Elements of Accountability Statements. Well-structured accountability statements contain several elements, which serve to clarify the nature of the end result expected. It takes practice to think clearly about accountabilities.

These are the major elements each accountability statement should contain:

- *End result*—a word or short phrase about what is to be achieved in a particular end-result area.
- *Nature of impact*— the role or function performed in relation to the end result.
- *Measures*—ways that achievement of the result can be quantified.
- *Action*—the activity performed to produce the desired result.
- *Constraints*—the boundaries or limits placed on the action taken in producing the result.

Table 8 shows some examples of accountability statements and their major elements.

Relative Importance of Accountabilities. Because not everything is equally important, some accountabilities will be of more significance than others. Consequently, it is sensible to review accountabilities in terms of importance and to identify those that are most critical.

- *Critical, or Primary.* These are accountabilities that are central to the basic function of the job—the "make or break" as-

Table 8. Examples of Accountability Statements and Their Major Elements.

Position	Accountability Statement	End Result	Accountability Elements			
			Nature of Impact	Suggested Measures	Action	Constraints
Manager, MasterCharge	Ensures generation of income from the sale of bank credit cards in assigned territory, through customer development and customer service activities, within market-share objectives	Generation of sales income	Ensures (primary)	• Sales mix • Sales volume • Market share	Customer development and service	• Assigned territory • Stated objectives
Purchasing agent	Contributes to cost reduction through constantly seeking alternative supply sources and materials, consistent with quality and performance specifications	Cost reduction	Contributes (contributory)	$ saved	Seeking sources and materials	Quality and performance specs
Secretary	Produces letters, memos, and reports, typed neatly and accurately and on time, from handwritten or dictated drafts	Typed letters, memos, and reports	Produces (primary)	• No. errors • No. times late • Neatness	Typing	Handwritten or dictated drafts

pects of the company, its units, or its people. A good test to
determine whether an accountability is critical is to ask, "If
this accountability is not fulfilled, is acceptable performance
still possible?" Every enterprise probably has at least two
critical accountabilities that represent the basic reasons it
exists. To make a profit and to provide a product or service
come readily to mind.

- *Secondary, or Supportive.* These accountabilities are necessary because they make it possible to achieve the primary
  accountabilities. Examples might be to grow in size or to
  provide an exciting place for people to work. At the management level, a secondary accountability might be "To provide accurate and timely financial statements." At the individual level it might be "To sell $10 million in pumps with-
  in the Midcontinent Division."

Changes in Importance. The importance of accountabilities can
change. A high-priority accountability one year may be less important the following year. The emphasis that managers place
on particular results varies even in the short term. Changing corporate needs should result in changes in emphasis in divisional
and personal accountabilities.

Agreement among top management, division heads, supervisors, and employees on which accountabilities are important will improve productivity and quality and reduce failed
expectations.

Measures of Performance

In any system of managing performance, important elements
are a language for communicating how much is expected and
tools for measuring results. We have seen in previous chapters
that the executive can choose from a variety of measures to
track performance, some quantifiable, others subjective.

Since there are several types of performance measures, it is
sometimes necessary to ask, "Which form of measurement is
best?"

Types of Measures. The four kinds of measures, ranging from the most subjective to the most objective, are as follows:

Most Subjective

- *General descriptions.* These are loosely defined subjective judgments—for example, (1) satisfaction expressed by management, (2) satisfaction expressed by customers, (3) favorable publicity.
- *Judgmental scales.* These are also subjective but are quantified. Their advantage over general descriptions is that it is possible to compare, add, and subtract judgments. Multiple judgments enhance objectivity. A judgment scale might range from 1 to 7, with 1 representing worst results and 7 representing best—for example, (1) value of data-processing services, low to high on 1–7 scale, (2) level of personnel support, low to high on 1–7 scale.

Most Objective

- *Direct counts.* These are quantified measures dealing with physical objects, specific occurrences, and other objective data—for example, (1) dollars of sales, (2) costs of operations, (3) number of units produced or sold.

   Sometimes it is easier to measure the exceptions than to measure the normal occurrences—for example, (1) number of errors, (2) number of complaints.
- *Ratios.* These are even more objective, since they report results in relative numbers: They match actual performance to available opportunities—for example, (1) percentage of product produced that meets quality-control standards, (2) employee turnover.

Guidelines for Identifying Measures. The executive who is trying to manage corporate performance has to be especially careful in choosing measures. It is here that participation is especially useful in making sure that those who must carry out your corporate strategy are capable of translating ideas into actions and results.

When measurement must be subjective, it is possible to increase accuracy and acceptance by using either (1) more than one indicator or criterion or (2) more than one judge. Multiple indicators are used more often than multiple judges. Specifying beforehand the criteria by which performance will be judged increases the probability of achieving the desired performance. For example, the quality of an analysis performed might be judged by such criteria as completeness and clarity of the analysis, sensibleness of conclusions, and the value of the recommendations. By starting with these criteria in advance, you have some idea about the differences between a quality report and a poor one.

Line performance is more readily measured than staff performance. When we think of accountabilities that involve sales volume or deposit growth, ratio measurements or direct counts quickly come to mind. Staff accountabilities, however, have end results that involve service or support.

If the staff performance area involves a service, some common measures are—

- Number of occasions on which schedules were missed.
- Number of hours (or budget) spent per user area.
- Quality of service as rated by user.
- Number of complaints or commendations from user about service.

This list is not exhaustive but suggests the kinds of measures that are frequently used. The proper measures should relate to the purpose of the function or the job. To identify sound measurements, ask, "Will these measurements show the degree to which required end results have been produced?"

For some result areas, there is more than one objective, quantitative way to measure performance. So the next question is "Which of these several possible measures should be used?" Managers should narrow the choice to one or two measures that best capture the nature of the end result to be achieved. This can be done by using a few selection criteria:

- *Relevant.* Good measures are related directly to the major results rather than to activities or less important results.
- *Unit-specific.* Good measures are those that are directly affected by the organizational unit or the person. For example, a sales manager should use sales volume as a measure but should not use profit. Even though profit is affected by volume, a sales manager does not control profit.
- *Obtainable.* A measure is of little use unless it is currently available or can be obtained without an elaborate effort.
- *Practical.* In most performance areas there are already common measures in use. Using these whenever possible makes good sense because they represent the natural, existing language of the company's business.

Table 9 gives examples of measures for three accountability areas. Some other measures are listed subsequently.

Profitability

- Actual versus budget
- Net income
- Return on equity
- Gross operating profit
- Return on sales
- Return on capital
- Earnings per share
- Net as a percentage of expense

Quality

- Complaints
- Audit results
- Actual versus standard errors
- Accuracy
- Rejects and returns
- Warranty claims and refunds
- Variance from standard

Productivity

- Dollar cost per unit of product
- Actual versus standard cost
- Equipment utilization
- Absenteeism
- Employees per dollar of sales
- Scrappage

Marketing

- Number of customers
- Number of new products
- Actual versus forecast
- Market share
- Volume
- Product mix

Table 9. Examples of Measures.

Position	Accountability Area	Possible Measures	Type of Measure
Bank branch manager	Achieve growth in new deposits	• Number of new deposits—time and demand	Direct count
		• Market share—percentage of area business	Ratio
Financial officer	Provide information about financial operating results	• Number of errors in report	Direct count
		• Number of late reports	Direct count
Head of personnel	Provide company with qualified staff	• Time to fill vacancies	Direct count
		• Placement cost per vacancy	Direct count

Cost Control

- Actual versus standard cost
- Actual cost versus forecast
- Worker's compensation costs
- Unemployment compensation costs
- Lost work hours
- Direct versus indirect labor

Standards

After the executive has determined what to do and how to measure it, he needs to decide *how much* of it needs to be done. Performance standards are previously established levels of performance that serve as a basis for determining "how much?" There are two types of standards. *Current-capability standards* are the current performance levels in a result area, expressed as last year's performance or the average level of performance over the past several periods. *Job-related standards* are the levels of performance expected of competent, commendable, excellent, or distinguished performers in a particular job function or unit. These standards would apply to any and all incumbents or businesses.

Sometimes it may not be possible to identify standards, as the nature of the effort and activity changes considerably from year to year or during the year. It may be necessary to decide what constitutes the average and to define the progress expected between the current situation and the standard.

For example, consider a production job with the following standard:

- Job-related standard for fully competent = 50 units per hour.
- Average time to reach this level = two years.
- Average performance expectations for fully competent:

Time in Job	Progress Expected
One month	20 units per hour
Six months	35 units per hour
One year	42 units per hour
Two years	50 units per hour

Standards are stated in terms of measures identified for the result area. If volume growth is an important measure, a current-capability standard might be actual average volume growth over the past three years. Table 10 shows examples of current-capability and job-related standards for the performance of a bank branch manager in one accountability area.

There are two ways to arrive at standards for fully competent performance. The first is to identify the extremes of performance that are least desirable and most desirable. It is easy to identify the completely unacceptable outcome as well as the outstanding end result. Once these outcomes are established, work toward the middle to identify the fully competent job-related standard. The second approach begins with a sense of the norm or average, the solid performance that meets requirements.

Where standards for fully competent performance are available, the executive still needs to decide whether these standards apply to her particular situation or whether different standards are better because the nature of her company's activity is really different.

Performance standards for fully competent performance reflect what the average company or unit or position can realistically be expected to achieve. The individual company's average performance may or may not be at a level considered to be fully competent by its chief executive or the board. There may be pressure to improve average performance, so that the standard should be set higher than the current average but be realistically attainable within a reasonable time.

It is highly desirable to have those accountable for achieving results participate in developing the standards for competent performance. People in a job usually have a pretty good idea what competent performance is. But, of course, it is the manager who must bear final responsibility for establishing the standard.

Once the standard has been set, it is important that everyone involved fully understand the standard and why it is important and appropriate. If you believe that people want to do a good job, standards will be helpful to them in knowing what "a

Table 10. Examples of Standards.

Position	Accountability Area	Possible Measures	Job-Related Standards (Levels of Performance)	Current-Capability Standards
Bank branch manager	Achieve growth in new deposits	Percentage increase in new deposits—time and demand	• Competent: Achieve growth equal to prior years'	Average new-deposit growth for the branch is 7 percent
			• Commendable: Achieve 9 percent growth	
			• Excellent: Achieve 11 percent	
			• Distinguished: Achieve 13 percent	
		Market share—percentage of branch area business	• Competent: Maintain current market share	Market share for the branch is 10 percent
			• Commendable: Increase market share by 1 percent	
			• Excellent: Increase market share by 3 percent	
			• Distinguished: Increase market share by 5 percent	

good job" means. If you prefer to believe people are lazy, at least they will know what they had better produce. Those not now performing to standard have something to shoot for. Those already performing at that level know how they can be rated above competent. In both cases, the result can be improved productivity.

Standards for fully competent performance will not change often. Only if there is a clear need to redefine "fully competent" for the average incumbent will the standard change. What could change from year to year is the individual goals in relation to the standards. Management should periodically review standards for "fully competent" to be sure they are still realistic and attainable by the average performer or unit.

Importance of Participatory Performance Management

This chapter has outlined the principal parts of a technique for managing corporate performance. The idea is to be very clear about the overall strategy and goals of the corporation and then to involve everyone—at least at the management and professional level but preferably all employees—in the process of implementing that strategy by division and function and by individual position. In this chapter the emphasis has been on describing the broader language of the process: accountabilities, goals, measures, and standards. The next two chapters describe in more detail the translation of corporate strategy into individual employee goals.

Performance management is not new. Readers will recognize concepts here that are shared with the well-known management-by-objectives technique popularized by Odiorne and others. MBO is a useful technique, and many companies have had positive experiences with it. The emphasis in PPM, however, is somewhat different. The key thought is total performance translated into individual goals. The critical process is *participation,* with the desired end result a shared understanding of the *corporate* mission and how a given unit or person plays an important part in helping achieve it. Management is asked to assume that it is dealing with an intelligent, sophisticated work force who, if managed properly, will want to achieve as much as top management. Of course, this will not always be the case. But PPM argues that it will be true more often than not. It says, for example, that auto workers read papers and watch TV. They can be expected to understand that Americans are buying more Japanese-made cars in part because they believe them to be superior in quality to American cars—that American workers are perceived to be producing an inferior-quality product while being paid more than their Japanese counterparts. Now, poor strategic planning by top auto makers has also hurt, but while the workers do not plan strategy, they do affect quality. So PPM says that top management will have quality as a major corporate goal and will work to make sure that everyone involved in making the car understands and is committed to improve quality. The argument can be reduced to simple economic terms. If we do not improve quality (as well as make better strategic decisions), all of us may be out of work before very long. But you, the workers, have to want it as much as we do. Do you agree that improved quality should be a major corporate goal for the next several years? So how do *we* get better quality? Let's try to measure it. What kinds of standards are available? How about setting some goals?

We may not yet have an organizational world of management by committees of coequals. But we do have one where there will be performance management by participation.

12

Translating Concepts into Specific Results

In the previous chapter an argument was made that organizational corporate performance is enhanced when employees participate in implementing strategy at the unit and individual levels. This opinion was offered because I have seen participation work both as a manager and as a consultant and because the research literature of the field of management psychology confirms it as a management style.

The word *participation* is chosen deliberately rather than *team work, consensus, quality circle, productivity, democratic, MBO, results-oriented, Theory Z,* or other words. Within the American business culture, executives have become suspicious, and rightly so, of the latest trends or fads in organizational development. Given the strong tradition of entrepreneurship and individualism in American business, workers are skeptical of teams, and managers are sometimes too impatient to achieve consensus. Consensus means general agreement or unanimity, agreed to by all parties—a state seldom if ever reached in most American companies. This management style, so successfully used by the Japanese, is a product of an Oriental culture and cannot be implanted without modification into an Occidental industrial and service society with its own values, traditions, and beliefs. But *participation* means "to take part in, to support, aid, help, and encourage." Democracy is a form of government by will of the majority and the style of political leadership still supported by most Americans. Though deeply democratic by nature, most Americans are also staunchly capitalistic in their views on business. They do not expect to be given an equal voice in making the decisions that affect the enterprise; they look instead to the source of capital, the head, the chief executive, the owners, to do that. Participatory performance management, then, lies in between an authoritarian style of leadership and the consensus leadership advocated by some adherents to Japanese practices or to the workers'-council practices by which some companies are managed in Socialist or Communist countries.

Participatory performance management definitely gives middle managers, supervisors, and individual workers a voice in the running of the business. Chief executive officers who encourage participation avoid issuing top-down orders. They focus their efforts on longer-range planning and establish goals for the corporation. They achieve improved productivity not through edict but through a common desire. They give employees a sense of intellectual ownership in the business by opening discussion of challenges, opportunities, and strategies and by seeking the advice of others. They are patient and do not expect to get results overnight. The guiding principle in participatory management is to ask, not tell; to reward, not punish; to support, not threaten.

This chapter deals with those elements of participatory performance management that directly affect the individual: goals, action plans, and appraisals. It presents a more common language and concepts that management can use to translate corporate strategy into specific results. The first of these ideas is the notion of goals.

Goals

Individual goals are specific levels of end results expected for a given time period (up to one year). They are individual performance targets. Goals lead to action plans, which trigger action.

The results of that action can then be compared against original goals. Goals state *what* will be achieved; action plans state *how* it will be achieved.

Goals are stated in terms of measurable levels of performance—for example, "Increase branch deposits by 10 percent." Goals are set at specific levels but have enough flexibility to be changed if underlying assumptions change.

Goals can come from any of the following sources: (1) strategic objectives, (2) corporate or departmental short-term objectives, (3) position accountabilities, (4) superior's goals, (5) current standards, (6) performance areas in which there are currently problems to overcome or opportunities on which to capitalize.

The number of individual performance goals should be small. It is impossible to focus attention on all the goals one could identify. It is better to identify the most important goals to be achieved in a particular time frame and to set priorities. About five is the realistic maximum number of individual goals that is meaningful. Focusing on two or three major goals may be even better.

To achieve consistency between goals set at various organizational levels and between functional units, individual goals should flow from guidelines provided by higher levels. They need to be in harmony with corporate strategy. Good integration is achieved when—

- Goals cover areas in which there is most need for performance improvement.
- Individual goals are consistent with higher-level goals (corporate, divisional, and so on).
- There is consistency between superior's and subordinates' goals.
- The focus is on major opportunities or problems.

To ensure achievement of the goals that are most critical, it is a good idea to set priorities among the goals identified for the performance period. Priorities will help determine the relative effort to be expended toward achieving the goals and will reflect their importance. The goals selected should be set realistically. At times, difficulty is experienced in trying to achieve goals. In most cases, this will require changing action plans, rather than changing the goal itself. Legitimate questions may arise about whether the original goal should be changed during the performance period. Alternative action plans for achieving the goal should be examined before changing it. Exhibit 3 is an example of a form used to monitor performance.

Individual and unit goals are identified through participation. A good way to do this is to meet with each individual to discuss personal and unit goals, modify them as necessary, and agree on final goals for the period. Performance measures are discussed at the same time. Planning the specific steps to be taken in order to reach the goals should be left largely to the goal setter.

These are the steps commonly used in getting people to set goals that support the corporate strategy and involve them in managing its performance:

1. Review general corporate strategy with employees. Make sure they understand the mission of the company.
2. List the critical accountabilities for each person's job.
3. Have the employees choose with you the measures to be used in determining their performance.
4. Identify the current standards.
5. Have the individuals set goals for themselves that are integrated with corporate goals.
6. Assign priorities to no more than five goals.
7. Fix a specific time period for achievement.

Action Plans

An action plan is a step-by-step outline of movement toward a goal, such that if all steps are taken properly, the goal will be achieved. Each action step is a subgoal, or means to an end. An action plan is an outline of assumptions, conditions, and steps to be taken toward goal achievement. It includes deciding on the timing of the steps and identifying the support required to achieve subgoals.

Action plans are not necessary for all goals, but they are

Exhibit 3. Goal Planning Worksheet.

Position ___Branch Manager___   Incumbent ___J. T. Doe___   Performance Period ___Jan.19___ to ___Dec. 19___

Accountability Area (Key Words)	Measures	Standards		Individual Goal	Actual Performance	Development Needs
		Job-Related (Fully Competent)	Current Capability			
1. Growth in new deposits	a. Number of new deposits- time and demand	Achieve growth equal to prior year's average	Now 7 percent for the branch	Achieve 10 percent increase in new deposits		

desirable for complex or especially difficult goals, and in a few cases goals may have to be measured in segments. Achieving the action plan means the goal is being achieved. Action plans mean thinking about what we are trying to get done and the series of things we must accomplish in sequence to get there.

An action plan has several parts:

- *Goal*—An action plan begins with a brief statement of the goal.
- *Why important*—A reminder of why the goal was set; how the goal supports the corporate strategy.
- *Assumptions*—The basic conditions on which the goal is based, either within the company or externally.
- *Possible obstacles*—The events or circumstances that could prevent goal achievement. Assumptions and obstacles overlap and are sometimes just opposite sides of the same coin. It is not critical whether an event is stated in the positive (assumption) or in the negative (obstacle), only that critical events are anticipated.
- *Action steps*—The conscious, planned actions that need to be taken and the dates by which they should be accomplished. Identifying needed actions often makes the difference between merely thinking about something and actually doing it. Action steps are a commitment to begin, continue, and finish. They divide tasks into manageable parts and give the individual a sense of accomplishment as he proceeds.
- *Type and nature of resource requirements*—Contributions needed from other areas: money, people, information, products, or services.

Almost every action plan requires that decisions be made at certain points and that remaining steps be reviewed on the basis of an evaluation of performance in progress. Milepost dates should be fixed to the action steps. An Action Planning Worksheet (see Exhibit 4) contains a restatement of the goal, why it is important, assumptions, possible obstacles to goal attainment, planned actions to be taken, and resource requirements needed. The purpose of developing an action plan is not

Exhibit 4. Action Planning Worksheet.

Position __Branch Manager__

Incumbent __L. Frank__

Date __October 1982__

Goal:

Reduce nonexempt employee turnover to below 30 percent by year end.

Branch Status:

Turnover = 40 percent
Bank average = 30 percent

Why Important:

Constant need for retraining is costly and reduces productivity.

Key Assumptions:

-- Company salary levels remain competitive.
-- No layoffs.

Possible Obstacles

-- F. Turner not available from Personnel.

Action Steps	Timing Start	Finish	Type and Nature of Resource Requirements (people, money, hours)	By Whom
1. Discuss turnover with employees	2/1	3/1	Personnel to conduct half the interviews	FT, LF
2. Discuss findings with Personnel interviewer	3/1	3/15	Personnel interviewer	FT, LF
3. Research exit-interview results for last three years	2/1	3/15	Personnel records or summary of results by Personnel	FT to arrange
4. Summarize all findings*	3/15	4/1		
5. Agree on action plan	4/1	5/1	Personnel representative to attend meeting	FT
6. Implement plan*	5/1	6/1		LF
7. Monitor results	Monthly			LF
8. Follow-up meeting with task force*		9/1		
* Key review dates 4/1, 6/1, 9/1				

to make goal achievement mechanical but to make the sequence of necessary events understandable and to permit periodic progress reviews. Participation is achieved by having people understand why their goals are important and by giving them structure in helping achieve them.

Participatory Goal Setting

One of the major benefits of participatory management is improved communications through goal setting. The process by which the executive determines the levels of desired results and reviews performance is often more important than the goals themselves. People are more willing to accept higher expectations and are more motivated to put forth the required effort to achieve those expectations if they participate in setting goals than if goals are imposed on them by others. Participatory management means communication, and communication means listening even more than telling.

Subordinates should keep three guidelines in mind in preparing for a discussion of their goals and performance expectations: (1) they will want to have a clear understanding of their job's accountabilities and be ready to discuss them with the manager; (2) they should decide on the order of importance of their goals; (3) they should have a clear action plan.

Although genuine accountabilities should not vary much from year to year, sometimes reporting relationships will shift or job responsibilities will change, causing a shift in job accountabilities. Even more probable, major accountabilities will remain intact from year to year, but their relative importance will change. The employee is the person most sensitive to shifts in relative importance of accountabilities. As part of preparation for a performance appraisal, subordinates should review their major accountabilities. If accountability changes appear to be in order, the jobholder and the executive should talk about how the alterations better support corporate objectives.

Before a goal-setting meeting, subordinates should be asked to list their most critical performance goals. They should suggest measures and standards. Because subordinates have the most knowledge about the opportunities and constraints that are present in meeting their goals, it is best if they can take the initiative. Managers and subordinates need to review together measures, standards, and goals, especially the degree of difficulty of the goals. Goals that one of the parties feels are too high may indicate that someone is not being realistic. Similarly, goals set too low may indicate that someone does not want to assume a normal amount of risk and is trying to protect himself. This matter of goal difficulty is one of the most important parts of truly participatory performance management. Superiors who insist on unrealistically high goals are simply issuing orders politely. Goal difficulty is one area of management in which there must be consensus. The boss may be authoritarian about strategy, but about individual goals it is better to seek consensus even at the risk that all personal goals, when summed, may be less than the corporate plan.

Individual action planning is one of the more important and difficult aspects of participatory performance management. It takes effort to think through what must be done in order to achieve something. Developing action steps is an exercise in tactical planning. By planning her action steps, the subordinate decides for herself what is required to accomplish her goals. She should not agree to be held accountable for those goals unless she has the necessary resources, both personal and corporate, to succeed.

Middle-management and professional employees set their individual goals by being sure to link them to corporate goals. In helping subordinates establish their goals, the top executives of the company communicate the overall mission, offer guidance, and encourage feedback about strategy. But top management refuses to do subordinates' thinking for them or to change the corporate plan. Of course, if enough employees express doubt about the strategy, accountabilities, measures, and overall goals of the company, an enlightened top management will reconsider the course it has set and how realistic is the speed by which it intends to sail.

Whereas the majority of top management's goals will be set for a twelve-month or even thirty-six-month period, for individual employees time frames of three to twelve months may be more appropriate. These shorter time frames may better reflect the tempo of individual jobs, while lasting corporate achievement can seldom be assumed in less than one year.

If corporate performance assurance is to be a participative process, all goals need to be integrated—corporate, unit, and individual. To achieve this, goal-setting guidelines need to be communicated downward to subordinates. This has been the intention of the past two chapters. Subordinates work on their goals after receiving guidance from superiors. This counsel can be quite goal-specific—for example, "I think you should focus on getting 20 percent net on sales"—or general: "How about quality as the emphasis next quarter?" The specificity of the guidance given will be a function of management style, the subordinate's capabilities, and the needs and opportunities of the department at the time. Ideally, people should be allowed the latitude to think through their own job accountabilities, formulate goals, measures, standards, and action plans, and discuss and modify their goals as necessary. The trick is to let them do this while ensuring that the company's basic business plan is accomplished. Some managers will use all the concepts of participatory management, seeing the advantage of understanding the pieces and sequence of performance. Others will prefer to cut through directly to specific goals without going through all the steps.

Management can usually see that one or two performance targets are critical for a given job and that the subordinate has to attend personally to these. There may be other important results in a person's functional area for which the person is responsible, but these are goals that can be delegated.

Once subordinates and managers have jointly identified what they consider important goals, they discuss them thoroughly. Do the goals provide realistic stretch in relation to current standards? Do the individual's goals support corporate, business-unit, or functional goals? Can the goals be achieved in the planned time frame? Are the goals stated specifically enough to determine whether they have been achieved? Will the action steps achieve the goal? Are assumptions and resource requirements sensible?

These guidelines will help tie individual goals into those

developed for the corporation and its major functional groups. All employees review their jobs, accountability by accountability, and select performance goals. They support these with measures, standards, and action plans. They explain their reasons for setting the goals, modify them as needed, and, finally, set time limits for achievement. What remains is to follow up periodically to help keep each person on schedule.

Performance Reviews

In the review, subordinates should be the ones to take the initiative in revising accountabilities, suggesting new measures, setting new goals, and creating action plans to achieve next quarter's and next year's goals. The manager's role in the review is to compare against her own perceptions what the subordinate has presented. Supervisors help subordinates set performance goals after they set their own goals to be sure that their subordinates' goals are consistent with their own.

Performance reviews are regularly scheduled, but *informal,* discussions with subordinates to review results against plan. The purpose is to work consistently over time to be sure that goals are achieved. In participatory management the focus is on conjoint problem solving, not blame fixing. It is during these reviews that assumptions are examined in relation to goals, action plans are modified, and any needed midcourse corrections are made. For most jobs, quarterly reviews are fine, but ideally performance, like quality assurance, should be a continuous process. Action plans provide logical mileposts of times when formal performance review sessions make the most sense.

At least annually, and preferably quarterly, have management and employees sit down for a formal review of performance. This includes reviewing actual performance against planned goals, looking at the general demonstrated capabilities a person has in relation to her current job, identifying development needs to meet current job requirements, and preparing for larger responsibilities in the future.

The performance appraisal meeting should be an exchange of viewpoints. Although the manager has the responsibility for the appraisal, the meeting is intended as an opportunity for both parties to work together to achieve goals at the highest level of performance that the talents of the two persons permit. The outcome of a performance appraisal usually determines the person's performance rating, which in turn may relate to salary increases, but discussion of salary action should be held at a different time than the performance appraisal discussion, to allow both parties to devote their full attention to improving productivity and to developing the next quarter's or the next year's goals and action plans.

Just as a well-managed company keeps a close watch on its financial operations through the records and reports generated by its accounting systems, it will also monitor the utilization and productivity of its human resources. An effective performance appraisal system periodically measures and records how well each employee is doing in relation to his goals. It tells the company how much improvement is needed in employee productivity to meet the corporate plan. It is human nature to want to know how we are doing in our jobs and how we can improve. When we have to guess at how we are doing, we may either worry needlessly or be unrealistically optimistic. If goals are clearly stated from the outset, people know how they are doing. Working together can improve performance by generating new ideas and renewing commitment to productivity.

During feedback, managers and workers discuss both performance strengths and problem areas so that they can identify ways to improve performance. Good feedback is relevant to expectations established at the beginning of the performance period and does not judge performance against expectations that were not clearly communicated to and understood by the subordinate.

Good feedback looks for the underlying causes of any performance problems, rather than dwelling on the symptoms. With specific goals it is easy to know where performance is falling short of expectations, but it is not always easy to understand why. To get at the whys takes trust and empathy, the ability to listen quietly to the other's views before making judgments. Thoughtful feedback does not worry about assigning blame when things go wrong. It tries to come up with an action plan that both parties agree will improve performance.

Giving good feedback (and accepting it in turn) is one of the hardest things a manager has to do. How can you be honest without damaging your relationship? Negative feedback is effective only when there are clear indications that the receiver is ready to hear it. Otherwise anger and hard feelings result. Tactful feedback is more descriptive than interpretive, more a reporting of the facts than an elaboration of their implications.

In giving feedback, the sooner the better. When feedback is given immediately, the receiver will more clearly comprehend exactly what is meant because the feelings associated with the event still exist and can be part of the meaning. Feedback should be given at times when there is a good chance it can be helpful, not when the receiver is absorbed in other things. Critical feedback always hurts and should be given privately. No purpose is served by negative feedback about things people cannot change. For this reason it is far better to give positive feedback than negative. When in doubt, do not criticize. Negative feedback is seldom as helpful as management thinks it will be. People hate to be criticized. If possible, ignore negative behavior and instead give positive feedback when the right behavior occurs or describe to the person the behavior that is preferred.

In giving feedback, executives tend to overdo it. This is especially true in communicating feedback about poor performance. People who are not performing well are likely to be sensitive to criticism. Count on it. It is best to keep negative comments brief and tactful.

Participatory performance management gives the executive a tool for managing his corporation's performance. In this and the previous chapters, the system has been defined in detail and examples shown of all parts of the process. The emphasis has been on its application down to the individual level. The next chapter is an extended case study illustrating the impact of PPM on a particular company and its people—First Bank of Tahoe.

13

Case Study: Implementing Performance Management from Top to Bottom

The following case study is the longest in the book because it is intended as a summary case—an example of the concepts and techniques presented in previous chapters. Here the goal is to improve performance from the corporate to the individual level in a medium-sized Western bank.

First Bank of Tahoe, with $650 million in deposits, operated throughout the state of Nevada from its headquarters at Lake Tahoe. The bank had twenty branches, including six in the Tahoe area, five in Las Vegas, and four in Reno.

The primary stockholder in First Bank of Tahoe was Hans Seeberg, a widower who lived at the lake in a secluded home. Though no longer active in the day-to-day operations of the bank, between himself, his two daughters, and a trust fund, Seeberg controlled over 50 percent of the bank's stock. Besides bank stock, Seeberg had a large portfolio of common stock, tax-free bonds, and extensive real estate holdings in commercial buildings and undeveloped land around Lake Tahoe. His real interest, however, was airplanes, and up until William Lear's

death he was a close associate of the inventor. Seeberg stayed
scrupulously clear of the bank's affairs. Although he retained
the title of chief executive officer (it was a family tradition to
do so), he let his man Ashford Greely run things.

Seeberg was Austrian. His grandfather Gottfried had
come to the Tahoe area from Vienna when he was twenty-
eight. Vienna, with its gray skies and baroque buildings, had
depressed Gottfried. He wanted adventure, but he also wanted
to live in the mountains. After learning the dry-goods business
from an uncle, Gottfried borrowed enough money from him to
buy a one-way steamship ticket to the United States, where he
headed straight for the gold and silver fields of the Sierra Nevada. The big California strikes of the 1840s and 1850s were over,
but there were still thousands of miners tearing the earth apart
searching for wealth.

Gottfried decided to take a quieter and less risky approach to making his fortune. He let others gamble on finding
silver and gold; he prospered by selling to the miners. From tent
stores out in the fields he peddled as much food, clothing, tobacco, dynamite, picks and shovels, firearms, and whisky as he
could get his hands on. He would give credit to men he knew
personally or who were referred to him by others, extending it
at a straight 20 percent per annum. Known as an extremely fair
man but not one to be trifled with, he built a large business.
Some of the miners asked him to invest in their claims, which he
did selectively. When bonanzas and busts were averaged out, he
earned 100 percent on his money. By 1896, when he had accumulated $200,000 in cash, he bought a little bank in Reno,
the Washoe National Bank. It had three branches and assets of
$5 million. His Victorian friends teasingly called it "Mr. See-
berg's bucolic bank." "Hey, Gottfried," they would ask, "What
you want with that run-down old thing? Better you should sell
hammers and nails."

Gottfried Seeberg had two sons. During World War I one
was killed in the trenches in Germany. The other saw action as a
pilot over France but was able to return home, with his brains
and limbs intact, to manage the bank. This was Hans Seeberg's
father, Karl. During Karl Seeberg's administration the bank

changed its name to First Bank of Tahoe and began a campaign of cautious expansion throughout Nevada. Hans worked with his father for several years. Finally, when Hans turned forty, he replaced his father as president. Seven years later, when his wife died, he decided to replace himself. His father had left him a $100 million bank, a portfolio worth $10 million, and a collection of twenty classic airplanes housed in two hangars, one in Lake Tahoe and the other a few miles outside Reno, in Sparks, near the car collection of a man who had made a fortune in casinos. Seeberg promoted himself to chairman and brought in Ashford Greely to be president. At that time Greely was a senior vice-president of personal banking with the North Star Bank, out of Minneapolis.

Before his responsibilities at North Star as head of personal banking, Greely had been planning officer. Few banks did formal planning in those days, and Greely made a minor name for himself by publishing a thin book called *Planning for Bankers.* Unfortunately, it reinforced his tendency toward pomposity, a trait that irritated many people but fortunately only amused Seeberg. Greely was deferential to rich people, and when around Seeberg, he hid his intellectual snobbery out of respect for Seeberg's money. It was a workable compromise.

The real test of their relationship came in 1978. From 1970 to 1977 the bank's earnings had improved from 60¢ per share to $1.50 per share. Return on average assets exceeded 1 percent. Then in 1978 disaster struck. Greely personally approved loans of $500,000 each to two prominent Basque sheep farmers in northern Nevada. There was not much collateral on the loans besides livestock scattered over the desolate, semiarid mountains of Nevada's interior. It was hard to understand how it could happen so fast, but in just thirty days 10,000 sheep died of what appeared to be Rocky Mountain spotted fever. There were allegations of radiation poisoning and government coverups, which were never proved.

It cost the bank one million dollars, 25¢ a share. Since Seeberg owned almost two million shares, it cost him personally half a million dollars. Greely, of course, knew this, and yet Seeberg never said a word about it. Seeberg was curious to see

Greely's reaction. Would Greely become depressed and overly cautious, would he lose his nerve? He didn't. He did, however, lose some of his smugness. A thin patina of humility tarnished his once highly polished conversation, his smugness burnished to an aura of quiet confidence. It became him. Seeberg felt it was almost worth the half million. Ten years with a Viennese psychoanalyst would have cost about the same and wouldn't have worked as well or qualified as a writeoff.

It was shortly after Greely lost the million dollars that he decided to implement a participatory performance management program. Before, he had always felt he didn't need any help in planning the bank's course or monitoring its performance. He had been the brains of the bank as well as its brawn. Now he decided he could use a little assistance.

Because he had surrounded himself with mediocre executives, Greely found himself working harder and experiencing more stress as the bank grew. Though still convinced he was the bank's best strategist, he decided to bring his people into the management process as a developmental experience. If they were going to run the bank after him (and he was running out of time to position his succession team), they had to learn to think for themselves. One of the best ways to help them was to let them go through a complete planning cycle and assume responsibility for setting corporate, as well as functional, goals.

An initial meeting date was established early in January 1979 to set overall corporate goals in the areas of financial, physical, marketing, and human resource objectives. The meeting took place away from the bank, at Seeberg's lakeside chalet. Seeberg conveniently managed to be away at a bi-wing plane race, flying across the Grand Canyon. Greely met at Seeberg's house with the bank's officers in charge of the northern region, the southern region, the Tahoe region, trust, administration, lending, and marketing. Two days were devoted to developing a corporate charter for the bank and establishing a long-term strategy with supporting one-year goals. The material that follows shows what Greely and his people developed at their executive retreat—their corporate strategy as well as their specific goals.

Figure 6. First Bank of Tahoe: Organizational Structure.

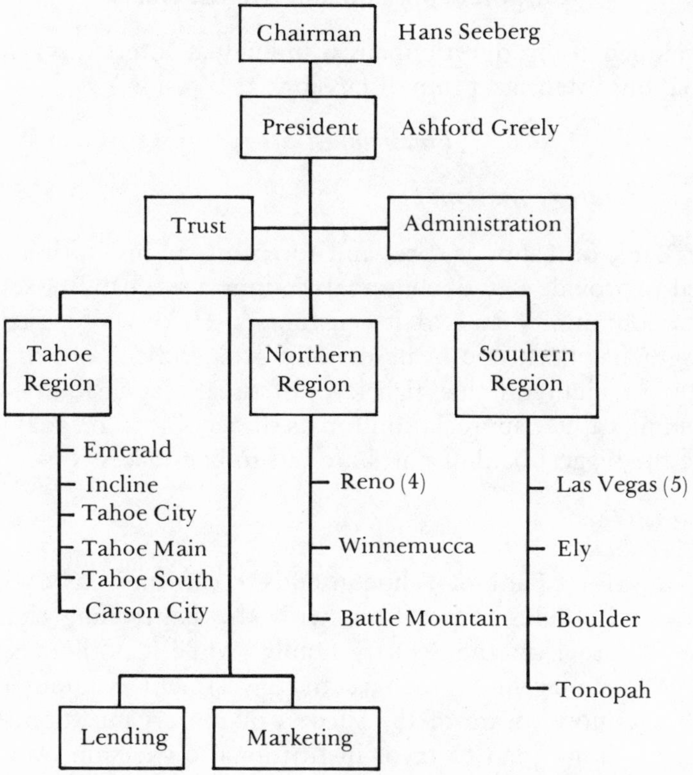

```
              ┌──────────┐
              │ Chairman │   Hans Seeberg
              └────┬─────┘
              ┌────┴─────┐
              │ President│   Ashford Greely
              └────┬─────┘
        ┌──────────┴──────────────┐
    ┌───┴───┐              ┌───────┴────────┐
    │ Trust │              │ Administration │
    └───┬───┘              └───────┬────────┘
 ┌──────┴──────────┬──────────────┐
 ┌────────┐   ┌──────────┐   ┌──────────┐
 │ Tahoe  │   │ Northern │   │ Southern │
 │ Region │   │ Region   │   │ Region   │
 └────────┘   └──────────┘   └──────────┘
```

Tahoe Region:
- Emerald
- Incline
- Tahoe City
- Tahoe Main
- Tahoe South
- Carson City

Northern Region:
- Reno (4)
- Winnemucca
- Battle Mountain

Southern Region:
- Las Vegas (5)
- Ely
- Boulder
- Tonopah

Northern Region (lower):
- Lending
- Marketing

FIRST BANK OF TAHOE
Corporate Mission and Annual Goals

(Developed using questionnaires, individual interviews, and informal but intensive group discussions at lakeside.)

Financial Strategy

General Strategy Statement

First Bank of Tahoe is, first and foremost, an institution established to provide sound, conservative, innovative banking services to its community and to its customers. Historically, financial strength has been one of its major assets, and the organization wishes to maintain this high level of fiscal responsibility while providing capital appreciation for its shareholders. Its goal is not to be the biggest bank in the state but to be the best.

1. *Structure*
    1.1 *Distribution*
        First Bank of Tahoe intends to continue to be a closely held corporation, with the controlling share of stock in the Seeberg family. While it is the desire of management to have the investment community be more aware of the success of the organization, there is no plan to favor institutional ownership over individual ownership.
    1.2 *Stock Exchange Listing*
        The stock of the bank is traded over the counter and listed on NASDAQ. A study is being conducted of the advantages and disadvantages of listing the bank's stock on a major exchange, such as the NYSE. There is a good chance that the bank will become listed on a major exchange within the next five years.
    1.3 *Price/Earnings Ratio*
        The bank's stock currently sells at a P/E ratio of 6 to 1. The bank has no particular goals regarding increasing the multiple on the price of its stock.
    1.4 *Dividends*
        Dividend payout is currently 17 percent of earnings. Dividend yield to shareholders is not a major concern

of the bank, and future dividend payouts will be determined by the bank's plan for growth. An important aspect of the financial structure of the bank is the equity-to-capital ratio. Ownership is willing to accept a reduction in dividends of up to 30 percent if this is needed to maintain necessary equity-to-capital ratios.

1.5   *Financial Analyst Evaluations*
The opinion of financial analysts is not currently viewed as a critical consideration for the bank as long as private placements are used and the bank continues to be a closely held corporation. At this time the bank has not set specific rating objectives for its various investment instruments. It is the intention of the bank to tell its story of achievement to the financial community as opportunities present themselves.

2.   *Growth*
2.1   *Deposits*
First Bank of Tahoe is a moderately growing financial institution. To serve the residents of the state of Nevada, justify the confidence of its stockholders, and provide challenging opportunities for its employees, the bank is committing itself to a strategy of growth.

The bank has about 12 percent of the market share in the state and has been growing at a rate approximately equal to that of other Nevada banks. The corporation wishes to improve its growth record while maintaining its reputation for fiscally sound management.

Traditionally, First Bank of Tahoe has grown in deposits at about 14 percent per year. Western banks in general have grown at 13.5 percent a year. Growth in deposits is in part predicated on equity-to-capital ratios, which in turn are predicated on dividend payouts. Goals for fiscal year 1980 are as follows for growth in deposits:

Competent	*Commendable*	*Excellent*	*Distinguished*
12%	13%	14%	15%

The goal of First Bank of Tahoe will be to secure 33 percent of the new savings and checking deposits of all the banks in Nevada over the next five years. The assumption underlying this goal is that the bank's growth will come from its ability to acquire an above-average share of new deposits in the state. It is in new-deposit growth that the bank is strongest, and this business is traditionally the most economical to acquire and the most stable. Taking market share away from competition has historically been difficult, expensive, and transitory.

2.2 *Assets*

A common measure of the size of a financial institution is the total assets under management. Although this measure is not necessarily the most precise or controllable variable in determining institutional size, it provides an easily understood yardstick by which the bank can compare itself against others. The industry average for asset growth has been approximately 14 percent compounded annually.

Tahoe Bank, for planning purposes and to provide an easily understood goal for the public as well as its employees, intends to become a $1 billion-asset institution by 1982. Specifically, the objective is as follows:

Year	Assets
1979	$ 650,000,000
1980	725,000,000
1981	850,000,000
1982	1,100,000,000
1983	1,500,000,000

2.3 *Loans*

The bank currently has guidelines on loans to deposits of a minimum of 65 percent and a maximum of 70 percent. This policy will be continued for the coming year. The bank will remain flexible in its portfolio mix and will attempt to emphasize shorter-term credits, such as commercial loans.

2.4   *Profitability*
First Bank of Tahoe has been a profitable bank, although the philosophy of ownership is to emphasize
quality more than profitability. Nevertheless, the
bank has historically performed, and is currently performing, in the top 20 percent of profitability for
banks its size as measured by return on average assets.
For the past five years the bank's ROA has averaged
.85, with specific annual performance as follows:

1979	1978	1977	1976	1975
.85	.875	.849	.82	.89

The bank intends to grow while protecting its
current profitability. Specifically, for 1980, ROA targeted levels of achievement have been set as follows:

Competent	Commendable	Excellent	Distinguished
.8	.825	.85	.9

Projected (budgeted plan) ROA for FY 1980 is .85.
2.5   *Other Financial Goals*
Additionally, the bank has established as high-priority
financial goals for the coming year two special programs: (1) cash management system and (2) financial
supporting system.

Marketing Strategy

General Strategy Statement

Tahoe Bank is committed to providing its customers with innovative banking services. It currently receives high marks for convenience and for its full range of service to customers. At the
same time, the bank's marketing strength has not developed to
its fullest degree. A major goal for FY 1980 is to upgrade the
overall quality of the bank's marketing activities.

1.   *Geography*
Tahoe Bank's service area is the state of Nevada. The bank
sees ample opportunity for growth and sufficient challenge
in serving the residents of the Silver State. The bank may
become active in the secondary mortgage market and in
this way could serve investors beyond the borders of the

state. There are no plans to have a physical presence outside the boundaries of Nevada.

The proper placement of the bank's branches has con-
tributed significantly to its past success. The bank will continue to concentrate on the metropolitan Reno area, the Las
Vegas area, and the Carson-Tahoe area. These areas currently account for approximately 90 percent of the population
of Nevada, and most new growth in the state will come from
here. The bank believes that it can best serve its customers
and its stockholders through carefully placed branches in major areas rather than through attempting to have a branch
in every small community in rural Nevada.

2. *Facilities*
The bank will continue to pursue its philosophy of providing
its customers with convenient locations and to build branch
facilities that complement the community and reflect the
bank's preference for high-quality buildings. To control
branch expansion, the bank will follow a policy guideline of
allowing a maximum of *6 percent net after tax* as the maximum of loss to be allowed for new branches.

To achieve its plan of growth, the bank will need to
expand its facilities in order to serve the public. The strategy will be to build or purchase buildings in carefully selected sites in its major service areas. A preference exists
for freestanding buildings whose visibility can continue to
promote the recognition of the bank in Nevada. Acceptable
but less preferable will be attached buildings located in
shopping centers. A few branches well placed in prime
areas, rather than geographical saturation, will be the predominant scheme.

Primary Service Area Branch Locations

Year	Las Vegas	Reno	Carson-Tahoe	Other	Total
1979	5	4	6	5	20
1980	6	5	6	5	22
1981	7	6	6	5	24
1982	8	6	7	5	26
1983	8	8	7	5	28

3. *Equipment*

   The bank currently relies on an outside data-processing service bureau to meet its data-processing needs. The bank plans to continue to rely on the services of an outside organization, and there is no plan to acquire its own computer.

   The 1980s will see rapid developments in operating equipment in financial institutions. The bank's strategy will be to buy new equipment only when the need for it has been demonstrated by the pioneering (and costly) efforts of other institutions and when the reliability of the equipment is proved.

4. *Corporate Identity*

   The various campaigns that have been used to advertise First Bank of Tahoe have been more institutionally oriented than product-oriented. The corporation's theme is "the Nevada bank for Nevada people." The organization is content with its theme, logo, and overall image and sees no need to change its corporate identity at this time.

   Tahoe Bank has a reputation for being a first-rate bank of the highest integrity with conservative fiscal management. It has been known as a banker's bank. The state Banking Department has frequently referred other banks to Tahoe Bank to study its personnel, operations, profitability, chargeoffs, and branching activities.

5. *Products*

   The organization is a full-service bank committed to providing its customers with the full range of bank services being offered in the state of Nevada. The bank will not simply offer its more profitable services if this should limit the organization's overall ability to serve its customers. The bank will remain aggressive and innovative in evaluating new bank products.

6. *Cross-Selling*

   The bank recognizes the value of having its employees knowledgeable about the services available to customers and wants them to assist in the bank's marketing efforts.

For fiscal year 1980 Tahoe Lake Bank will reemphasize its cross-selling program so that it becomes an effective tool at all levels. Sales training will be offered for new-account representatives, loan officers, assistant branch managers, and branch managers.

7. *Advertising*
The organization currently spends 2 percent of its gross income on marketing, while an operating rule of thumb for banks is to budget approximately 1 percent of net income for marketing. Tahoe Bank will continue to spend twice the national average in its marketing budget but expects to receive better results from its efforts. As part of its goal to upgrade marketing this year, the bank is undertaking a thorough review of the function.

8. *Community Involvement*
To be sure that the bank is involved in its various communities, the corporation has a formal policy of encouraging employees to participate in community organizations. Participation is viewed as more important than a position of leadership.

Meetings with Officers

After the corporate mission and annual goals had been established at the executive retreat, other meetings were held to link top, middle, and supervisory management together to carry out the organization's objectives. The program, called *Tahoe Lake Participatory Performance Management,* was intended to get all managers involved in assuring corporate performance by making sure (1) they understood the bank's mission and goals, (2) they understood the role of their unit in the success of the overall corporate plan, (3) they had an opportunity to participate in the implementation process and, through this, refine and improve the plan, (4) they developed the necessary skills to develop goals with their employees and appraise their performance. A conscientious effort was made to keep the concepts, procedures, and forms simple and to encourage genuine participation.

The meetings with the branch managers were particularly important because they represented the greatest number of profit centers within the bank. Obviously the totals of the goals of the branches had to equal or exceed the corporate goals, or the bank would fall short of its objectives. It is at these operating-level meetings that conflicts over goal difficulty are the most serious and intense. Feelings that corporate goals are unrealistically aggressive or that operating managers are really powerless to achieve what is being asked of them often surface and have to be resolved if a true sense of ownership is to result.

The training sessions with other bank officers responsible for managing people were held after those with the branch managers. Corporate missions and annual goals were reviewed openly and in detail, suggestions solicited, and the message "This is *our* program" emphasized and reemphasized. The concepts of participatory performance management were presented, and each manager, with the help of the workshop leaders, developed goals for his unit that tied in to the overall corporate plan. This was the final knot in the rope lashing each unit snugly in the corporate vessel. The last step was to train supervisors in the psychology of goal setting and performance appraisal.

Training in Participatory Management

After the corporate strategy meeting a two-day workshop was held with the bank's branch managers to train them in goal setting and performance appraisal. The meetings were led by Jed Smith, vice-president of personnel. Greely approved the course content but did not attend himself. He wanted to see whether personnel could make the program work. At this meeting the general corporate mission and the annual corporate goals were communicated and discussed. The branch managers felt that the bank's goals were too aggressive, since they were the ones who would carry the burden of achieving the cumulative deposit growth and gross profit objectives. The Northern Region, led by a positive and energetic senior vice-president, quickly became deeply involved in the workshop and easily set branch-by-branch objectives for deposit growth, gross profit, and turnover reduction.

The Southern Region workshop was initially a failure. The senior vice-president, a younger, cautious man, was tentative in his support of participatory management. Then the vice-president in charge of the largest Las Vegas branch began to attack the credibility of participatory management as a concept. Finally, it became apparent that the Southern Region felt under extreme pressure to make its numbers. There had been an unusual amount of rain in southern Nevada that year, and flash flooding plus a fire in downtown Las Vegas had ruined the street-level main casino rooms of several large hotels.

The day with the Southern Region went poorly, and at the conclusion of the session, the vice-president of personnel decided that Greely had to be informed of the problem. Reached that night by telephone, he listened but refused to lower the goals for the Southern Region. Instead, he called the senior vice-president and told him in the bluntest terms that he was to support the corporate goals and no lower targets for his region would be considered. Another workshop day was set for Southern Region branch managers, and this time it was more successful. The region eventually made its volume goal but missed the distinguished profit level because of the branch manager in

Tonopah. He disappeared while he was hunting deer as the bank's auditors were investigating a default on a $100,000 unsecured loan he had made to the owner of a small casino in town. The manager was eventually found near his jeep, dead of a gunshot wound, an apparent suicide. Without the $100,000 writeoff the region would have exceeded its goal.

Besides the branch managers and the heads of the regions, meetings were also held with all other bank officers who were responsible for managing people. During their meetings they were given training in participatory goal setting. What follows is a fictionalized transcript of a tape recording of the meeting. The vice-president of personnel is addressing a group of about thirty bank officers in the training room of the bank's headquarters. He is paraphrasing a prepared text. Periodically he departs from the text and delivers a little aside or homily. In the back row, two men are dozing. The purpose of the meeting is to teach managers how to conduct a formal performance appraisal.

A Performance Appraisal Workshop
Lake Tahoe, November 1979

Now we want you to give each employee the opportunity to develop his own performance review before meeting with him. Make it clear that this is his chance to review and think through his part in achieving the corporate plan. Help him understand his own performance and how it is important to the bank. If you're smart, you'll ask for a chance to review his self-appraisal before the meeting, so you can prepare for the meeting.

The performance appraisal should be based on facts—specific examples—about the person's performance. Using examples will help to avoid disagreement and keep you from making general statements you can't back up. Also, better review your notes from other meetings. Has the person made progress since the last review? Make sure you have all the necessary materials at hand—you know, the job description, relevant numbers, appraisal forms, personnel records, and so on.

One thing we want all you folks to learn is how to get people really involved in making this bank go. You have to help by creating the proper interview climate. One style is the direct approach in which you assume "My job is to inform the employee how well he has done." A second style is the indirect participatory approach. Here you assume "My role is to listen a lot, talk a little, and ask the right questions."

The indirect approach is preferable because we want employees to become more independent, to show initiative and to accept responsibilities, to participate in the management of the bank. Some people call this style participatory management, but it seems like just good common sense. This participatory style helps the manager get more facts about how to improve productivity. Participatory management has many advantages: it gets people involved; it tells you about the interviewee's motives, problems, needs, and expectations; and it can lead to better understanding between management and employees. In participatory management, the manager listens with an accepting, understanding attitude. This reduces defensiveness and increases cooperation. The person is usually more willing to be frank about problems or ambitions and to take a more active interest in helping Mr. Seeberg and Mr. Greely meet the bank's goals. Now, participatory management requires more planning, greater skill, and generally more interview time. But it's worth it.

Performance is rated here on the basis of whether you and your people have reached the goals that have been agreed to. Progress toward a goal is encouraging, but it is only the achievement that finally counts. There are situations where this is an oversimplification. For example, in a long-term project you may have to measure the degree to which the overall goals are being met over a long period of time. But here too, specific time targets are set by which certain things are to be accomplished.

The overall evaluation should reflect the individual's performance over the whole period of time covered by the review. One month of above-average performance, even if it was the month immediately preceding the review, does not offset eleven months of mediocre performance.

Don't let performance ratings on one goal affect ratings on other goals. Most people do well in some areas and not so well in others, so try to make each rating independent. Do your darnedest to be fair and objective. Avoid these halo effects, as we call them.

Now what if your people also do work for other folks here in the bank? Maybe some other supervisor has important insights to contribute concerning the person's job performance. So consult the other supervisor before the performance review. The same thing goes when you got someone who has regular dealings with other departments or units and whose work affects them significantly. In a case like this, it is a good idea to go get the views of the other departments.

Now, what with all these government programs and everything, I can't tell you how important it is not to be prejudiced. Every single human being in the world has some bias or prejudice about something or someone. If we are aware of our feelings, we are in a better position to control them. So if you got a thing about old men or Indians or whatever, you'd better be damn careful! Give the rating the individual has earned. Be sure you can back up everything and be careful of what you say and how you say it.

We want to be fair, but that doesn't mean to be easy. Some of us hate to tell people they are only average. But if we are too easy, the standards of performance we have set for the bank will be cheapened. Lowering standards reduces the bank's chances of attaining its goals. And we actually hurt people because we are lying to them, pretending they are better than they are. Be strict and fair to everyone. Don't play favorites and don't make excuses.

Now I want you all to listen up good, especially you two fellas there in the back row, because I'm getting to the real important stuff.

[Goes to flip chart and writes.]

Ten Aids to Conducting a Successful Performance Appraisal

Be Prepared

It is important that you be thoroughly prepared for the review meeting. There are a number of reasons for this. You'll feel more comfortable and secure if you have done your homework.

The person being appraised wants to know you are prepared. If it is clear to him that you are ready for the meeting, he will listen better and cooperate with you more.

Have the Right Attitude

The performance appraisal session is, above all, a communication meeting. This discussion needs to be two-way. Both parties should be free to talk to each other about anything that is relevant. This is not simply a corrective session. All aspects of on-the-job performance must be discussed. Negative aspects must be covered, but they should not be emphasized to the exclusion of positive aspects of performance.

Sit Properly

[Someone laughs; Smith frowns.]

There are at least two points of view here. The first is simply "Be natural." Seating arrangements for an appraisal session should be no different from those for any other meeting. Let things be familiar. The second view is to ask the interviewee to sit on the same side of the desk so that you can go over the appraisal together, working side by side at a table. This is a friendlier way to sit, and it suggests a more informal meeting, which may lead to more open communication.

Get Off on the Right Foot

[Smith turns and scowls. No one laughs.]

Begin by briefly structuring the meeting for the employee. Outline the objectives of the get-together and the manner in which it will proceed. This allows the individual to see an overview of what will happen.

Let the Employee Go First

Ask the employee to present his goal review first. Have him go through each accountability separately, explaining how he did on his goals.

That psychologist fella we have working with us says that research shows people feel better when you let them go first.

You get into less arguments that way. It's harder for your people to speak up if you talk first. If you want to know what your people really think, let them talk.

React Thoughtfully

It is best to react slowly to what the other person says. As the manager, you don't even need to give your appraisal formally. Just respond conversationally to what the person says. As the person brings up information you may not have considered, you can think about it.

Emphasize Improvement

The whole purpose of this program is to improve performance. What can you do to help the person meet his goals? Does the person have any practical suggestions along these lines? The performance appraisal process is successful when it leads to a practical plan of action to build on the person's strengths and help him correct weaknesses.

Stress Performance, Not Personality

No matter how amiable and longstanding the relationship between you and the other person, a performance review session can be tricky, so go carefully. Try to focus the discussion on the job and on results. These are the things to be covered during the review meeting. Sometimes it's hard not to have the discussion move into the area of the individual's personal problems. This is okay, but again, try to stick to goals and how they fit into the corporate plan.

Finish What You Start

You've got to keep the meeting moving along. Don't let it drift. One way to close is to restate the objectives of the session, which were set at the beginning. Ask the employee to summarize his understanding of the evaluation. The purpose is to be sure that communications have been clear. You and the employee don't have to see eye to eye on the evaluation, but you should both be clear about what was said.

Shoot Wide of the Traps

Although each employee is different and no two performance interviews are exactly the same, there are certain types of behavior that are frequently encountered and represent traps to be avoided. Here are a few of those traps. Take a minute and read this.

[Uncovers charts prepared earlier.]

- Poor preparation.
- Lecturing people.
- Jumping to conclusions.
- Always have to be right.
- Not letting employee talk.
- Assuming employee understands.
- Reacting defensively.
- Being rigid.
- Dealing in generalities.
- Getting personal.
- Being insensitive to problems.
- Making accusations.
- Dwelling on past problems.
- Going around in circles.
- Missing hidden agendas.
- Causing employee to lose face.
- Playing God.
- Arguing.
- Being hostile.
- Poor follow-up.

Now, while most folks look forward to receiving feedback about themselves, occasionally you get some that act ornery. Here are some suggestions on how to deal with them.

First, you've got to be realistic and expect some disagreement when you discuss an employee's performance. After all, each person sees the job from his side, so don't expect complete agreement. Just try to get agreement on the major points.

When disagreement occurs, say to yourself, "Whoa!" And ask what's really going on here. Is the disagreement factual or emotional? Get the individual talking. Ask questions and listen while he explains his position. This provides an opportunity to evaluate his point of view and compare it with your own. It also provides information to help decide on the best approach for resolving the difference of opinion.

You may discover things during the interview that change your view of the situation. You may even want to postpone the interview until you can investigate further. It may be advisable to end the interview and set a future date to finish discussing the matter. But remember that you've got the responsibility for making the final decisions about the employee's performance. Employees will not always agree with those decisions, no matter how reasonable you think they are. But that's what you're getting paid for, to be tough when you have to.

Don't assume, either, that a person really agrees with you just because he says he does. Agreement that isn't genuine is due either to ignorance or to wanting to avoid a fight. Maybe he's too embarrassed to tell you he doesn't really understand what you said, or he's keeping the disagreement to himself because he's afraid if he argues with you he'll get fired. This problem is a real tough one. About the best thing you can do is play it easy and try to draw out his real feelings. It doesn't do any good, really, to browbeat anyone into agreeing, because he is just going to go off and do what he can anyway.

We've all met people who get madder than hell when told about their weaknesses, no matter how polite we try to be. Things are only made worse if you lose your temper too. Instead, listen patiently. Don't argue with someone when he's spitting fire. Wait until he cools off and suggest that you meet again in a few days to talk, after you've both had time to think things over. Don't let the person leave while he is still upset.

It's natural to be a little nervous during a performance appraisal interview, particularly at the beginning. If the employee is real nervous, calm him down and tell him to just take it easy. Remind him that the major purpose of the get-together is to review and set goals.

Now, I know you're all going to like this part, because I can see some of you are getting fidgety and are wishing I would hurry up and end this thing.

The next type of person is the impatient one—the person

who is not realistic in his expectations. This is particularly true of the younger folks who are anxious to progress quickly. Where they have been doing a good job and show potential, it is important that you counsel them to be patient. Explain that sustained performance over time is required to demonstrate readiness for an increase or promotion. Assure them that they will be considered along with others for future opportunities, provided their work continues to be of high quality. Suggest, also, what steps they can take in the meantime to improve or develop job-related skills.

Once in a while in the course of an interview, an employee may indicate that he intends to leave the company. If his performance has been good, find out why he wants to quit. Ask whether the evaluation session stimulated this decision, although it is unlikely that this would be the sole reason. By getting the person to talk, you may find clues to the causes of dissatisfaction. If the reason for leaving is to obtain a higher salary or a position with another company, be sure to emphasize opportunities for future growth. Ask whether the employee may not be giving up a better long-term situation for a temporary advantage. If the reason for leaving has resulted from any misunderstanding, try to set the record straight. Few people take lightly an announcement of their intention to resign. By the time they declare their intentions, they have usually worked through, in their minds, all the advantages and disadvantages of leaving. It is emotionally painful to separate from a company, and once the decision has been made, it is accompanied by a sense of relief and peace. Not many employees will reverse themselves, but for good people it's worth the try.

Well, I can see that we are almost out of time, so I'd better see if I can summarize the main points of the president's program for you here.

[Uncovers final flip chart.]

Summary of Participatory Management
Individual Goal Setting

1. Review specific accountability statements, revised as needed.

Review measures, standards, and so on to develop complete and accurate statements.
2. Provide general goal guidelines.
   • Suggest measures and standards.
   • Rank importance of goals.
3. Get employee's agreement.
4. Meet periodically to review progress.

[Closes chart. Faces group. Reads paragraph.]

Remember that participatory management is an annual ongoing process that begins each year with our corporate planning cycle and ends with a performance appraisal meeting between you and your employees. This meeting will coincide with the planning of goals for the next period. Participatory management is First Bank of Tahoe's vehicle for translating corporate plans and goals into action so that each employee can help the chief executive manage corporate performance.

All right. I'm through talking. Who'll buy me a drink?

Postscript

On December 31, 1980, Hans Seeberg left Lake Tahoe Airport on his way to a New Year's Eve party with friends in Santa Barbara, California. His flight plan called for him to fly out of the Lake Tahoe basin to Reno, then south along the eastern slope of the Sierra Nevada until he reached Lone Pine, near Mt. Whitney. From there he would vector southwest across the mountains until he found the coast. Seeberg's last radio signal was heard as he climbed over the crest near Whitney. Search-and-rescue teams failed to find any trace of him or his Cessna.

The terms of his will called for First Bank of Tahoe to be sold to the first organization that would pay three times the bank's book value. The buyers were two brothers from Kuwait who paid cash. Under the terms of the agreement, Ashford Greely's stock was worth $1.1 million, roughly twice what his sheep loans had cost his former employer and benefactor.

14

Trends in Managing Performance and Implications for Productivity

Reef Points: The Annual Handbook of the Brigade of Midshipmen of the U.S. Naval Academy explains: "*Reef Points* are pieces of small stuff used to reduce the area of a sail in strong winds, making for smoother sailing." As a plebe at Annapolis in the summer of 1961, I was required to study the 279 pages of the handbook and to commit some of it to memory. This was sometimes done while sitting in the dark under a blanket with a flashlight in prereveille hours spit-shining shoes and reading items like: "On the sea there is a tradition older even than the tradition of the country itself. . . . It is the tradition that with responsibility goes authority and with it goes accountability. . . . The captain of a ship, like the captain of a state, is given honor and privilege and trust beyond other men" (S. Edwards, "Image of Command," quoted in *Reef Points*, pp. 263-264).

It is customary sometimes to have a final chapter be a summation of the previous chapters. Such a chapter is useful to

310

those who have not read the entire book but are seeking an easily accessible place to find the main points of content. For the reader who has plowed steadfastly through the complete text of the book, however, such a treatment tends to be repetitious and unnecessary.

Another tradition for the final chapter is to have it serve as a glimpse into the future. Here the idea is to identify the most up-to-the-minute trends, make a judgment about which of these is likely to last long enough to have an impact on the next several years, and finally to imagine the nature and consequences of that impact. Such an effort has been made here. Some of the more recent concepts in planning, corporate image, not-for-profit organizations, performance appraisal, Japanese-style management, and productivity are described and projected forward into time. This promises to be more useful and interesting for the reader than a simple recapitulation of what has come before.

The past chapters of this book have been *sailing directions*—"guides . . . charts, and reports, furnished to mariners to aid them in safely reaching their destinations" (*Reef Points,* p. 245). This last chapter contains the reef points, final bits of information and thought intended to get the book's mariner safely into port.

The book began with discussions of strategy, image, and climate. It went on to review measures of corporate performance, both quantitative and qualitative, major and minor. Then not-for-profit institutions were looked at, including the special problems of performance assurance in government and in hospitals. Finally, performance appraisal and its psychology became the topic. The theme of the management of the performance of an organization was examined vertically from the CEO to the hourly worker, from deciding on corporate strategy to setting production standards. Planning, measuring, and controlling performance were the subject matter—gone at as an archeologist digs a site: a layer at a time, starting from the top, going deep rather than broad, treating the material vertically, not horizontally.

The question we sought to answer was "How can management make the connection between corporate strategy and the

implementation of that strategy?" In response to increased
world competition, stagflation, declining productivity, uncom-
mitted workers, and a myriad of other problems, how do you
induce other managers, supervisors, and employees to carry out
corporate strategy? The answers we gave were, in part:

1. Have a sensible strategy. Don't try to be all things to all
    people. Figure out the few things that you can do best, and
    do only those.
2. Find out what your image is. Is that how you want to be
    seen? Get to work at making your image match your strat-
    egy.
3. Create the right climate. Successful companies make and
    maintain special environments. Make your own weather.
4. Define performance in both quantitative and qualitative
    terms. Develop measures, standards, and goals that spell out
    the "how much" and the "how soon" of your strategy.
5. Spread the word. Be apostolic. Get everyone involved. You
    can't do it yourself, so you'd better get everyone involved.
    The emphasis is on the word *everyone*.
6. People may be human resources, but first they are people.
    Take the time to learn a little performance psychology.
    Participation is the key. It's the people on the assembly line
    or in the teller cages or working in the intensive care unit
    who have to carry out the corporate plan. You'd better be
    sure they know what you are trying to do. Much more im-
    portant, you've got to make sure they care. A corporate
    strategy, no matter how well conceived, will fail if it isn't
    implemented at all levels of the organization.

This last point is one of the classic problems of management—
how to get everyone in the corporation working to achieve corporate goals. How do you link corporate strategy with individual performance? The arguments and explanations bearing on
these questions have been made at length in the preceding pages
from the viewpoint of *measuring* and *controlling* performance.
Managing productive people—the individual psychology of corporate success—will have to wait for another book. There I will

take one stratum of this book's subject matter, the productive-people stratum, and cover it broadly, horizontally.

Now it is appropriate to move on. Some of the tools described here—planning and goal setting, for example—have evolved considerably since they were first introduced to the organization executive. But it would be naive to expect them to remain static. What should we expect to see, to encounter, over the next ten years and beyond?

Strategic Strategy

The meaning of the word *strategy* includes the concept of projecting, of looking ahead. Can we look ahead at looking ahead? Can we have a strategy about strategic planning? The authors of at least one study believe you can. Gluck, Kaufman, and Wallick (1980) believe that the planning function evolves in most companies that plan for any length of time. Gluck and his associates see four phases in planning. Phase I is essentially financial planning. It usually consists of making and meeting the budget, plus perhaps a few other financial objectives. Future projections are restricted to an earnings growth rate. Phase II is forecast-based planning. The objective is to predict the future. This phase can be a routine process of merely projecting forward last year's plan, or you can roll out the heavy guns and use computerized economic models. In Phase III you make a conceptual leap and really begin to think strategically. You analyze the competition, evaluate your alternatives, and commit your resources. You begin to try to manage the future, but there is still one higher level to which you can evolve: Phase IV, which is true strategic management. Here you work to create your own future by orchestrating resources (financial, physical, and human) to gain and secure a lasting competitive edge. You combine strategy and image. You decide what you want to be and then manage that scenario. You write the script rather than read it.

An advanced corporate strategy tool is called portfolio planning. Many companies reach a size at which they find they can no longer continue to grow at desired rates by sticking to their past. It's like the shoemaker who makes shoes for everyone in his home town and all the surrounding towns. He finds he has to diversify to get any bigger. Should it be vertical diversification—start acquiring suppliers, such as leather companies and cattle ranches? Or would horizontal be better? If he can work well in leather, how about trying wood or maybe glass? Once you decide to leave your past, you are faced with the challenge of managing diversity.

Portfolio planning can be defined as a technique for managing a collection of diversified businesses, each of which contributes to the overall performance of the corporation (Haspeslagh, 1982). According to a survey sponsored by the *Harvard Business Review* in 1979, this technique was used by 45 percent of the *Fortune* 500 and 36 percent of the *Fortune* 1,000 (see Haspeslagh, 1982). There are questions about the true value of the technique and whether, in fact, the approach may be part of the problem with American business rather than the solution. A review of the technique can nevertheless be helpful to the executive who expects that in the future managing diversity is going to be one of his jobs.

Portfolio planning is often done by consultants using grids, or matrices. By *grid* or *matrix,* corporate planners mean a device, a conceptual framework that places a business, defined as a strategic business unit (SBU), according to its competitive position and the attractiveness of its market. The grid framework is used to assign objectives for growth, profit, and resource allocation. Typically, the outcome variable is *cash flow.* The idea is to maximize it. The Boston Consulting Group popularized a growth/share matrix. General Electric and McKinsey put forward the idea of industry attractiveness/business position. Arthur D. Little liked industry maturity/competitive position.

What lessons are to be learned by those who see diversity in their future? First, there is no magic in the grid. The wizardry is in assigning a mission to a business, knowing how the business fits into the industry generally, visualizing its potential. The alchemy is to use the philosopher's stone of goal setting to turn each SBU into gold. "Good portfolio planning often requires the ability to treat SBUs as portfolio segments. Companies with a tradition of management by objectives easily introduce the appropriate set of objectives specific to each segment and thereby mold the review process so it incorporates both an aggregate and detailed view" (Haspeslagh, 1982, p. 70).

Haspeslagh offered these eleven commandments for strategic planning for diversified companies after studying how the process worked or did not work in large, diversified companies:

1. Divide and conquer—push the process all the way through one unit rather than taking on all units at once.
2. Involve and educate line managers.
3. Define your strategic business units.
4. Forget the grids. Focus on the missions.
5. Cluster similar SBUs into portfolios.
6. Review strategic plans as well as operating plans.
7. Have no across-the-board treatment. Like people, businesses are different.
8. Put your money where your plans are.
9. Plan for people as carefully as you plan for capital.
10. Develop explicit plans for new businesses.
11. Make clear commitments to a few technologies or markets. Do this early; then be patient.

If you expect to go from a single-business company to a diverse-business company, you should also expect your planning priorities to change. Again from the work of Haspeslagh, Table 11 shows how you will probably rank the individual parts of your overall business plan as you shift into planning for diversity.

Are there other trends that are beginning to emerge in business planning, other reef points we can tie to our strategy sail? There is a small body of work that is trying to get directly at the issue of making strategy operational, of implementing corporate goals at the individual level. Sasser and Leonard (1980) believe that to solve this classic management dilemma, corporations should pay more attention to first-level supervisors. These warrant officers, to continue the naval metaphor, are the link between management and the worker. They face

Table 11. Suggested Priorities in Strategic Planning for
Single-Business and Diverse-Business Companies.

Part of Plan	Rank	
	Single Business	Diverse Business
1-year profit	1	6
3–5-year profit	2	1
1-year capital	3	4
1-year volume	4	8
3–5-year volume	5	3
3–5-year capital	6	2
Competition and environment	7	5
Milestones	8	7
Contingencies	9	9

workers who are better educated, more diverse, and less interested in their jobs than before. Sasser and Leonard feel that top management should give first-line supervisors better tools—more technical know-how and skill in human relations. The byword is *participation.* Tell supervisors the goals of the corporation. Train them in the technical aspects of their jobs. Give them feedback on how well they are meeting the corporation's expectations. Take company time to let them discuss common problems affecting their jobs. Keep them informed. Train them in basic and advanced management psychology, and encourage them to speak their minds.

To this list can be added a few more admonishments, tips for supervisors on how to supervise (Sartain and Baker, 1972): Don't oversupervise. Help your people take pride in their work. Be both people-centered and task-centered, but emphasize people the most. Keep your workers informed, ask their opinions, take an interest in them, develop an atmosphere of trust. Supervising this way, say Sartain and Baker, leads to higher productivity.

Beyond strategic planning techniques and making strategy operational, the corporate executive can expect a continuation of the debate about pay and performance. Companies will spend more time trying to devise compensation plans that support the corporate strategy. Particularly, the compensation committee of the board will want programs that pay top managers for achieving a balance between long- and short-term results (Stata and Maidique, 1980). Single-dimension plans will fall from favor. Multiple-variable incentive approaches will become widely used in not-for-profit organizations. Do bonus plans improve performance? Maybe; maybe not. But they have other uses.

"Bonus" plans are generally viewed as a means of motivating performance. But one of the main impacts is to educate, although it is clear management needs to clarify better how business and personal goals are interrelated (Stata and Maidique, 1980). The message seems to be that to link corporate strategy and individual performance, you should tell people the strategy and pay them to help you achieve it.

Corporate Image Is Corporate Differentiation

The success of any company depends on its ability to grow and to make a profit. In the beginning growth is likely to come from a single product or service. You get larger by doing more volume in the same place. But sooner or later you obtain as much market share in that place as is practical; so you go into a new geographical area and grow some more that way. Eventually you have all the volume you can get from that product or service in as many places as it is efficient to operate. You have to start a new venture. Are there any reef points for growth and diversification? For example, to take the latter concern first, how can you grow through new ventures?

Roberts (1980) has some advice. First, be patient. Be prepared, if you invest in a new (for you) business, to stay with it at least five years. Ten years is better. Second, find an entrepreneur to run the business, and let him manage it entrepreneurially. Third, remember that no single strategy works for everyone. Fourth, keep in mind that new ventures work best when they involve new technology. Go for that when you can.

But what if the business you have is rather humdrum? Suppose that not only don't you have a proprietary new technology, you don't even have a technology at all. What if your product is a commodity or a service, which is the same thing as a commodity because all you are selling is knowledge and time?

The key to success here is *differentiation.* The task of the executive in managing corporate image will be to create differences in the minds of the company's customers—even if the product is a commodity.

How can this be? Levitt (1980) offers some aphorisms about differentiation that the mariner may want to stash in his sea chest for later or, if the sailing is already rough, he may want to tie immediately to the corporate-image sail.

> "There is no such thing as a commodity. All goods and services are differentiable" (p. 83).

> "The *offered* product is differentiated, though the *generic* product is identical" (p. 83).

> "*The way in which he operates* becomes an extension of the idea of product differentiation itself" (p. 91).

> "The product is a promise" (p. 84).

If your product is a service, there are at least four ways you can make it different from your competitors': Make the product different in terms of delivery, terms, service, or new ideas. The last characteristic sounds like technology but really means giving more than you contracted for, usually in the form of information or advice.

The United States already has essentially a service economy. Those service companies that will survive beyond the 1980s and on past the year 2000 will be those that decide on a strategy and an image and manage themselves consistently with it. According to Hall (1980), executives who want to ensure corporate performance had better strive to achieve either the lowest cost or the most differentiated position. This means that the strategy/image issue can be reduced to one of two options.

In successful strategy = *cost,* the goal is to achieve the lowest delivered-cost position relative to competition. Management combines this with an acceptable level of quality and a pricing policy designed to give the company a market share it can live with.

In successful strategy = *point of difference,* management works to achieve a differentiated position based on one of three things: (1) *products,* (2) *quality,* or (3) *service.* The company couples this with acceptable cost and a pricing policy that has sufficient margin to find reinvestment in that aspect of the product or service that differentiates it. Success in the future will require companies to have a high degree of differentiation. This could mean selling a single product to a single market. Imagine real estate agents who only sell condos to retirees, or stockbrokers who only sell bonds to doctors.

A consultant company might position itself to specialize in incentive compensation for hospitals or management by objectives for public administrators. Specialization is already commonplace in the medical, legal, and academic professions. In the future, companies that are diverse may be merely holding companies, managing portfolios of highly differentiated or lowest-cost businesses. You can sell price, or you can sell features. You will have a hard time in the future being all things to all people.

Coming of Age in the Not-for-Profit

In the future, while for-profit companies will get better at implementing corporate strategy at all levels of the organization, the not-for-profits will learn the importance of strategic planning, marketing and corporate image, and goal setting. Books written especially for the managers of nonprofits are beginning to include chapters on these subjects. (See Connors, 1980, for strategy and marketing; see Zaltman, 1979, for strategy; see McFarland, 1979, for marketing; see Rados, 1981, for marketing for nonprofits.)

Strategic planning will become increasingly popular with not-for-profits. In a survey of over 100 not-for-profit organizations, Unterman and Davis (1982) found a major void in the formulation and implementation of strategy. NFPs need to learn to plan strategically. "Not only have NFP organizations failed to reach the strategic management stage of development, but many of them have failed to reach even the strategic planning stages that for-profit enterprises initiated fifteen to twenty years ago" (p. 30). With strategy will also, ideally, come surplus. It will be recognized that nonprofit organizations established under the guidelines of section 501.c.3 of the Internal Revenue Code should be allowed to finance growth and replace aging assets (Young, 1982). Or, argue others (Long, 1976), surpluses should be used to provide extra services for the disadvantaged in the community.

Hospitals serve as a model for showing the gradual growth of management sophistication in a still-emerging business. What is happening to health care illustrates the challenge and change typical of organizations evolving over time. In 1978 there were over 7,000 hospitals in the United States, with combined budgets in excess of $70 billion, employing over 3.2 million people (U.S. Department of Labor, 1978). Of these 7,000 hospitals, 5,000 were community hospitals, 3,300 were private but not-for-profit institutions, and 1,800 were public (state and local government). (Note that some categories overlap.) Of the 5,000 community hospitals, 30 percent belonged to a larger system of some kind. All this will most likely change. The system of fragmented, isolated, freestanding community hospitals will evolve into a health care industry dominated by large multihospital corporations and systems. These will be both voluntary and proprietary (Goldsmith, 1981).

Growth will come to some hospitals through acquisition. They will absorb or merge with their neighbors. Others will manage to keep their independence by adapting to a changing world. By the year 2000, captains of hospital ships will be sailing in still-stormier seas. Physicians will have increased power. There will be many new forms of health care delivery, including more prepaid health plans. The regulatory environment will become even more onerous. Goldsmith (1980) says that the hospitals that survive will have learned to do strategic planning and to build their image by marketing. They will compete for physicians, promote their services, and reduce their costs. And they will diversify out of acute care and into a broader mix of medical services. Diversification can be horizontal into other health care services—outpatient care, outpatient surgery, freestanding emergency rooms, and health maintenance organizations. Diversification can also be vertical in materials or personnel (razor blades, nursing schools). Hospital administrators and their boards will also learn to manage corporate image by advertising, in line with the professional goal of "a better-informed public or improved patient care" (American Hospital Association, 1977).

The Future of Performance Appraisal

These are, then, a few portended changes and trends in strategy and image. They deal with the broad part of the book's funnel-like approach to organizational management. What about specifics at the narrow end, at the level of individual performance? How about some reef points on people?

Years ago (1957) Douglas McGregor expressed the opinion that most managers did not have the skill to appraise performance effectively. Decades later the situation had not improved materially, and articles were still being written (Ronan and Schwartz, 1974) that maintained that most performance ratings did not accurately describe performance and therefore should not be used.

In 1980 over 30 million working people in the United States were covered by a performance appraisal program (Winstanley, 1980). Factors other than actual performance can influence one's rating. These factors include personality, occupation, relative salary, position in the organization, purpose of the appraisal, mandatory feedback, length of service, age, race, and sex. It is unlikely that in the future executives will encounter greatly improved methods of measuring individual performance. Organizations may continue to experiment with MBO-type systems. This is because, as the "father" of MBO himself says, "The genius of the U.S. Constitution will be extended more and more into the workplace, especially as charges and protestations of discrimination for various reasons such as sex, age, race, national origin, and religion are stated more and more emphatically" (Odiorne, 1979, p. 27).

Expect performance appraisal to become more litigious. Encouraged by studies (Holley and Field, 1975; Basnight and Wolkinson, 1977) that have found performance appraisal to be sometimes inappropriate, illegal, or actually discriminatory and by a "what have I got to lose" legal system, more employees will probably sue their employers. One possible solution is the increased use of arbitration in settling performance disputes.

On the positive side of performance appraisal are employers who are going out of their way to publicly recognize those whom they consider outstanding performers. Although this cannot yet be called a trend, it is an example of how organizations can overtly reinforce the type of participatory performance that they want to encourage in employees.

Although the programs go by various names, a common nomenclature is *Special Award Program.* The purpose is to recognize contributions by the rank and file to the management of organizational performance. Such programs are intended to improve operations, recognize excellence, acknowledge constructive suggestions, and encourage dedication on the part of the average worker to the pursuit of goals of the total enterprise.

Forms of recognition can vary and include invitations to participate in training experiences that offer status, variety, and paid time away from work. A variation on this is an assignment to a special project or committee. Tokens of special recognition, such as medals, pins, plaques, and certificates, are often involved, but the best programs usually provide cash in addition to, or in place of, the token of esteem.

To cite just a few examples in the private sector: Goodyear Tire has a Spirit Award recognizing exemplary personal qualities exhibited at work or in the community. The Aluminum Company of America gives a technical award to employees who receive a patent. General Motors has a Cost Improvement Award for employees who contribute to cost reduction and product and profit improvement. These are positive behaviors by top management to reward and increase the frequency of positive behaviors by employees—all with the goal of managing the organization more effectively. Beyond improved productivity, the benefits that accrue to the company are said to be im-

proved morale, increased feelings of participation and ownership, and upbeat publicity.

Another example of a valuable approach to performance
appraisal is the employee suggestion program. A *suggestion* is
defined as a constructive idea submitted in writing by an employee to management to improve methods, working conditions, equipment, or procedures or to improve productivity by
reducing time and expenses. Such programs, while useful in any
organization, can be particularly helpful in ones where payroll
costs are the major expense or where the enterprise is budget-
driven. The federal government has a formal program, described
in the *Federal Personnel Manual*; in 1979, $3.8 million in
awards, or $123.10 per employee, was paid under an employee
suggestion program. Cost savings were estimated at $147 million.

Here are some guidelines for organizations that want to
encourage participatory management directly by sharing with
employees the dollars of improved productivity: (1) Try to get
at least one employee in six to submit a suggestion. (2) A good
program will result in acceptance of about one out of every four
suggestions. (3) A fairly standard incentive award is 10 percent
of savings, up to some maximum. (4) Keep the turnaround time
between employee suggestion and management response to the
absolute minimum.

Special award programs are just one method management
can use to make its people more productive. Although such incentive plans have been shown to work, they are not the only,
or even the best, method of managing productive people. Quality employee relations may be even more important.

Managing Productive People

Assuming we can agree on a definition of competent performance, can we manage people so they are productive? After sixty years of research, going back at least to the Hawthorne experiments, we have yet to achieve much success in managing
productive people. It's not that we haven't tried. According to
Skinner (1981), none of the following has produced either a
breakthrough or lasting results: supervisory training, organiza-

tional development, T-groups, sensitivity training, job enrichment, attitude surveys, flextime, flex benefits, communications, or a return to the work ethic. Why? Too much conflicting theory, for one thing, says Skinner—too many experts in human relations, labor relations, personnel management, and industrial engineering, all with their own brand of advice. Another reason for failure is managers with unrealistic expectations, ambivalent feelings about personnel, and attitudes toward employees that undermine efforts to motivate them. Nor are the workers without fault, say others: "Many workers view their jobs as necessary evils to provide the resources for filling their lives with leisure time, which they are pressing harder and harder to increase" (Sasser & Leonard, 1980, p. 114).

Even though some would argue that workers do not care much for their jobs, increased efforts will be made to be sure that they get to keep them. Management can expect more and more legislation forbidding employers to discharge employees for unjust cause. At present, about 70 percent of private-sector workers have neither a contractual agreement nor a protected-class status to keep them from unjust discharge. This is likely to change (Summers, 1980), more people being covered.

Job security is the leading edge of a developing employee-rights movement that is increasing in size and momentum. The larger the organization, or the more emphasis placed on service, the more attention you will need to pay to employee rights. For example, the Bank of America, which employs 70,000 people, has six elaborate programs to keep open communications and to be sure employee rights are recognized (Clausen, 1980).

In the future more executives will share the goals of one (Zaphiropoulos, 1980) who said that he founded his company with two objectives. One was to make money. The other was to create an environment in which people looked forward to coming to work. "The essence of any kind of success is to be able to say that a person's talents, natural talents, fit the requirements of the job. This is what I would say is working in an effortless manner. That is, you naturally fit what you're asked to do" (p. 115).

In a study of twenty-six large corporations that were either predominantly or entirely nonunion, Foulkes found a set of common attributes, policies, and attitudes that represent "creative approaches to employee relations [that] can improve productivity" (Foulkes, 1981, p. 91):

1. A sense of caring—egalitarian benefits, minimal executive perquisites, common eating quarters.
2. Carefully considered surroundings—small plants in rural or suburban areas.
3. Good profits and fast growth.
4. Family ties.
5. Employment security—ensuring full or nearly full employment. Not laying people off. Instead, using temporary help in good times and salary freezes or cuts and vacation stockpiling in bad times.
6. Promotion from within.
7. Influential personnel departments.
8. Competitive pay and benefits.
9. Careful grooming of managers.

The company with productive people will clearly try to create a climate of cooperation between employees and management. In doing so it will continually listen, explain, anticipate, and care. Managers will view employees as stockholders in the enterprise, with as much sense of ownership as financial investors. They will pay attention to the basics and get them right: recruit, compensate, motivate. They will realize that they do not have a monopoly on management, that employees also have a right to participate in corporate management. Employee participation in corporate management has been encouraged by Americans who believe it helps improve productivity (Graham and Titus, 1979). But it is the Japanese executive who has developed the partnership between managers and workers into a fine art.

The Lessons of Japan

One of the curiosities of business theory and practice in the last quarter of the twentieth century is the emergence of Japanese-style management as a paradigm of excellence. Rebuilding with astonishing rapidity since the Second World War, within a generation Japan regained a position of preeminence among the world's industrial powers. Its rise has been all the more noticeable because it contrasts sharply with the nearly as precipitous decline of American performance.

Whether the fascination with Japanese management methods will last into the next century is impossible to predict. But after about a decade of study, American academicians are certain that the United States can learn some lessons from Japan. What are the secrets of the Japanese? Do simple things well. Include everyone on the management team. Push strategic thinking down to the operations level by giving workers a view of the big picture and making sure they understand that they are all working together for the same company, that everyone shares the same goals.

Harvard's Robert Hayes (1981), one of the most respected and frequently cited researchers on the subject of Japanese management, studied the manufacturing facilities of six Japanese companies. He expected to see the following because of common misconceptions about the key to Japanese success: (1) extreme automation, (2) ubiquitous quality circles, and (3) uniform compensation systems. He did not find these things. Instead, he discovered that successful Japanese manufacturers shared nine characteristics: (1) clean, orderly workplaces, (2) little inventory or work in progress on the plant floor, (3) a no-crisis atmosphere, (4) monitoring systems, (5) striving for absolute perfection, (6) thinking in terms of quality, (7) long-term commitments, (8) partnerships, co-destinies, lifetime suppliers, and (9) (some) lifetime employment.

For the executive working to get everyone in the organization to implement the goals of the organization the watchwords from Japan are *strategic operations.* Strategic operations is a management philosophy practiced by the Japanese that recognizes that every act of every employee affects the strategy of the company. This is especially true in operations. Wheelwright (1981) believes that this general philosophy of managing corporate performance can be broken down into eight specific behavioral recommendations.

1. Link longer-term and short-term objectives.
2. Refuse to accept false dichotomies such as "Low costs or high quality—take your choice."
3. Integrate corporate goals with individual goals.
4. Set goals for improving operations.
5. Measure group performance on a regular basis.
6. Pay attention to detail.
7. Stress continually the need for planning and review.
8. Have patience.

About the mysteries of the Nipponese, Hayes (1981) has this to say: "Improving our . . . competitiveness does not lie with . . . the 'technological fixes' or the 'strategic coups' that we love so much. Instead we must compete . . . by always putting our best resources and talent to work doing the basic things a little better every day over a long period of time. It is that simple—and that difficult" (p. 66).

Productivity

Much of the material presented so far has dealt indirectly with the issue of productivity. For high performance, companies must be productive, capable of producing quality goods or services within budget and on time. Yet, productivity is a special measure of corporate performance, one that stimulates interest in many quarters. "Productivity is in fact the buzzword of the decade. One can scarcely pick up any publication without being barraged by articles on the topic written from every possible perspective" (Byrne, 1981, pp. 36–37).

Productivity is important because lower productivity, all other things being equal, means a lower standard of living (Thurow, 1980). The Productivity Index of the Bureau of Labor Statistics defines productivity simply as output per hour of work. But the concept of productivity encompasses a broad spectrum, not merely the production inputs and outputs usually discussed in terms of technology and capital. It also covers human resources and their efficiency. A definition of productivity in people terms is value added per employee (Gale, 1980). This, in turn, is defined as the net of sales less purchases, divided by the total number of employees.

According to the Strategic Planning Institute, a nonprofit organization based in Boston, value added in the typical manufacturing company will vary from about $10 million to $60 million. SPI's data base is called PIMS, for Profit Impact of Market Strategy. It covers 1,700 companies and includes 200 variables. In seeking answers to productivity problems, the SPI data base can be used to address these questions:

- Which of our businesses should be automated?
- How does our output per employee compare with that of other companies?
- What is the best measure of operating effectiveness for us to use?
- Can portfolio management improve our productivity?

The federal government is naturally concerned with productivity and is a good source of information about it. There are at least three government sources of published data:

1. The Office of Productivity and Technology of the Bureau of Labor Statistics publishes a bibliography on productivity (U.S. Bureau of Labor Statistics, 1980).
2. The Board of Governors of the Federal Reserve System publishes the *Federal Reserve Bulletin,* listing monthly figures on production by industry and market.
3. The Bureau of Economic Analysis of the Department of Commerce publishes monthly industrial production statistics.

Measurement has been a central theme in the preceding chapters. Accurate measurement is fundamental in evaluating productivity. Yet, according to the National Academy of Sciences, there is no generally accepted standard for productivity, and improved measures are needed (National Research Council, 1979). Measures of current profit and growth are the most frequently used indicators of corporate performance, but they are not necessarily the best (Hayes and Garvin, 1982). There is a danger for executives that overemphasizing current growth and profit can result in "a serious underinvestment in the capital stock (the productive capacity, technology, and worker skills) on which their companies rest. As a result they have unintentionally jeopardized their companies' futures" (Hayes and Garvin, 1982, p. 71).

The facts seem undisputable that the United States has suffered a drop in productivity relative to other major industrial nations. Since 1970 Germany's production is up four times as much as the United States's, and France's gain is three times ours (Hayes and Abernathey, 1980). Various causes have been ascribed: inflation, government, management, workers.

Executives in the United States may overemphasize short-term financial results, placing too much faith in such concepts as portfolio management. They are called market-oriented, not customer-oriented. Of late chief executive officers have come from financial or legal backgrounds rather than from careers in research and development, marketing, or manufacturing. Hayes and Garvin (1982) argue that United States corporations are more concerned with near-term profitability than their German or Japanese counterparts. Many American managers are less willing to invest in their own business. "Managers must be willing to reinvest at the very time such action appears least attractive. They must stop pouring funds into refurbishing their images and upgrade their factories instead. They must resist the lure of the unfamiliar business and mind their own" (p. 79).

Most researchers on productivity have concluded that the problem is real and serious. There are exceptions. Henrici (1981) believes that the Productivity Index of the Bureau of Labor Statistics is not error-free and that it is unwise to overreact to small (1 percent) changes in the index. But, more important, it is mainly journalists, economists, politicians, and academicians who "harp on our productivity disease." If the phenomenon were real, wouldn't more business executives be concerned? Consequently, it is possible to conclude that the so-called productivity ailment is imaginary and that as a nation the United States is suffering from productivity hypochondria.

Clearly there is a need for more frequent and effective communication between scholars and management practitioners (Dogramaci, 1981). Accepting productivity as a legitimate problem with dangerous consequences, why has there been a drop in this important measure of corporate performance? One argument is that the United States has abandoned its technical superiority out of preference for serving existing markets, not new ones, and is infatuated with short-term results and management by the numbers. Executives worry too much about using existing resources effectively and not enough about producing superior products over the long term.

Hayes and Abernathy (1980) suggest six major causes for the decline in productivity in United States corporations:

1. They have shifted away from trying to compete by offering superior technical products.
2. They emphasize numerical analysis too much and intuition too little.
3. Too much stress is put on maximizing short-term profits.
4. They are not as entrepreneurial as they once were.
5. They are too interested in return on investment and not interested enough in products and customers.
6. They are investing less in research and development and manufacturing, while foreign companies are investing more.

In the past much of America's industrial edge has been due to its technical lead. This calved cash cows that U.S. companies are still milking. U.S. corporations are spending less on research and development and receiving fewer patents. No longer can American executives afford to overlook the technical innovations of other countries or to assume that they still have a lead-time advantage because of their previous technical superiority (Vernon, 1980).

If these are the causes of lessened productivity, what are the solutions? Typical recommendations include cost cutting, mechanization, and raising prices (Gale, 1980). Two of the management techniques argued for in preceding chapters have value in helping improve productivity: goal setting and participation

(Hinricks, 1978). But these techniques need to be fully integrated into the organization rather than treated as programs. Research has found a drop to previous levels of performance when attention was no longer paid to setting goals and participatory performance management. The direct relationship between management-by-objectives style and productivity has been proved and recognized as useful also for not-for-profit organizations and public administrations (Mali, 1978).

Money helps too. There is little doubt that an increase in capital investment can ultimately improve productivity if the company has certain characteristics. A large share of the current market, a low rate of new-product introduction, and a high utilization of current manufacturing capacity are the best correlates of improved productivity resulting from more capital (Gale, 1980). The importance of more capital investment and new technology cannot be overemphasized. "The recovery of productivity and the ability to do better in world competition need not wait for our representatives in Washington . . . of crucial importance in companies large and small are distinctive technology-driven strategies. If these are to be effective, capital must be attracted to reequip established industry and launch new ventures; employees at all levels, particularly on the shop floor, must be engaged in creative cooperation in quality and cost control" (Andrews, 1982, p. 1).

Not all companies are technology-based, nor, even if they were, could they necessarily invest more capital in their business. And so the solution most readily applicable to the broadest range of organizations is to manage better and to increase productivity through more effective people. O'Toole (1981) believes so strongly in the need for more worker participation in management that he not only sees involvement as the most important single criterion leading to improved productivity, he also thinks it is essential for the survival of the political and economic system of the United States. In the future he envisions workers as true owners of their companies. Forget the sops of employee stock ownership plans and the nonsense about how employees already own industrial America through their pension funds. Have true ownership. Have more and smaller com panies. Close trade schools. Teach the four Rs: reading, writing, arithmetic, and responsibility.

Others would not go so far. In Judson's (1982) study of the productivity problem, managers laid the blame for America's declining productivity at their own feet. As the main cause of the problem, 30 percent cited management ineffectiveness and 30 percent cited management's concern with short-term results. The 236 top-level executives from 195 companies surveyed reported some success in improving productivity. More capital was a big plus, but other frequently mentioned methods of improvement lie within any concerned executive's grasp: capital investment, cited by 72 percent as a reason for their own success; top-management commitment, cited by 61 percent; good controls (45 percent); good employee relations (38 percent); and good communications (35 percent). Except for capital investment, all these practices are forms of the techniques covered in previous chapters: strategy, measures, controls, involvement—really working to implement the corporate mission at all levels of the organization.

Reveille

The year is the future. The scene is Bancroft Hall at the U.S. Naval Academy. The time is 4 A.M. A fourth-class midshipman is huddled under a blanket in a closet with a flashlight, shining shoes and reading silently.

Plebe: [To himself] "The successful corporate officer worries first about having a good product and then about ROI . . ."

Officer of the Watch: What's this? What's going on here? [Pulls back blanket. Sees plebe.] All right, sandblower, hit the bulkhead!

Plebe: Yes, sir.

Officer: What the hell are you doing?!

Plebe: Working, sir.

Officer: At 4 A.M.?

Plebe: Yes, sir.

Officer: Why?

Plebe: So I can get a head start, sir. I'm trying to get through plebe summer with no demerits. Sort of like the Japanese idea of zero defects, sir.

Officer: You know I could ruin the whole thing and give you five demerits for being out of your rack before reveille?

Plebe: Yes, sir.

Officer: What are you reading, sweat?

Plebe: Managing Organizational Performance. The last chapter, sir. About how the United States is falling behind Japan and Germany and other countries when once we were the leaders, sir.

Officer: What should we do about it, plebe?

Plebe: Well, sir, Andrews (1980, p. 1) says: "A universal idea is reasserting its power; persistent investment in quality, cost, product differentiation, and durability—under the guidance of a consistent and valid strategy—will win customers regardless of race, color, creed, or country of origin . . . ." Sir.

Officer: No kidding? [Yawns.]

Plebe: No, sir.

Officer: Anything else?

Plebe: Yes, sir. Vernon (1980, p. 155) says, "The race will be won by those enterprises with the best price, the best quality, and the best after-sales service . . . changes in attitude come slowly, but I am betting many U.S. enterprises will be able to make the shift." Sir.

Officer: That's pretty interesting stuff. Come around today, 1800 hours, Room 464. Frank and Mary will get a big kick out of hearing you recite that while standing on your head. Dismissed. Hit the rack.

Plebe: Sir?

Officer: What is it now, mister?

Plebe: Request permission to speak, sir.

Officer: Well, what is it?

Plebe: Beat Army, sir.

Officer: Yeah. You bet. Let's beat Army.

References

Alderfer, C. "Theory and Practice in O.D." *Contemporary Psychology,* 1982, *27*(1), 37–38.

Allan, P. "Managers at Work: A Large-Scale Study of the Managerial Job in New York City Government." *Academy of Management Journal,* 1981, *24*(3), 613–619.

American Hospital Association. *Advertising by Hospitals—Guidelines.* Chicago: American Hospital, 1977.

American Institute of Management. *Manual of Excellent Managements.* (11th ed.) New York: American Institute of Management, 1970.

Andrews, K. R. "Letter from the Editor." *Harvard Business Review,* 1980, *58*(6), 1.

Andrews, K. R. "Letter from the Editor." *Harvard Business Review,* 1982, *60*(1), 1.

Ansoff, H. I., Declerck, R. P., and Hayes, R. L. *From Strategic Planning to Strategic Management.* London: Wiley, 1976.

Argenti, J. *Corporate Planning: A Practical Guide.* Homewood, Ill.: Dow Jones–Irwin, 1969.

Argenti, J. *Systematic Corporate Planning.* New York: Wiley, 1974.

335

Argyris, C. "Organizational Effectiveness Under Stress." *Harvard Business Review,* May–June 1960, *38*(3), 137–146.

Atkinson, J. W., and Feather, N. T. (Eds.). *A Theory of Achievement Motivation.* New York: Wiley, 1966.

Basnight, T. A., and Wolkinson, B. W. "Evaluating Managerial Performance: Is Your Appraisal System Legal?" *Employee Relations Law Journal,* 1977, *3,* 240–254.

Bass, B. M. "Further Evidence of the Dynamic Character of Criteria." *Personnel Psychology,* 1962, *15,* 93–97.

Bass, B. M. "When Planning for Others." In B. M. Bass and S. D. Deep (Eds.), *Current Perspectives for Managing Organizations.* Englewood Cliffs, N.J.: Prentice-Hall, 1970.

Bass, B. M., Shackleton, V. J., and Rosenstein, E. "Industrial Democracy and Participative Management: What's the Difference?" *International Review of Applied Psychology,* 1979, *28*(2), 81–92.

Basset, G. A., and Meyer, H. H. "Performance Appraisal Based on Self-Review." *Personnel Psychology,* 1968, *21,* 421–430.

Becker, S. W. *The Efficient Organization.* New York: Elsevier, 1975.

Beer, M. *Organizational Change and Development: A Systems View.* Santa Monica, Calif.: Goodyear, 1980.

Belcher, D. *Compensation Administration.* Englewood Cliffs, N.J.: Prentice-Hall, 1974.

Bennis, W. G. "Chairman MAC in Perspective." *Harvard Business Review,* Sept.–Oct. 1972, *50*(5), 140–147.

Bower, J. "Effective Public Management." *Harvard Business Review,* 1977, *55*(2), 131–141.

Branch, M. C. *The Corporate Planning Process.* New York: American Management Association, 1962.

Bryan, J. F., and Locke, E. A. "Goal Setting as a Means of Increasing Motivation." *Journal of Applied Psychology,* 1967a, *51,* 274–277.

Bryan, J. F., and Locke, E. A. "Parkinson's Law as a Goal-Setting Phenomenon." *Organizational Behavior and Human Performance,* 1967b, *2,* 258–275.

Bryan, L. A. "The Japanese and the American First-Line Supervisor." *Training Development Journal,* 1982, *36*(1), 62–68.

Buchholz, R. A. "The Belief Structure of Managers Relative to Work Concepts Measured by a Factor Analytic Model." *Personnel Psychology,* 1977, *30*(4), 567–587.

Budde, J. F. *Measuring Performance in Human Service Systems: Planning, Organization and Control.* New York: Amacom, 1979.

Burke, R. J. "Characteristics of Effective Appraisal Interviews: 1) Open Communication and Acceptance of Subordinate Disagreements." *Training and Development Journal,* 1970, *24,* 9-12.

Byrne, R. S. "Sources on Productivity." *Harvard Business Review,* 1981, *59*(5), 36.

Cammann, C., and Nadler, D. A. "Fit Control Systems to Your Managerial Style." *Harvard Business Review,* 1976, *54,* 65-72.

Campbell, J. P., and others. *Managerial Behavior, Performance and Effectiveness.* New York: McGraw-Hill, 1970.

Cantley, M. F. "The Choice of Corporate Objectives." In B. Taylor and K. Hawkins (Eds.), *A Handbook of Strategic Planning.* London: Longman, 1972.

Carr, A. F., and others. "Outcome Measures of Police Performance: Some Steps Toward Positive Accountability." *Journal of Community Psychology,* 1980, *8*(2), 165-171.

Carroll, S. J., and Tosi, H. L. "Goal Characteristics and Personality Factors in a Management by Objectives Program." *Administrative Science Quarterly,* 1970, *15,* 295-305.

Cascio, W. F., and Bernardin, H. J. "Implications of Performance Appraisal Litigation for Personnel Decisions." *Personnel Psychology,* 1981, *34*(2), 211-226.

Cascio, W. F., and Valenzi, E. "Behaviorally Anchored Rating Scales: Effects of Education and Job Experience of Raters and Ratees." *Journal of Applied Psychology,* 1977, *62*(3), 278-282.

Chamberlin, J. *The Enterprising Americans: A Business History of the United States.* New York: Harper & Row, 1967.

Cherns, A. B. "Can Behavioral Science Help Design Organizations?" *Organizational Dynamics,* 1977, *5*(4), 44-64.

Clausen, A. W. "Listening and Responding to Employees' Concerns." *Harvard Business Review,* 1980, *58*(1), 101-114.

Cleveland, J. N., and Landy, F. J. "The Influence of Rater and Ratee Age on Two Performance Judgments." *Personnel Psychology,* 1981, *34*(1), 19-29.

Cochran, T. C., and Miller, W. *The Age of Enterprise.* New York: Macmillan, 1942.

Collier, J. R. *Effective Long Range Business Planning.* Englewood Cliffs, N.J.: Prentice-Hall, 1968.

Connollan, T. *How to Improve Human Performance.* New York: Harper & Row, 1978.

Connors, T. D. (Ed.). *The Nonprofit Organization Handbook.* New York: McGraw-Hill, 1980.

Controllership Foundation. *Planning, Managing and Measuring the Business: A Case Study of Planning and Control at General Electric.* New York: Controllership Foundation, 1955.

Cooper-Jones, D. *Business Planning and Forecasting.* New York: Wiley, 1974.

Cotton, D. B. *Company-wide Planning, Concept and Process.* New York: Macmillan, 1970.

Crawford, K. S., Thomas, E. D., and Fink, J. J. "Pygmalion at Sea: Improving the Work Effectiveness of Low Performers." *Journal of Applied Behavioral Science,* 1980, *16*(4), 482–505.

Cummings, T. G. (Ed.). *Systems Theory for Organization Development.* Chichester, England: Wiley, 1980.

Denning, B. W. (Ed.). *Corporate Planning: Selected Concepts.* London: McGraw-Hill, 1971.

Dipboye, R. L., and de Pontbriand, R. "Correlates of Employee Relations to Performance Appraisals and Appraisal Systems." *Journal of Applied Psychology,* 1981, *66*(2), 248–251.

Dogramaci, A. (Ed.). *Productivity Analysis: A Range of Perspectives.* Boston: Martinus Nijhoff, 1981.

Dossett, D. L., and Greenberg, C. L. "Goal Setting and Performance Evaluation: An Attributional Analysis." *Academy of Management Journal,* 1981, *24*(4), 767–779.

Dowd, J. "The Board of Directors Looks at Long Range Planning." In D. W. Ewing (Ed.), *Long Range Planning for Management.* (3rd ed.) New York: Harper & Row, 1972.

Drucker, P. F. *The Practice of Management.* New York: Harper & Row, 1954.

Drucker, P. F. *Managing for Results.* New York: Harper & Row, 1964.

Drucker, P. F. "Long Range Planning Means Risk Taking." In D. W. Ewing (Ed.), *Long Range Planning for Management.* (3rd ed.) New York: Harper & Row, 1972.

Drucker, P. F. *Management: Tasks, Responsibilities, Practices.* New York: Harper & Row, 1973.

Evans, P., and Bartolomé, F. *Must Success Cost so Much?* New York: Basic Books, 1980.

Ewing, D. W. *Long-Range Planning for Management.* (3rd ed.) New York: Harper & Row, 1972.

Ferguson, C. R. *Measuring Corporate Strategy.* Homewood, Ill.: Dow Jones-Irwin, 1974.

Field, H. S., and Holley, W. H. "Subordinates' Characteristics, Supervisors' Ratings, and Decision to Discuss Appraisal Results." *Academy of Management Journal,* 1977, *20*(2), 315–321.

Field, H. S., and Ridenheur, C. B. "Presentation of Positive and Negative Policy Changes: What Effects on Members' Satisfaction with Their Organization?" *Personnel Psychology*, 1975, *28*(4), 525–532.

Fineman, S. "The Influence of Perceived Job Climate Upon Relationship of Managerial Achievement Motivation and Performance." *Journal of Occupational Psychology*, 1975, *48*, 113–124.

Forbes, B. C. *Men Who Are Making America Great.* New York: B. C. Forbes Publishing Co., 1917.

Forsyth, G. C., and Thomas, G. D. "Models for Financially Healthy Hospitals." *Harvard Business Review*, 1971, *49*(4), 106–118.

Foulkes, F. K. *Personnel Policies in Large Nonunion Companies.* Englewood Cliffs, N.J.: Prentice-Hall, 1980.

Foulkes, F. K. "How Top Nonunion Companies Manage Employees." *Harvard Business Review*, 1981, *59*(5), 90–97.

Friedman, M., and Friedman, R. *Free to Choose.* New York: Harcourt Brace Jovanovich, 1979.

Furukawa, H. "Effects of Management Objective upon Leadership Behavior." *Japanese Journal of Experimental Social Psychology*, 1979, *19*(1), 15–24.

Gale, B. T. "Can More Capital Buy Higher Productivity?" *Harvard Business Review*, 1980, *58*(4), 79–86.

Geffin, A. B. "Human Resource Accounting and Modern Day Theorists." *Psychologia Africana*, 1980a, *19*, 41–52.

Geffin, A. B. "Human Resource Accounting (HRA) and the Ability of Management to Report on Social Benefits to Stockholders." *Psychologia Africana*, 1980b, *19*, 53–59.

Gibson, C. F. *Managing Organizational Behavior: Achieving Results Through Understanding and Action.* Homewood, Ill.: Irwin, 1980.

Gilbert, A. C., and Downey, R. G. "Validity of Peer Ratings Obtained During Ranger Training." *U.S. Army Research Institute for the Behavioral and Social Sciences*, 1978, *344*, 18.

Gilbert, T. *Human Competence.* New York: McGraw-Hill, 1978.

Glasgow, Z., Simkins, M. L., and Guerrieri, J. A. "Job Performance Appraisal System Training Program." *USAFHRL Technical Report*, Jan. 1981, *80-56*, 30 pp.

Glover, J. D., and Simon, G. A. *Chief Executives' Handbook.* Homewood, Ill.: Dow Jones–Irwin, 1976.

Gluck, F. W., Kaufman, S. D., and Wallick, S. A. "Strategic Management for Competitive Advantage." *Harvard Business Review*, 1980, *58*(4), 134–142.

Goetz, B. E. *Management Planning and Control.* New York: McGraw-Hill, 1949.

Goldsmith, J. C. "The Health Care Market: Can Hospitals Survive?" *Harvard Business Review,* 1980, *58*(5), 100–112.

Goldsmith, J. C. "Outlook for Hospitals: Systems Are the Solution." *Harvard Business Review,* 1981, *59*(5), 130–142.

Gordon, G. G., and Cummins, W. *Managing Management Climate.* Lexington, Mass.: Lexington Books/Heath, 1979.

Graham, B. S., and Titus, P. S. *The Amazing Oversight: Total Participation for Productivity.* New York: Amacom, 1979.

Greller, M. M. "Subordinate Participation and Reactions to the Appraisal Interview." *Journal of Applied Psychology,* 1975, *60,* 544–549.

Gruber, W. H. *The New Management: Line Executive and Staff Professional in the Future Firm.* New York: McGraw-Hill, 1976.

Gruneberg, M. M. *Understanding Job Satisfaction.* New York: Halsted Press, 1979.

Gutman, P. M. "Strategies for Growth." *California Management Review,* 1964, *6.*

Hall, W. K. "Survival Strategies in a Hostile Environment." *Harvard Business Review,* 1980, *58*(5), 75–85.

Hamner, W. C. *Organizational Shock.* New York: Wiley, 1980.

Haspeslagh, P. "Portfolio Planning: Uses and Limits." *Harvard Business Review,* 1982, *60*(1), 58–74.

Hayes, R. H. "Why Japanese Factories Work." *Harvard Business Review,* 1981, *59*(4), 56–67.

Hayes, R. H., and Abernathey, W. J. "Managing Our Way to Economic Decline." *Harvard Business Review,* 1980, *58*(4), 67–77.

Hayes, R. H., and Garvin, D. A. "Managing as if Tomorrow Mattered." *Harvard Business Review,* 1982, *60*(3), 70–80.

Henderson, R. I. *Compensation Management: Rewarding Performance.* (2nd ed.) Reston, Va.: Reston Publishing, 1979.

Heneman, H. G. "Comparisons of Self and Superior Ratings of Managerial Performance." *Journal of Applied Psychology,* 1974, *59,* 638–642.

Henrici, S. B. "How Deadly Is the Productivity Disease?" *Harvard Business Review,* 1981, *59*(6), 123–130.

Hersey, P. *Management of Organizational Behavior: Utilizing Human Resources.* Englewood Cliffs, N.J.: Prentice-Hall, 1977.

Herzberg, F., and others. *Job Attitudes: Review of Research and Opinion.* Pittsburgh: Psychological Service of Pittsburgh, 1957.

Hinricks, J. R. *Practical Management for Productivity.* New York: Van Nostrand Reinhold, 1978.

Holley, W. H., and Field, H. S. "Performance Appraisal and the Law." *Labor Law Journal,* 1975, *26,* 423–430.

Holtz, H. *Profit-Line Management: Managing a Growing Business Successfully.* New York: Amacom, 1981.

Holzbach, R. L. "Rater Bias in Performance Ratings: Superior, Self- and Peer Ratings." *Journal of Applied Psychology,* 1979, *63*(3), 579–588.

Humble, J. W. (Ed.). *Management by Objectives in Action.* London: McGraw-Hill, 1970.

Humble, J. W. *How to Manage by Objectives.* New York: Amacom, 1973.

Hutchinson, J. G. *Management Strategy and Tactics.* New York: Hall, 1971.

Ilgen, D. R., and others. "Supervisor and Subordinate Reactions to Performance Appraisal Sessions." *Organizational Behavior and Human Performance,* 1981, *28*(3), 311–330.

Ivancevich, J. M. "Effects of Goal Setting on Performance and Job Satisfaction." *Journal of Applied Psychology,* 1976, *61,* 605–612.

Ivancevich, J. M. "Different Goal Setting Treatments and Their Effects on Performance and Job Satisfaction." *Academy of Management Journal,* 1977, *20*(3), 406–419.

Ivancevich, J. M., and McMahon, J. T. "Education as a Moderator of Goal Setting Effectiveness." *Journal of Vocational Behavior,* 1977, *11,* 83–94.

Ivancevich, J. M., and Smith, S. V. "Goal Setting Interview Skills Training: Simulated and On-the-Job Analyses." *Journal of Applied Psychology,* 1981, *66*(6), 697–705.

Ivancevich, J. M., Szilagyi, A. D., and Wallace, M. J. *Organizational Behavior and Performance.* Santa Monica, Calif.: Goodyear, 1977.

Judson, A. S. "The Awkward Truth About Productivity." *Harvard Business Review,* 1982, *60*(5), 93–98.

Keeley, M. "Subjective Performance Evaluation and Person-Role Conflict Under Conditions of Uncertainty." *Academy of Management Journal,* 1977, *20*(2), 301–314.

Kellogg, M. *Closing the Performance Gap.* New York: American Management Association, 1967.

Kelly, P. R. "Reappraisal of Appraisals." *Harvard Business Review,* May–June, 1958, *36*(3), 59–69.

Kerr, S. (Ed.). *Organizational Behavior.* Columbus, Ohio: Grid Publishing, 1979.

Kim, J. S., and Hamner, W. C. "Effect of Performance Feedback and Goal Setting on Productivity and Satisfaction in an Organizational Setting." *Journal of Applied Psychology,* 1976, *61,* 48–57.

Kimberly, J. R., Miles, R. H., and Associates. *The Organizational Life Cycle: Issues in the Creation, Transformation, and Decline of Organizations.* San Francisco: Jossey-Bass, 1980.

Kins, W. R. *Strategic Planning and Policy.* New York: Van Nostrand Reinhold, 1978.

Kipnis, D., and others. "Why Do I Like Thee: Is It Your Performance or My Orders?" *Journal of Applied Psychology,* 1981, *66*(3), 324–328.

Koontz, H., and O'Donnell, C. *Principles of Management.* New York: McGraw-Hill, 1968.

Korman, A. K. "Self-Esteem, Social Influence, and Task Performance: Some Tests of Theory." In *Proceedings of the 76th Annual Convention of the American Psychological Association,* 1976, pp. 567–568.

Kozak, R. E., and Cangemi, J. P. "Individual and Corporate Objectives: Determinants of Human Behavior." *Psychology,* 1977, *14*(3), 33–44.

Kraus, W. A. *Collaboration in Organizations: Alternatives to Hierarchy.* New York: Human Sciences Press, 1980.

Labaw, P. J. *Advanced Questionnaire Design.* Cambridge, Mass.: ABT Books, 1980.

Landy, F. J., Barnes, J. L., and Murphy, K. R. "Correlates of Perceived Fairness and Accuracy of Performance Evaluation." *Journal of Applied Psychology,* 1978, *63*(6), 751–754.

Latham, G. P., and Kinne, S. B. "Improving Job Performance Through Training and Goal Setting." *Journal of Applied Psychology,* 1974, *59,* 187–191.

Law, A. W., and Parett, C. M. "The Nature of Managerial Work: A Comparison of Public and Private-Sector Managers." *Group and Organization Studies,* 1980, *5*(4), 453–466.

Lawler, E. E., III. *Pay and Organizational Effectiveness.* New York: McGraw-Hill, 1971.

Lazarev, V. S. "Planning as the Main Direction and Fundamental Principle of Research in the Psychology of Management." *Voprosy Psikhologii,* 1980, *6,* 25–33.

Leon, F. R. "Does the Peruvian Worker Like the Authoritarian Style of Supervision?" *Revista Latinoamericana de Psicología,* 1980, *12*(1), 79–94.

Levinson, H. "Management by Whose Objectives?" *Harvard Business Review,* July–Aug. 1970, *48*(4), 125–135.

Levitt, T. "Marketing Success Through Differentiation of Anything." *Harvard Business Review,* 1980, *58*(1), 83–91.

Likert, R. "Measuring Organizational Performance." *Harvard Business Review,* 1958, *36*(2), 41–51.

Lippincott, E., and Aannestad, E. "Management of Voluntary Welfare Agencies." *Harvard Business Review,* 1964, *42*(6), 87–99.

Litschert, R. J. "Some Characteristics of Long-Range Planning: An Industry Study." In D. W. Ewing (Ed.), *Long Range Planning for Management.* (3rd ed.) New York: Harper & Row, 1972.

Litwin, G. H. "Climate and Motivation: An Experimental Study." In R.

Tagiuri and G. H. Litwin (Eds.), *Organizational Climate: Exploration of Concept.* Cambridge, Mass.: Harvard University Press, 1968.

Locke, E. A. "Relationship of Success and Expectation to Affect on Goal-Seeking Tasks." *Journal of Personnel Social Psychology,* 1967, *7,* 125–134.

Locke, E. A., and Bryan, J. "The Directing Function of Goals in Task Performance." *Organizational Behavior and Human Performance,* 1969, *4,* 35–42.

Locke, E. A., Cartledge, N., and Koeppel, J. "Motivational Effects of Knowledge of Results: A Goal-Setting Phenomenon?" *Psychological Bulletin,* 1968, *70,* 474–485.

Long, H. W. "Valuation as a Criterion in Not-for-Profit Decision Making." *Health Care Management Review,* 1976, *1*(3), 40.

Lynn, L. E., Jr., and Seidl, J. M. "Bottom-Line Management for Public Agencies." *Harvard Business Review,* 1977, *55*(1), 144–160.

McClelland, D. C. *The Achieving Society.* New York: Van Nostrand, 1961.

McConkey, D. D. *Management by Objectives for Staff Managers.* New York: Vantage Press, 1972.

McConkey, D. D. *MBO for Nonprofit Organizations.* New York: Amacom, 1975.

McConkey, D. D. *How to Manage by Results.* New York: Amacom, 1976.

MacDonald, C. R. *MBO Can Work!* New York: McGraw-Hill, 1982.

McDonald, J. "Sears Makes It Look Easy." *Fortune,* 1964, *69,* 120–127.

McFarland, D. E. *Managerial Innovation in the Metropolitan Hospital.* New York: Praeger, 1979.

McGregor, D. "An Uneasy Look at Performance Appraisal." *Harvard Business Review,* 1957, 89, *35*(3), 89–95.

McGregor, D. *The Human Side of Enterprise.* New York: McGraw-Hill, 1960.

Macy, J. W. *Public Service: The Human Side of Government.* New York: Harper & Row, 1971.

Mahler, W. R. *Twenty Years of Merit Rating, 1926–1946.* New York: Psychological Corporation, 1947.

Mahler, W. R. *Structure, Power and Results: How to Organize Your Company for Optimum Performance.* Homewood, Ill.: Dow Jones–Irwin, 1975.

Mali, P. *Improving Total Productivity: M.B.O. Strategies for Business, Government, and Not-for-Profit Organizations.* New York: Wiley, 1978.

Mali, P. *Managing by Objectives: An Operating Guide to Faster and More Profitable Results.* New York: Wiley-Interscience, 1972.

Martin, T. N., Price, J. L., and Mueller, C. W. "Job Performance and Turnover." *Journal of Applied Psychology,* 1981, *66*(1), 116–119.

Marvin, P. R. *Management Goals: Guidelines and Accountability.* Homewood, Ill.: Dow Jones–Irwin, 1968.

Massey, R. H., Mullins, C. J., and Earles, J. A. "Performance Appraisal Ratings: The Content Issue." *USAFHRL Technical Report,* Dec. 1978, *78-69,* 18 pp.

Matsui, T., Okada, A., and Mizuguchi, R. "Expectancy Theory Prediction of the Goal Theory Postulate, The Harder the Goals, the Higher the Performance." *Journal of Applied Psychology,* 1981, *66*(1), 54–58.

Miles, R. H. *Macro Organizational Behaviors.* Santa Monica, Calif.: Goodyear, 1980.

Miller, L. *Behavior Management.* New York: Wiley, 1978.

Misumi, J., Sugiman, T., and Kubota, Y. K. "Empirical Studies on Leadership of Middle Management in Private Enterprises." *Japanese Journal of Experimental Social Psychology,* 1979, *19*(1), 1–14.

Mitchell, T. R., and Wood, R. E. "Supervisor's Responses to Subordinate Poor Performance: A Test of an Attritional Model." *Organizational Behavior and Human Performance,* 1980, *25*(1), 123–138.

Mobley, W. H. "A Link Between M.B.O. and Merit Compensation." *Personnel Journal,* 1974, *53,* 423–427.

Mockler, R. J. *Business Planning and Policy Formulation.* New York: Appleton-Century-Crofts, 1971, 1972.

Moore, P. D., and Stauton, T. "Management by Objectives in American Cities." *Public Personnel Management,* 1981, *10*(2), 223–232.

Moreno, I. G. *Top Management Long-Range Planning.* New York: Vantage Press, 1963.

Morrisey, G. L. *Management by Objectives and Results for Business and Industry.* Reading, Mass.: Addison-Wesley, 1977.

Mossholder, K. W., and Dewhirst, H. D. "The Appropriateness of Management-by-Objectives for Development and Research Personnel." *Journal of Management,* 1980, *6*(2), 145–156.

Murray, R. K. "Behavioral Management Objectives." *Personnel Journal,* 1973, *52,* 304–306.

Nadler, G. *Work Systems Design: The IDEAL Concept.* Homewood, Ill.: Irwin, 1967.

National Research Council. *Panel to Review Productivity Statistics.* Washington, D.C.: National Academy of Sciences, 1979.

Naylor, J. C., Pritchard, R. D., and Ilgen, D. R. *A Theory of Behavior in Organizations.* New York: Academic Press, 1980.

Oberg, W. "Making Performance Appraisal Relevant." *Harvard Business Review,* Jan.–Feb. 1982.

Odiorne, G. S. *Management by Objectives: A System of Management Leadership.* New York: Pitman, 1965.

Odiorne, G. S. *MBO II: A System of Managerial Leadership for the 80's.* Belmont, Calif.: Fearon, 1979.

Olson, R. F. *Performance Appraisal: A Guide to Greater Productivity.* New York: Wiley, 1981.

O'Toole, J. *Making America Work: Productivity and Responsibility.* New York: Continuum, 1981.

Patten, T. H., Jr. *Pay: Employee Compensation and Incentive Plans.* New York: Free Press, 1977.

Patton, A. "How to Appraise Executive Performance." *Harvard Business Review,* Jan.–Feb. 1960, *38*(1), 63–71.

Pestonjee, D. M., Singh, A. P., and Singh, S. P. "Productivity in Relation to Morale, Participation and Alienation." *Psychologia: An International Journal of Psychology in the Orient,* 1981, *24*(3), 171–175.

Porter, L. W., Lawler, E. E., III, and Hackman, J. R. *Behavior in Organizations.* New York: McGraw-Hill, 1975.

Potter, B. *Turning Around: The Behavioral Approach to Managing People.* New York: Amacom, 1980.

Potter, E. H., and Fielder, F. E. "The Utilization of Staff Member Intelligence and Experience Under High and Low Stress." *Academy of Management Journal,* 1981, *24*(2), 361–376.

Pritchard, R. D., Montagno, R. V., and Moore, J. R. "Enhancing Productivity Through Feedback and Job Design." *USAFHRL Technical Report,* Aug. 1978, *78-44,* 45 pp.

Rados, D. L. *Marketing for Non-Profit Organizations.* Boston: Auburn House, 1981.

Raia, A. P. *Managing by Objectives.* Glenview, Ill.: Scott, Foresman, 1974.

Ralph, P. M. "Performance Evaluation: One More Try." *Public Personnel Management,* 1980, *9*(3), 145–153.

Redding, W. J. *Effective Management by Objectives.* New York: McGraw-Hill, 1971.

Roberts, E. B. "New Ventures for Corporate Growth." *Harvard Business Review,* 1980, *38*(4), 134–142.

Ronan, W. W. "Effects of Goal Setting and Supervision on Worker Behavior in an Industrial Situation." *Journal of Applied Psychology,* 1973, *58,* 302–307.

Ronan, W. W., and Schwartz, A. P. "Ratings as Performance Criteria." *International Review of Applied Psychology,* 1974, *23*(2), 71.

Rosen, B., and Jerdee, T. H. "Effects of Decision Performance on Managerial Willingness to Use Participation." *Academy of Management Journal,* 1978, *21*(4), 722–725.

Rosen, B., Jerdee, T. H., and Lynn, R. O. "Effects of Performance Appraisal Format, Age, and Performance Level on Retirement Decisions." *Journal of Applied Psychology,* 1981, *66*(4), 515–519.

Ross, J., and Ferris, K. R. "Interpersonal Attractions and Organizational Outcomes: A Field Examination." *Administrative Science Quarterly,* 1981, *26*(4), 617–632.

Rothschild, W. E. *Putting It All Together.* New York: Amacom, 1976.

Rothschild, W. E. *Strategic Alternatives: Selection, Development, and Implementation.* New York: Amacom, 1979.

Sartain, A. Q., and Baker, A. W. *The Supervisor and His Job.* New York: McGraw-Hill, 1972.

Sasser, W. E., and Leonard, F. "Let First-Level Supervisors Do Their Job." *Harvard Business Review,* 1980, *58*(2), 113–121.

Schein, E. H. *Organizational Psychology.* (3rd ed.) Englewood Cliffs, N.J.: Prentice-Hall, 1980.

Schmitt, N., and Hill, T. E. "Sex and Race Composition of Assessment Center Groups as a Determinant of Peer and Assessor Ratings." *Journal of Applied Psychology,* 1977, *62*(3), 261–264.

Schneider, B. "Organizational Climates: An Essay." *Personnel Psychology,* 1975, *28*(4), 447–479.

Selby, C. C. "Better Performance from Nonprofits." *Harvard Business Review,* 1978, *56*(5), 92–99.

Shubin, J. A. *Business Management.* New York: Barnes and Noble, 1954.

Skinner, W. "Big Hat, No Cattle: Managing Human Resources." *Harvard Business Review,* 1981, *59*(5), 106–115.

Sloan, A. P., Jr. *My Years with General Motors.* New York: Doubleday, 1963.

Sloan, S., and Johnson, A. C. "New Context of Personnel Appraisal." *Harvard Business Review,* Nov.–Dec. 1968, *46*(6), 14–15.

Smalter, D. J., and Ruggles, R. L. "Six Business Lessons from the Pentagon." *Harvard Business Review,* 1966, *44*(2), 64–76.

Smircich, L., and Chesser, R. J. "Superiors' and Subordinates' Perceptions of Performance: Beyond Disagreement." *Academy of Management Journal,* 1981, *24*(1), 198–205.

Smith, H. P. *Performance Appraisal and Human Development: A Practical Guide to Effective Managing.* Reading, Mass.: Addison-Wesley, 1977.

Spiegel, A. H., III. "How Outsiders Overhauled a Public Agency." *Harvard Business Review,* 1975, *53*(1).

Srinivas, K. M., and Long, R. J. "Organizational Climate and Effectiveness of M.B.O." *Interpersonal Development,* 1975–76, *6*(1), 8–24.

Srivastava, A. K., and Krishna, A. "The Effect of Job-Anxiety on Job Performance." *Indian Journal of Social Work,* 1980, *41*(3), 255–260.

Stata, R., and Maidique, M. "Bonus System for Balanced Strategy." *Harvard Business Review,* 1980, *58*(6), 156–163.

Steers, R. M. *Introduction to Organizational Behavior.* Santa Monica, Calif.: Goodyear, 1981.

Steiner, G. A. *Job Management Planning.* New York: Macmillan, 1969.

Summers, C. W. "Protecting All Employees Against Unjust Dismissal." *Harvard Business Review,* 1980, *58,* 101–114.

Sutton, F., Harris, S. E., Kaysen, C., and Tobin, J. *The American Business Creed.* New York: Schocken Books, 1962.

Szilagyi, A. D., and Wallace, M. *Organizational Behavior and Performance.* Santa Monica, Calif.: Goodyear, 1980.

Taylor, B., and Hawkins, K. *A Handbook of Strategic Planning.* London: Longman, 1972.

Taylor, F. W. *Principles of Scientific Management.* New York: Harper, 1911.

Taylor, J. C., and Bower, D. G. *Survey of Organizations.* Ann Arbor: University of Michigan, 1972.

Taylor, R. L., and Zawacki, R. A. "Collaborative Goal Setting in Performance Appraisal: A Field Experiment." *Public Personnel Management,* 1978, *7*(3), 162–170.

Thayer, F. C. "Civil Service Reform and Performance Appraisal: A Policy Disaster." *Public Personnel Management,* 1981, *10*(1), 20–28.

Thayer, P. W. "Personnel Challenges in the Eighties." *Public Personnel Management,* 1980, *9*(4), 327–335.

Thompson, D. "Performance Appraisal and the Civil Service Reform Act." *Public Personnel Management,* 1981, *10*(3), 281–288.

Thompson, K. R., Luthans, F., and Terpening, W. D. "The Effects of M.B.O. on Performance and Satisfaction in a Public Sector Organization." *Journal of Management,* 1981, 7(1), 53–68.

Thune, S. S., and House, R. J. "Where Long Range Planning Pays Off." In B. Taylor and K. Hawkins (Eds.), *A Handbook of Strategic Planning.* London: Longman, 1972.

Thurow, L. "The Productivity Problem." *Technology Review,* 1980, 40 pp.

Tilles, S. "How to Evaluate Corporate Strategy." *Harvard Business Review,* 1963, *41*(4), 111–112.

Trainor, J. L. "Government Use of Nonprofit Companies." *Harvard Business Review,* 1966, *44,* 38–52.

Umstot, D. D., and others. "Effects of Job Enrichment and Task Goals on Satisfaction and Productivity: Implications for Job Design." *Journal of Applied Psychology,* 1976, *61,* 379–394.

U.S. Bureau of Labor Statistics. *Productivity: A Selected, Annotated Bibliography, 1976–1978.* Bulletin 2051. Washington, D.C.: Bureau of Labor Statistics, 1980.

U.S. Department of Labor. *Handbook of Labor Statistics.* Washington, D.C.: U.S. Department of of Labor, 1978.

Unterman, I., and Davis, R. H. "The Strategy Gap in Not-for-Profits." *Harvard Business Review,* 1982, *60*(3), 30–40.

Veninga, R. L., and Spradley, J. D. *The Work/Stress Connection: How to Cope with Job Burnout.* Boston: Little, Brown, 1981.

Vernon, R. "Gone Are the Cash Cows of Yesteryear." *Harvard Business Review,* 1980, *58*(6), 150–155.

Walsh, A. H. *The Public's Business: The Politics and Practices of Government Corporations.* Cambridge, Mass.: M.I.T. Press, 1978.

Webster's Dictionary for Everyday Use. Baltimore: Literary Press/Ottenheimer, 1981.

Weick, K. E. "Executive As Analyst." *Contemporary Psychology,* 1982, *27*(3), 195–197.

Weinwurn, E. H. *Long-Term Profit Planning.* New York: American Management Association, 1971.

Welsch, H. P., and Lavan, H. "Inter-relationships Between Organizational Commitment and Job Characteristics, Job Satisfaction, Professional Behavior, and Organizational Climate." *Human Relations,* 1981, *34*(12), 1079–1089.

Wheelwright, S. C. "Japan—Where Operations Really Are Strategic." *Harvard Business Review,* 1981, *59*(4), 67–75.

Wholking, W., and others. "Management by Objective." *Training and Development Journal,* 1972, *26,* 2–19.

Wickert, F. R., and McFarland, D. E. *Measuring Executive Performance.* New York: Appleton-Century-Crofts, 1967.

Wilkens, J. D. "Corporate Strategy and Management by Objectives." In B. Taylor and K. Hawkins (Eds.), *A Handbook of Strategic Planning.* London: Longman, 1972.

Williams, M. R. *Performance Appraisal in Management.* London: Heineman, 1971.

Winstanley, N. B. "Legal and Ethical Issues in Performance Appraisals." *Harvard Business Review,* 1980, *58*(6), 186–192.

Yager, E. "A Critique of Performance Appraisal Systems." *Personnel Journal,* 1981, *60*(2), 129–133.

Young, D. W. " 'Non Profits' Need Surplus Too." *Harvard Business Review,* 1982, *60*(1), 124–132.

Yukl, G. A., and Latham, G. P. "Interrelationships Among Employee Participation, Individual Differences, Goal Difficulty, Goal Acceptance, Goal Instrumentality, and Performance." *Personnel Psychology,* 1978, *31*(2), 305–323.

Zaltman, G. (Ed.). *Management Principles for Non-Profit Agencies and Organizations.* New York: Amacom, 1979.

Zaphiropoulos, R. "It's Not Lonely Upstairs." *Harvard Business Review,* 1980, *58*(6), 111.

Index